THE KING'S GRAMMAR

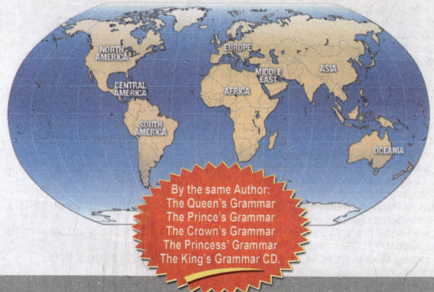

By the same Author:
The Queen's Grammar
The Prince's Grammar
The Crown's Grammar
The Princess' Grammar
The King's Grammar CD.

SANJAY KUMAR SINHA

- Guinness World Record Holder
- The Longest Grammar Teaching in the World for 73 Hours and 37 Minutes
- The Fastest Grammar Teaching in the World (LBR)

S. CHAND & COMPANY LTD.

(AN ISO 9001 : 2000 COMPANY)
RAM NAGAR, NEW DELHI -110 055

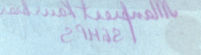

S. CHAND & COMPANY LTD.

(An ISO 9001 : 2000 Company)

Head Office : 7361, RAM NAGAR, NEW DELHI - 110 055

Phones : 23672080-81-82, 9899107446, 9911310888

Fax : 91-11-23677446

Shop at: **schandgroup.com**; E-mail: **schand@vsnl.com**

Branches :

- 1st Floor, Heritage, Near Gujarat Vidhyapeeth, Ashram Road, **Ahmedabad**-380 014. Ph. 27541965, 27542369, ahmedabad@schandgroup.com
- No. 6, Ahuja Chambers, 1st Cross, Kumara Krupa Road, **Bangalore**-560 001. Ph : 22268048, 22354008, bangalore@schandgroup.com
- 238-A M.P. Nagar, Zone 1, **Bhopal** - 462 011. Ph : 4274723. bhopal@schandgroup.com
- 152, Anna Salai, **Chennai**-600 002. Ph : 28460026, chennai@schandgroup.com
- S.C.O. 2419-20, First Floor, Sector- 22-C (Near Aroma Hotel), **Chandigarh**-160022, Ph-2725443, 2725446, chandigarh@schandgroup.com
- 1st Floor, Bhartia Tower, Badambadi, **Cuttack**-753 009, Ph-2332580; 2332581, cuttack@schandgroup.com
- 1st Floor, 52-A, Rajpur Road, **Dehradun**-248 001. Ph : 2740889, 2740861, dehradun@schandgroup.com
- Pan Bazar, **Guwahati**-781 001. Ph : 2738811, guwahati@schandgroup.com
- Sultan Bazar, **Hyderabad**-500 195. Ph : 24651135, 24744815, hyderabad@schandgroup.com
- Mai Hiran Gate, **Jalandhar** - 144008. Ph. 2401630, 5000630, jalandhar@schandgroup.com
- A-14 Janta Store Shopping Complex, University Marg, Bapu Nagar, **Jaipur** - 302 015, Phone : 2719126, jaipur@schandgroup.com
- 613-7, M.G. Road, Ernakulam, **Kochi**-682 035. Ph : 2381740, cochin@schandgroup.com
- 285/J, Bipin Bihari Ganguli Street, **Kolkata**-700 012. Ph : 22367459, 22373914, kolkata@schandgroup.com
- Mahabeer Market, 25 Gwynne Road, Aminabad, **Lucknow**-226 018. Ph : 2626801, 2284815, lucknow@schandgroup.com
- Blackie House, 103/5, Walchand Hirachand Marg , Opp. G.P.O., **Mumbai**-400 001. Ph : 22690881, 22610885, mumbai@schandgroup.com
- Karnal Bag, Model Mill Chowk, Umrer Road, **Nagpur**-440 032. Ph : 2723901, 2777666 nagpur@schandgroup.com
- 104, Citicentre Ashok, Govind Mitra Road, **Patna**-800 004. Ph : 2300489, 2302100, patna@schandgroup.com
- 291/1, Ganesh Gayatri Complex, 1st Floor, Somwarpeth, Near Jain Mandir, **Pune**-411011. Ph : 64017298, pune@schandgroup.com
- Flat No. 104, Sri Draupadi Smriti Apartment, East of Jaipal Singh Stadium, Neel Ratan Street, Upper Bazar, **Ranchi**-834001. Ph : 2208761, ranchi@schandgroup.com

First Edition 2008

ISBN : 81-219-2905-9

Code : 111 013

PRINTED IN INDIA

By Rajendra Ravindra Printers (Pvt.) Ltd., 7361, Ram Nagar, New Delhi-110 055 and published by S. Chand & Company Ltd., 7361, Ram Nagar, New Delhi-110 055

PREFACE

Human being is the most beautiful creation of God because of the power of speaking and expression in the form of languages. My knowledge is not more than a drop in the ocean. This book is an attempt to trap the ocean of knowledge into a drop. Now you have to justify my attempt and guide me towards the pinnacle of wisdom.

My effort is a never ending attempt in search of pearls from the ocean of knowledge and prepare the crown of "The King's Grammar." You deserve the crown but always remember that there are uncountable jewels still need to be added to its glittering beauty.

The path of greatness is never a road of roses. The flower that struggles through out mud and blooms as lotus only deserves the blessings of deity Saraswatiji & Laxmiji.

Those, who accept insult and curse with positive attitude, glitter in the golden pages of history. The monument of greatness have been built with the stones thrown by critics.

If you have such attitude, please open this book and join us in this mission to achieve the crown and rule the world of language and become "The King Of Grammar."

Finally, I would thank Mr. Nageshwar Pandeyji for inspiring me to write this book.

INSPIRATIONS TO MY LIFE

1. **Thakur V. K. Singh** : Chairman - Thakur Educational Trust
2. **Thakur Jitendra Singh** : Trustee - Thakur Educational Trust
3. **S. M. Lall** : Founder - S. M. Lall College
4. **Mr . Yogesh Patel** : Trustee - Vivekanand International School
5. **Dr. P. V. Pradhan** : Director - Thakur Educational Trust
6. **G. D. Sinha** : Parent
7. **Gangeshwar Rai :** Head of the English Department University of Gorakhpur
8. **Dr. Nelofer Bhaducha** : Head of the Eng. Dept. University of Mumbai.
9. **Mr. C. T. Chakrabory** : Thakur College of Science and Commerce
10. **Mrs. R. Chakraborty** : Principal - Vivekanand International School
11. **Dr. R. M. Badode** : Reader - Eng Dept. University of Mumbai
12. **Mr. R. S. Singh** : Principal - Gyanoaya Vidya Mandir High School
13. **Mr. Pandey** : Principal - Bansidher Agrawal High School
14. **Sister Naurah** : Principal - Convent Girls High School
15. **Sharma** : Principal - G. D. Somani High School
16. **Mr. R. D. Mishra** : Trustee - Divine Child High school
17. **Mr. N. B. Singh** : Principal - Vivekanand High School
18. **V. M. Naik** : Principal Fatimadevi English High school
19. **Mrs J . Sharma** : Principal Navjivan Vidyalaya High School
20. **R. K. Singh** : Principal Film City High School
21. **B. C. Singh** : Principal N. L. High school
22. **Mr. Dinesh Prased Singh**
23. **Jagjit Singh Shanshanwal**
24. **Mr & Mrs V. Devan**
25. **P. K. Jain** : Civil Engineer
26. **Dr. Kavita Patker** : Vivekanand International School
27. **Mr. Jai Prakash Naik** : Lecturer - M. P. Inter College
28. **Mrs Urmila Singh :** Unnav

CONTENTS

CHAPTERS   **PAGES**

DEFINITIONS 1–13

NOUN 14–16

SUBJECT / PREDICATE / OBJECT / COMPLEMENT 17–22

GRAMMAR BASED ON LETTERS 23–45

TENSE 46–76

CHANGE THE VOICE 77–100

DIRECT & INDIRECT SPEECH 101–127

PUNCTUATION MARKS 128–145

DEGREE OF COMPARISON 146–156

QUESTION TAG 157–165

ARTICLE 166–173

FIGURES OF SPEECH 174–191

CLAUSE 192–207

PHRASE 208–214

SIMPLE, COMPLEX & COMPOUND SENTENCES 215–243

SYNTHESIS 244–274

SEQUENCE OF TENSES 275–278

TRANSFORMATION OF SENTENCES 279–286

MODAL AUXILIARIES 287–296

USES OF HELPING VERBS & MAIN VERBS 297–316

USES OF TENSES 317–326

PRONOUN 327–332

ADJECTIVE 333–337

ADVERB 338–341

CONJUNCTION 342–347

INTERJECTION & EXCLAMATION 348–349

TRANSFORMATION OF SENTENCES II 350–358

PARTICIPLE 359–364

UNFULFILLED CONDITION 365–367

PREPOSITION 368–393

COMPOSITION 394–426

Definitions

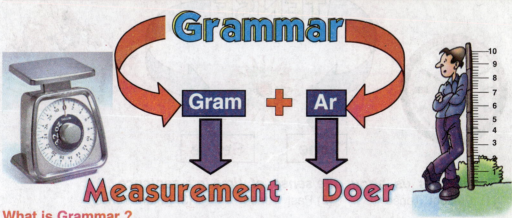

Grammar

Gram + **Ar**

Measurement   **Doer**

What is Grammar ?

You know kilo-*gram*, hecto- *gram*, mili-*gram*, **etc.** very well.

 KG.   HG.   MG. | Gram = Measurement or Scale |

A person who drives a car is a *driver*.
A person who manages is a *manager.*
A person who teaches is a *teacher*.
 ar / er = doer

Definition of Grammar : | Grammar is the measurement of language. |

Grammar can only tell you whether *the language* is correctly spoken or written.

It is the only *scale* for a correct *language*.

WHAT IS A DEFINITION ?

Definition

De + **Fine**

Introduction: | De | = | Down | Going down into the depth of anything, getting the finest part and presenting it . This presentation is the | Definition | .

 (or) Presenting the finest part of anything is the *Definition*

According to the greatest philosopher | Sir Plato |:

"**A definition** must have | a Genus | and a | Differentia | . "

Genus means class . The thing, person, etc. belongs to which *group* or *class*.

Differentia means different . How is the thing different from other things in its own group? Note: **Thing** means all that you can think about. (Noun, Pronoun etc.)

WHAT IS TENSE ?

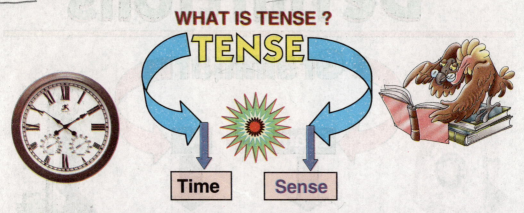

Tense tells us about the sense of time in a sentence.
(1) Present Tense (2) Past Tense (3) Future Tense

WHAT IS SENTENCE ?

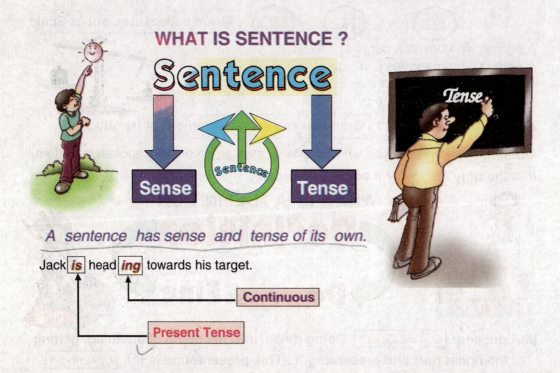

A sentence has sense and tense of its own.

Jack **is** head **ing** towards his target.

Continuous

Present Tense

Subject

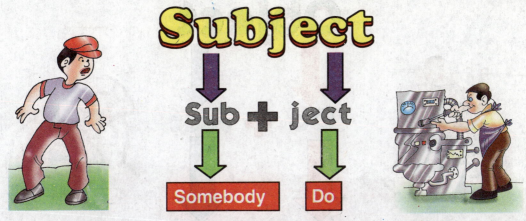

Sub + ject

Somebody **Do**

Somebody who does work is a subject in a sentence.

Henry writes a letter to his parents.

↑

Subject

Sometimes subject can be seen in a state.

In fact, Ject has two meanings: (1) throw (2) do (action)

Predicate

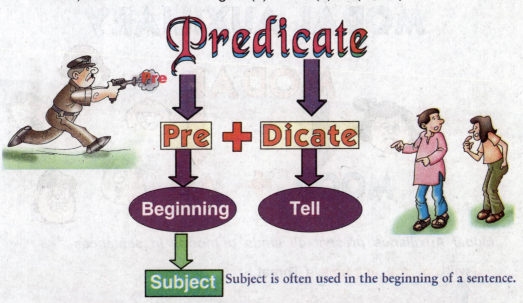

Pre + Dicate

Beginning **Tell**

Subject Subject is often used in the beginning of a sentence.

Predicate tells us about the action or state of the subject in a sentence.

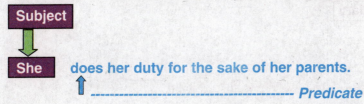

Subject

↓

She does her duty for the sake of her parents.

↑ --- *Predicate*

Object

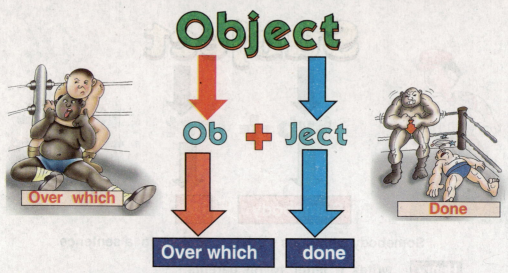

Ob + Ject

Over which + done

Over which a work is done is called an object in a sentence.

Shelly cracks *plates* in the hall.

Object

MODAL AUXILIARY

MODAL

MOOD + ALL

Modal Auxiliaries present all kinds of moods in sentences.

I *will* kill you any time. [Threat]

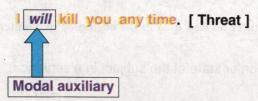

Modal auxiliary

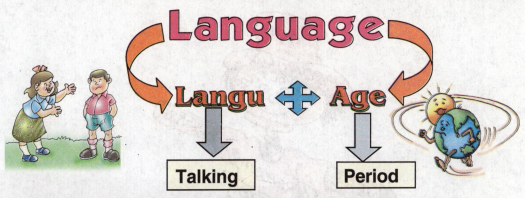

Language

Langu ⬌ Age

Talking   Period

Talking of common people is called *Language.*
Language should be simple, easy and understandable to the common people.

LITERATURE

Literate means *learned* :

The language of learned people is called '*Literature*.'

Whatever learned people speak, write, or present thought, etc.: the work comes under '*Literature*.'

That is the reason why – conversation, speech, poem, play, story, diary, etc. of *learned people* can be found in *the books of Literature*.

DIFFERENCE BETWEEN *LANGUAGE* & *LITERATURE*

Writing, speaking, etc. of common people is a *Language.*

Writing, speaking, etc. of the learned people is a *Literature*.

PARTS OF SPEECH

Parts   Of   Speech

Partition   Sentence

Partition of a sentence according its uses is called "Parts of Speech".

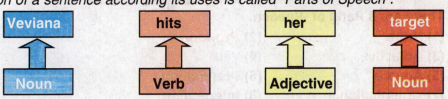

Veviana	hits	her	target
Noun	Verb	Adjective	Noun

Parts of Speech				Figures of Speech
He	is	a	devil.	He is a devil.
PRONOUN	VERB	ADJECTIVE (Article)	NOUN	METAPHOR
Partition of a sentence according to its uses is **Parts of Speech**				Telling about the quality or uses of the whole figure of a sentence is **Figures of Speech**

Parts Of Speech

There are 8 **Parts of Speech**.

(1) **Noun**
(2) **Pronoun**
(3) **Adjective**
(4) **Verb**
(5) **Adverb**
(6) **Preposition**
(7) **Conjunction**
(8) **Interjection**

NOUN

All that you can **see, feel or** *think* is a *Noun*,

E.g. Sam, Paris, pen, happiness, etc.

You can see : **a car, a peacock, an umbrella, a house, a man, a bird, etc.**

You can feel : **air, sorrow, happiness, pain, etc.**

You can think : **Psychology, Physics, life, fortune, et**c.

Common definition of Noun : A Noun is a naming word.

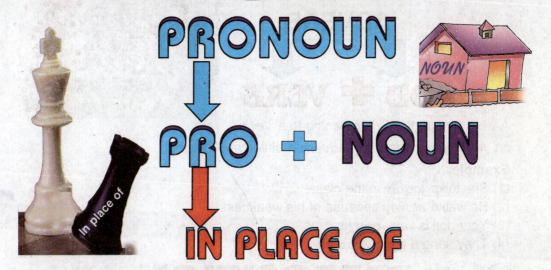

PRONOUN
↓
PRO + NOUN
↓
IN PLACE OF

A word that is used in place of a 'Noun' is called a ' Pronoun'.
Ex : He, she, it, him, her, its, etc.

ADJECTIVE

An **Adjective** adds some meaning to a **Noun** or a **Pronoun**.

Example :

(1) She knows the **black** magic of Bengal.

(2) He has lost **his** money.

(3) You have done a **silly** mistake.

(4) You must not ignore the **poor** students.

VERB

You know the words : Oral Verbal .

Verb : It means to tell.

A Verb is a word that tells about the action or state of Subject, Object (Agent) etc.

Example :

1. She writes a letter to her friends. [Action]

2. She is a teacher in a school. [State]

ADVERB

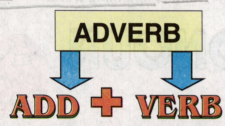

ADD + VERB

A word that adds some meaning to a *Verb* ,

an *Adjective*, or another *Adverb* is called an Adverb.

Example:

(1) She talks *loudly* in the class.

(2) He walks *slowly* because of his weakness.

(3) Your doll is very *costly*.

(4) They sang a song *properly*.

PREPOSITION

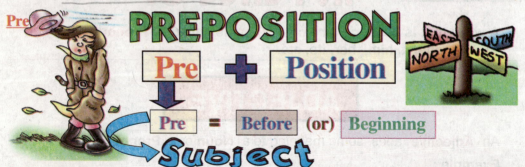

Pre + Position

Pre = Before (or) Beginning

Subject

Definition : Preposition tells us about the position of subject /agent in a sentence.

SUBJECT

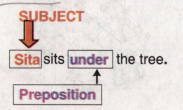

Sita sits under the tree.

Preposition

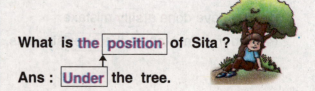

What is the position of Sita ?

Ans : Under the tree.

(B) | Preposition | tells us about the **position** of the **word** [**Subject**] which is used in the beginning of a sentence.

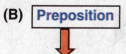

| Pre | = **in the beginning** of a sentence

| Subject | is used in the beginning of a sentence.

Example:

(1) The book has been kept | in | the **drawer**.
　　　　　　　　　　　Preposition-↑　　　↑**- Noun**

(2) The Earth moves **round** the **Sun**.
　　　　　　Preposition-↑　　　↑**-Noun**

(3) He is waiting | at | the **bus stop**.
　Preposition-↑　　↑**- Noun**

(4) She advised us and went **on**. [Exception]
　　　　　　　　　　　　↑**-Preposition**

Example: (1) | The book | has been kept | under | the table.

　　　　　　　　　　　　　　| Pre |　　　　　　　| Preposition |

What is the position of **Pre** = **the book** ? **Ans :** Under the table.

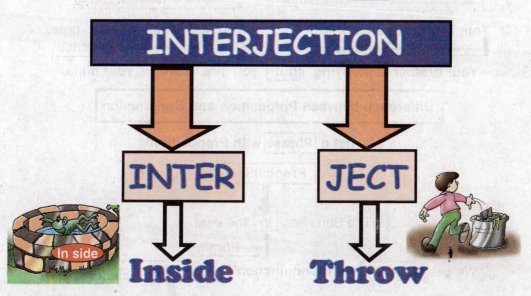

INTERJECTION

INTER　　　JECT

Inside　　　Throw

It is a word that helps you to throw your **sudden feeling** out that you have inside your heart or in your sentiment.

Example: (1) **Alas!** He is dead.　　(2) **Hurrah** ! We have won the match.

Ject has two meanings: (1) throw,　(2) do (some action)

CONJUNCTION

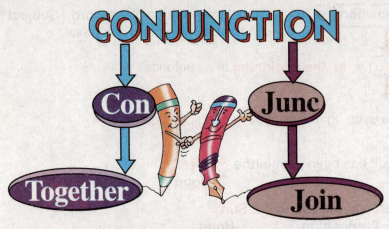

Con **Junc**

Together **Join**

A word that joins **two or more** words , phrases , clauses or sentences is called a Conjunction.

Example:

(1) **Robby** and **Sam** are waiting for you. **[Two words]**
↑**Word** ↑**Word**

(2) I met him **near the temple** and under the tree .
↑------Phrase ↑------- Phrase

(3) **She always creates problems** because **she is a cheat.**
↑--------------------------- Clause ↑----------------------Clause

(4) **Your brother is studying.** **You are wasting your time.**
↑---------------Sentence ↑----------------------Sentence

Your brother is studying but **you are wasting your time.**

Difference between Preposition and Conjunction

We get a Phrase **with Preposition**

Preposition

Example :

(1)The Sun rises in the east.
↑---- Phrase

We get a Clause **with 'Conjunction'** Conjunction

Example :

(1) I have helped you because you are honest.
↑---------------------- Clause

PHRASE

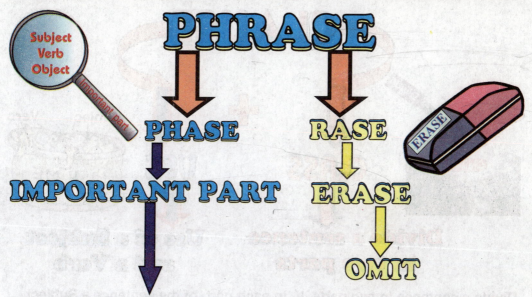

PHASE → **IMPORTANT PART**

RASE → **ERASE** → **OMIT**

SUBJECT / VERB / OBJECT / COMPLEMENT

If you omit (or) erase Subject Verb Object etc. from a sentence, rest part will be a Phrase.

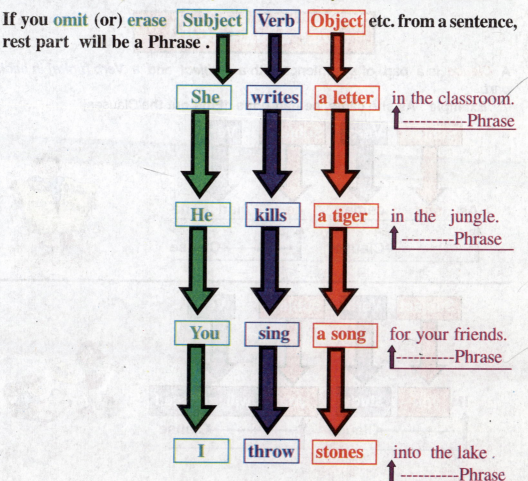

Subject	Verb	Object	
She	writes	a letter	in the classroom. ↑-----------Phrase
He	kills	a tiger	in the jungle. ↑---------Phrase
You	sing	a song	for your friends. ↑-----------Phrase
I	throw	stones	into the lake. ↑-----------Phrase

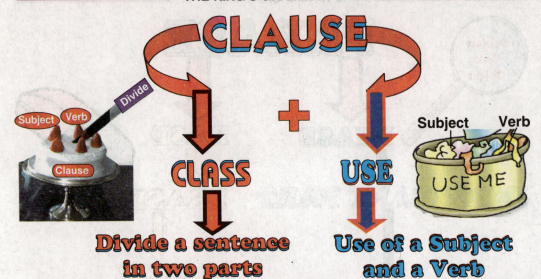

CLASS

USE

Divide a sentence in two parts

Use of a Subject and a Verb

Divide a sentence in two parts. If in each part of the sentence *a Subject* and *a Verb* is used, each part is *a Clause*.

DEFINITION

A *Clause* is a part of a sentence with a *Subject* and *a Verb [finite] in each part.*

Example : As she came, he had gone. [**Find out the** Clauses]

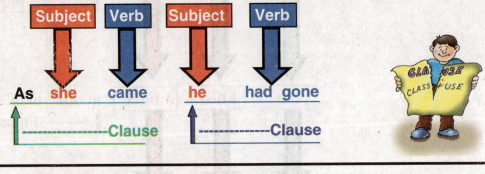

| Subject | Verb | Subject | Verb |

As **she** **came** **he** **had gone**

-------------Clause   -------------Clause

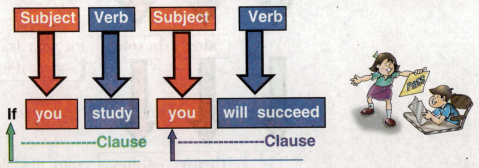

| Subject | Verb | Subject | Verb |

If **you** **study** **you** **will succeed**

-------------Clause   -------------Clause

EXERCISE NO. 1

1 A : Learn and write down the definitions of :

1. Grammar   2. Clause   3. Phrase   4. Interjection   5. Conjunction   6. Preposition   7. Pronoun   8. Noun   9. Verb   10. Adverb   11. Modal Auxiliary 12. Object   13. Subject   14. Sentence   15. Predicate .

1 B : Name the Parts of Speech of the underlined words :

1. **Help** the poor students .

2. Let us continue the **study**.

3. **Little** Jack **Horner sat** in a corner.

4. **Karna** was a **great** warrior.

5. **Wisdom** is better than **strength**.

6. **Anger** is one **letter** short of **danger**.

7. **Temper** is the most valuable thing, don't lose **it**.

8. **Humpty Dumpty** sat on a **wall.**

9. **Sincerity** never **goes** waste.

10. **Life** is a **challenge**, face it.

11. She **wept** an **ocean** of **tears.**

12. **Napoleon** was a very great Emperor.

13. Wherever **you** go, I shall **meet** you.

14. **Accept** the truth of life **or** you may suffer.

15. You should **cross** the river.

16. A person who manages is a **manager.**

17. A person who teaches is a **teacher.**

Note : Thing means all that you can think about. (Noun, Pronoun etc.)

NOUN

All that you can **see**, **feel** or **think** is a **Noun**,

E.g., Ricky, Paris, paper, sadness, etc.

You can *see* : a taxi, a cock, a banana, a mouse, a

mango, a girl, etc.

You can *feel* : air, sorrow, happiness, pain, etc.

You can *think* : Psychology, Physics, life, fortune, etc.

Common definition of *Noun* : A Noun is a naming word.

KINDS OF NOUNS

There are **5** kinds of **Nouns** :

1. Common Noun   2. Proper Noun   3. Collective Noun

4. Material Noun   5. Abstract Noun

HOW TO CLARIFY

Example No. 1

Suppose you have **a goat** which is **a common animal** :

(A) A goat is a **Common Noun.**

(B) If you name your goat as ‘Sony’, it will be a **Proper Noun** for you.

(C) If your goat enters into a flock of goats, it will be a **Collective Noun.**

(D) If you cut the goat, mutton will be a **Material Noun.**

(E) As you cook mutton and find delicacy in taste, it is **an Abstract Noun.**

[Words in the boxes are **Nouns**].

Example No. 2

(A) A Man is a **Common Noun.** [A name of a common person.]

(B) If his name is **Peter**, it will be a **Proper Noun** as it is the name of a **particular man.**

(C) If **Peter**, being a student, enters into a **class**, it will be a **Collective Noun.**

(D) If **Peter** goes through a forest and a tiger kills him, **the flesh** of his body will be a **Material Noun.**

(E) If you feel **sorrow** at his death, it will be an **Abstract Noun.**

[Nouns are underlined in the above sentences.]

IMP

KINDS OF NOUNS IN DETAIL

COMMON NOUN

A **Common Noun** is the name of a common person, place, animal, thing, etc.

Example: 1. Carol is a beautiful _girl_.

2. Mohan is a good **_boy_**.

3. Mumbai is a big _city_.

4. Nepal is our neighbouring _country_.

In the above sentences, underlined words are **_Common Nouns_**.

PROPER NOUN

A **Proper Noun** is the name of a particular person, animal, place, thing, etc.

Example: 1. **_Delhi_** is the capital city of **_India_**.

2. **_Krishna_** had to work hard.

3. **_Napoleon_** was a great commander.

4. **_Hamlet_** is a famous play.

COLLECTIVE NOUN

A **Collective Noun** is the name of a collection or group of persons, places, things, etc.

Example: 1. **A crowd** has created all these problems.

2. **The jury** has decided to send him to the jail.

3. **A flock of sheep** is grazing in the field.

4. **A bunch of keys** has been lost.

SOME MORE EXAMPLES

1. A committee of members
2. A flock of sheep
3. A herd of cattle
4. A swarm of insects
5. A bevy of girls
6. A galaxy of stars
7. A gang of bandits
8. A class of students
9. A fleet of ships
10. An archipelago of islands

IMP

MATERIAL NOUN

A Material Noun is the name of **a material** existing in the nature.

Example:
1. The ornament is made of **gold**.
2. **Cotton** is good for skin.
3. I like **rice** and **pulse**.
4. Take this **milk** before you go to bed.
5. We cannot live without **water**.

ABSTRACT NOUN

An Abstract Noun is the name of **a quality, action, state, etc.**

Quality : Bravery, kindness, goodness, honesty, etc.

Action : Laughter, hatred, behaviour, theft, etc.

State : Brotherhood, boyhood, death, sleep, youth, slavery, etc.

EXERCISE NO. 2

1. Find out 'Nouns' from the following sentences and tell their kinds also.

1. A burnt child dreads the fire. *common noun*
2. Little Jack Horner sat in a corner. *proper*
3. Napoleon, who is the most honourable French, died at Helena. *proper*
4. A rolling stone gathers no moss. *common noun*
5. Do noble deeds, don't only dream them. *common*
6. Rome was not built in a day . *common*
7. Religion does not banish mirth.
8. Time and tide wait for none. *common*
9. If you live well, you may die well. *common*
10. Hunger is the best sauce. *common*
11. Death is preferable to disgrace.
12. Uneasy lies the head that wears the crown.
13. Columbus discovered America. *proper*
14. Prayer does not cause inconvenience to anybody.
15. Those, who seek only for faults, cannot see anything. *common*
16. Bread and butter is our necessity. *common*
17. People, who are too sharp, cut their own fingers. *common*

SUBJECT/ PREDICATE/ OBJECT/ COMPLEMENT

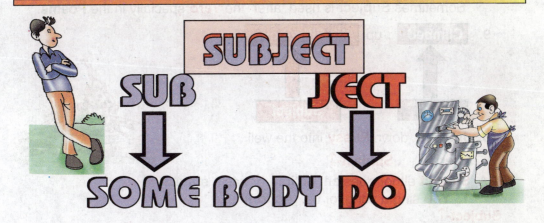

SUBJECT

SUB ⬇ JECT ⬇

SOME BODY DO

Sub = Somebody　　　　　　　**Ject = do**

Somebody who does work or has a state is a **Subject** in a sentence.

1. **She** is waiting for you. **[Action]**
2. **She** is a good student. **[State]**

Example :

1. **She** teaches English properly. **[Action]**
   ⬆----- **Subject**

2. **She** is a teacher in a Primary School. **[State]**
   ⬆-------**Subject**

3. **You** create so many problems.
   ⬆------**Subject**

4. **The bravery of villagers** saved the child from a wolf.
   ⬆------------------**Subject**

5. **Your brother** speaks English very well.
   ⬆-----**Subject**

6. **All the teachers of my school** have been to U.K.
   ⬆--------------------------**Subject**

In **Order** and **Request**, **'You'** is the **"Hidden Subject"**.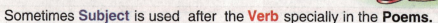

7. Get out from here.

You [Hidden Subject]

8. Please give me some money.

You [Hidden Subject]

Sometimes **Subject** is used after the **Verb** specially in the **Poems**.

9. **Climbed** up **the filthy boy.**

Verb   **Subject**

10. **Jumped** down **Pussy** into the well .

Verb-↑   **Subject**-↑

A **Subject** either does **an action** or has **a state**.

1. **You** sing a song for us. **[Action]**

Subject-↑

2. **She** is an honest lady. **[State]**

Subject-↑

EXERCISE NO. 3-A

Find out 'Subjects' from the following sentences :

1. Wordsworth is a well-known poet.
2. Socrates was a great Greek philosopher.
3. Plato used to preach about the truth of life.
4. Life means activity.
5. Mr. K. Rama Rao has written 100 poems in Tamil language.
6. The lion is said to be a man-eater.
7. Action is a supernatural power of life.
8. "Jurassic Park" was produced by a great producer.
9. Adversity is a better guide than prosperity.
10. Homer wrote Illiad and Odyssey.
11. Silence is the language of soul.
12. The C.B.I. has caught a notorious criminal at Centaur Hotel.
13. John is telling a cock and bull story.
14. Hamlet is one of the well-known plays in English.
15. White gold is the most precious metal.
16. No one can remain speechless in the hen's party.
17. She is talking like a turkey in a cage.

PREDICATE

PRE → **DICATE**

BEGINNING → **TELL**

Pre = beginning / in front of.

Dicate [dictate] = **tells.**

Predicate is a part of a sentence that tells us about **Subject / Agent** used in the beginning of a sentence.

Note : Each **Predicate** must have a **Finite Verb.** **(Finite means Limit.)**

A Verb, which is limited to the subject, is a **Finite Verb.**

Example:

She | **walks in the garden.**

Subject ← **Predicate**

Finite Verb

Finite Verb

I | **can** **live** **without food till 2 o'clock.**

Subject | **Predicate**

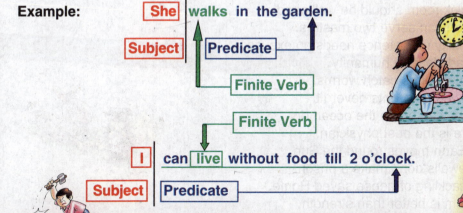

She cooks food in the kitchen. **[Subject]**

Food is cooked by her in the kitchen. **[Agent]**

Example:

1. Diamond **cuts diamond** .
   ↑ -----Predicate

2. Truth **needs no evidence.**
   ↑ -------------Predicate

3. The Earth **moves round the Sun.**
   ↑ ----------------- Predicate

4. Honesty **is the best policy.**
   ↑ -----------Predicate

EXERCISE NO. 3-B

Find out the '*Subjects*' and '*Predicates*' from the following sentences:

1. No one can help a dying duck in thunderstorm.
2. God helps those who help others.
3. Truth never dies.
4. Every man is the maker of his own destiny.
5. Opportunity never knocks the door.
6. He is facing a chicken and egg problem .
7. No pains, no gains.
8. Solomon was a wise king.
9. Her eyes are homes of silent prayer.
10. God is invisible.
11. This music is as dull as ditch water.
12. Plastic bags are widely used now a days.
13. A little knowledge is a dangerous thing.
14. You have to move heaven and earth to get a place in the Guinness Book of World Records.
15. Cleanliness is next to godliness.

EXERCISE NO. 3-C

Find out '*Subjects*' and '*Predicates*' from the following sentences:

1. The dew drops glitter in the morning.
2. The sick room should be well aired.
3. No man can serve two masters.
4. The guilty conscience needs no excuse.
5. All roads lead to humanity.
6. The early birds catch worms.
7. Borrowed garments never fit.
8. Nobody can pump the ocean dry.
9. Nature is the best physician.
10. The Earth moves round the Sun.
11. Stonewalls don't make a prison.
12. The cackling of geese saved Rome.
13. Wisdom is better than strength.
14. Each dog has his day.
15. A live ass is better than a dead lion.
16. A small leak may sink a great ship.
17. Good wine needs no bush.
18. Hunger is the best sauce.
19. A simple word acts like an oath.
20. Of two evils, choose the lesser one.
21. Lead is heavier than any other metal.
22. Open rebuke is better than secret love.
23. Prevention is better than cure.

OBJECT

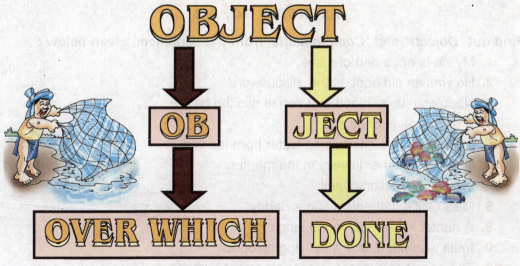

OB → **OVER WHICH**

JECT → **DONE**

Definition : **Over which a work is done is called an 'Object'** .
Object receives effect and is often placed after the **'Main Verb'** [**finite verb**].

Example:

1. She **kills** **a tiger** in the jungle.

↑ **Object**

↕ **Main Verb**

2. You **play** **football** in the garden.

↑ **Object**

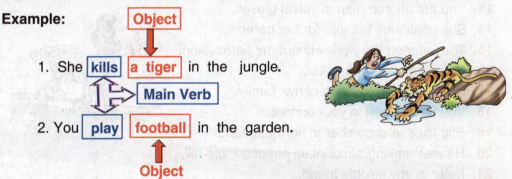

COMPLEMENT

A Sentence has a complete meaning if a **Subject** and a **Verb** are used in it.

If they cannot complete the meaning, **Complement** is used to complete it .

She **is** **Incomplete meaning**

Sub **Verb** **Complement**

She **is** **a teacher** . = **Complete Meaning**

You **have** **a book** . = **Complete Meaning**

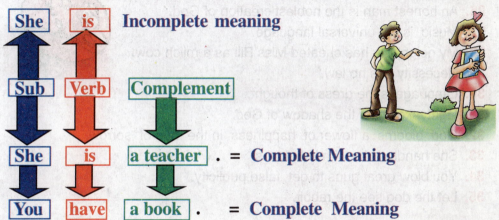

EXERCISE NO. 3-D

Find out 'Objects' and 'Complements' from the sentences given below :

1. My life is not a bed of roses.
2. He was an old boot in the discussion.
3. Napoleon used blood and iron to win the battle.
4. A ship sank into the sea.
5. Your brother fetched some water from the well.
6. She has sold her jewelry in the market.
7. Monty is the son of soil.
8. Miss Oak's father is a sugar daddy.
9. A hunter kills a tiger in the jungle.
10. India won the match with flying colours.
11. The secret of success is consistency of purpose.
12. Brain is a good teacher.
13. You are an iron man in velvet gloves.
14. She continues her job for her parents.
15. They started the work without my permission.
16. He is hot under the collar.
17. She is the black sheep of my family.
18. You have a bee in your bonnet.
19. She likes a cucumber in her breakfast.
20. He was making a mountain out of a mole hill.
21. Peter is my flexible friend.
22. Miss Cyral has killed the green-eyed monster.
23. You cannot find milk in the coconut.
24. Pitchers have ears.
25. Glory follows virtue like a shadow.
26. An honest man is the noblest creation of God.
27. Music is the universal language.
28. My neighbour has cheated Miss Bill as a milch cow.
29. Necessity has no law.
30. Language is the dress of thought.
31. Light sketches the shadow of God.
32. God blooms a flower of happiness in the mud of sorrow.
33. She handles him with kid gloves.
34. You blow great guns to get false publicity.
35. Let the dog see the rabbit.

GRAMMAR BASED ON LETTERS

Verbs End with "S" [letter] **= Singular Verbs**

Helping Verbs End with (S) / (E)

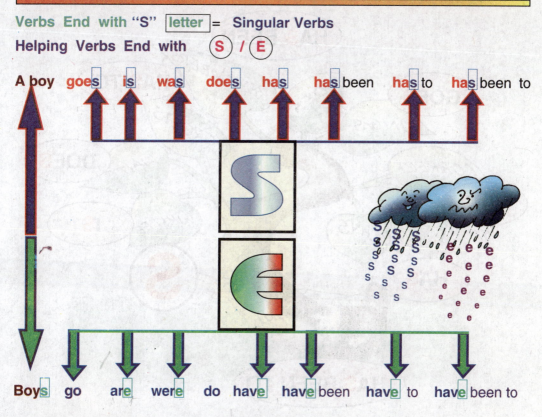

A boy goes is was does has has been has to has been to

S

E

Boys go are were do have have been have to have been to

Go / Goes = Main Verb

(A) Helping verbs that end with **"S"** letter are **Singular Verbs** .

(B) Helping verbs that end with **"S"** letter are used with **Singular Subjects** & Pronouns : He / She / It.

(C) Helping verbs that end with **"S"** letter are used in **Present Tense** only [Exception : Was = Past Tense]

Example :

1. He does his job for himself. [Simple Present Tense]
2. She is trying to speak loudly. [Present Continuous Tense]
3. It has been raining heavily. [Present Perfect Continuous Tense]

Helping Verbs ending with "E" are Plural Verbs

1. Helping Verbs ending with "E" are used with Plural Nouns & Pronouns:

   I / We / You / They

(2) Helping Verbs ending with "E" are used in Present Tense only .

Exception : Were = Past Tense .

Example :

(1) **All the students are** annoyed to see you.   [Simple **Present** Tense]

(2) **My friends have** been waiting for me. [Present **Perfect Continuous Tense**]

(3) **They have** done their home work.   [Present **Perfect Tense**]

(4) **You are** not doing your work properly.   [Present **Continuous Tense**]

Verbs that End with "**S**" letter = Singular Verbs

Rules : Verbs that end with "**S**" can only be used with Pronoun *He, She, It* & **Singular Nouns.**

(A) Helping verbs that end with "**S**" letter are **Singular Verbs**.

(B) Helping verbs that end with "**S**" letter are used with **Singular Subjects** & **Pronoun : He / She / It.**

(C) Helping verbs that end with "**S**" letter are used in **Present Tense** only.
    [Exception : Was = Past Tense]

Example :

He does his job for himself. **[Simple Present Tense]**

She is trying to speak loudly. **[Present Continuous Tense]**

It has been raining heavily. **[Present Perfect Continuous Tense]**

EXERCISE NO. 4-A

Fill suitable 'Subjects' in the blanks.

1. _____ sing**s** a sonorous song.

2. _____ doe**s** everything for the society.

3. _____ i**s** willing to meet you.

4. _____ wa**s** thinking about the whole world.

5. _____ ha**s** done so many mistakes.

6. _____ ha**s** been creating so many problems.

7. _____ ha**s** to complete the work in time.

8. _____ ha**s** been to London.

9. _____ play**s** in the garden.

10. _____ wa**s** feeling better.

EXERCISE NO. 4-B

Use the 'Verbs' given below in your own sentences.

1. does	**2.** has	**3.** has to	**4.** was	**5.** writes
6. has been	**7.** is	**8.** prays	**9.** has been to	**10.** teaches
11. reads	**12.** watches	**13.** plays	**14.** sings	**15.** gives

Verbs that End with "E" Letter = Plural Verbs

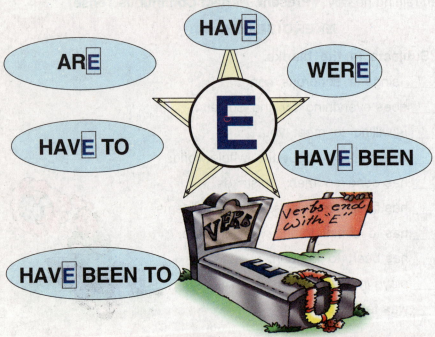

HAVE

ARE   WERE

E

HAVE TO   HAVE BEEN

HAVE BEEN TO

1. Are 2. Have 3. Have to 4. Have been 5. Have been to 6. Were

1. **Helping Verbs** ending with **"E"** are <u>Plural Verbs</u>.

2. **Helping Verbs** ending with **"E"** are used with <u>Plural Nouns</u> &
   Pronouns <u>I</u> , <u>We</u> , <u>You</u> & <u>They</u>.

3. **Helping Verbs** ending with **"E"** are used in <u>Present tense</u> only .

4. **Plural Verbs** <u>are</u> used with <u>I</u> / <u>We</u> / <u>You</u> / <u>They</u> / <u>Plural Nouns</u> , etc.

Exception : Were = Past Tense.

Example : (1) Your teachers **<u>are</u>** very strict regarding your studies.

[Simple Present Tense]

(2) My enemies **have** been waiting for compromise.

[Present Perfect Continuous Tense]

(3) You **have** made a silly mistake. [Present Perfect Tense]

EXERCISE NO. 4-C

Fill in the blanks with suitable *'Subjects'* in the following sentences:

1. _____ are looking for a better chance.
2. _____ were doing funny activities.
3. _____ have lost my books.
4. _____ have been doing my homework.
5. _____ have to go to your friend's party.
6. _____ have been to Paris.
7. _____ do not try to understand me.
8. _____ go to the temple daily after 2 o'clock.
9. _____ write letters to their parents.
10. _____ have sold your gold ornaments.
11. _____ were correcting the mistakes.
12. _____ are very anxious to meet you.

EXERCISE NO. 4-D

Use the 'Verbs' given below in your own sentences:

1. do	2. are	3. were	4. have	5. have been
6. have to	7. have been to	8. sleep	9. swim	10. cross
11. worry	12. drink	13. speak	14. climb	15. die.

EXERCISE NO. 4-E

Choose the proper alternative from the brackets and fill in the blanks:

1. She_____ [do / does] not enjoy the movie.
2. They _____ [play / plays] to win the trophy.
3. I _____ [sing / sings] a song for everybody.
4. You _____ [write / writes] a story about yourself.
5. It _____ [rain / rains] very heavily.
6. All the flowers _____ [blooms / bloom] in the garden.
7. Your teacher _____ [speak / speaks] about the truth of life.
8. Suraj _____ [work / works] hard to get a better result.

9. Her children _____ [is / are] crying for milk.

10. My father _____ [has / have] created so many problems because of you.

11. The Indian newspapers _____ [has been / have been] banned in Sri Lanka.

12. His parents_____ [was / were] waiting for me.

13. Miss Oak _____ [has / have] met me at the railway platform.

14. Your friends _____ [look / looks] very eager to meet you.

15. Shweta _____ [knows / know] my character very well.

16. She _____[look / looks] very aggressive.

17. You _____[collect / collects] your money from the bank.

18. They _____[has / have] to prepare a plan anyway.

19. It _____[rains / rain] heavily in Mumbai.

20. I _____[was/ were] willing to get my destination.

21. Miss Paul _____[has / have] lost her patience.

22. She _____[is / are] looking like a bat out of hell after receiving the result.

23. Miss Lilly _____[has been / have been] behaving like an angel with a magic stick.

24. The crowd _____[was/ were] shouting slogans like dogs bark for a full moon.

25. He _____[has been / have been] enjoying milk and honey after getting uncle's property.

Verbs End with "D" letter

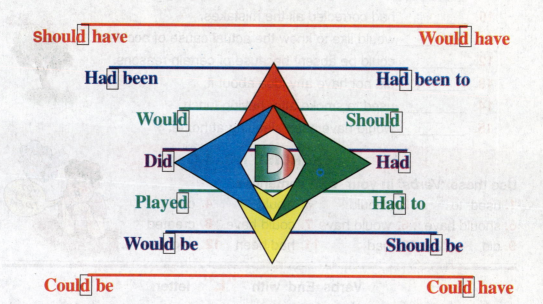

Should have

Had been

Would

Did

Played

Would be

Could be

Would have

Had been to

Should

Had

Had to

Should be

Could have

Used to

1. Verbs ending with "D" indicate **Past Tense**.
2. Verbs ending with "D" are used with all the **Subjects**.

[All subjects are correct.]

Example:

1. He **had gone to school.**
2. They **had gone to school.**
3. A boy **had gone to school.**
4. All the girls **had gone to school.**
5. I **had gone to school.**

I had gone to school

EXERCISE NO. 4-F

Fill in the blanks with suitable *'Subjects'* according to the sentences:

1. _____did his homework in time.
2. _____should try to eradicate poverty.
3. _____ would be happy to see you.
4. _____ used to go to the temple.
5. _____did not catch the thief.
6. _____could have prepared breakfast.
7. _____was looking for a better and a brighter opportunity.

8. _____ should have reached there in time.

9. _____ climbed up to the top of the tree to get some fruits.

10. _____ had corrected all the mistakes.

11. _____ would like to know the actual cause of accident.

12. _____ could be absent because of certain reasons.

13. _____ did not have any idea about it.

14. _____ used to smoke after having lunch.

15. _____ would have been sleeping at home.

EXERCISE NO. 4-G

Use these *'Verbs'* **in your own sentences:**

1. used to
2. should
3. would
4. could
5. should have
6. would have
7. could have
8. created
9. did
10. had
11. had been
12. might have.

Verbs End with "L" letter

Shall

Shall have been

Will have been to

Shall have to

Will have to

Shall have

Will have

Shall be

Will be

Will

L = Future Tense

Shall / Will / Shall be / Will be / Shall have / Will have / Shall have to / Will have to / Shall have been / Will have been / Shall have been to / Will have been to.

Generally – I / We = shall / Rest all Subjects = will

Example : **I shall write a letter to y**ou.
        We shall win the match.
In case of **Command / Threat / Challenge/ Determination**.
        I / We = will
        Rest all Subjects = shall
Example : I will kill you. [Threat]

EXERCISE NO. 4-H

Fill in the blanks with suitable 'Subjects' in the following sentences:

1. _____shall be trying to help him.
2. _____will understand my problem.
3. _____shall prepare your food.
4. _____will have directed a movie.
5. _____shall be trying to achieve success.
6. _____will have been snatching the ball.
7. _____will have to know the truth.
8. _____will teach English properly.
9. _____shall have been looking for a better friend.
10. _____will discontinue his work.
11. _____ shall be unhappy to see him.
12. _____will have been very busy.
13. _____shall do the night duty.
14. _____will be waiting at the bus stop.
15. _____ will show me the clear evidence of crime.
16. _____will be a famous writer.

EXERCISE NO. 4-I

Use the 'Verbs' given below in your own sentences :

1. shall   2. will   3. shall be   4. will be
5. will have   6. shall have   7. will have been   8. shall have been
9. shall have to   10. will have been to.

EXERCISE NO. 4-J

Fill in the blanks with either 'shall' or 'will':

1. You_____have to be very sincere.
2. She_____ try to know about you.
3. It_____rain.
4. They_____have been playing flute.
5. Rakesh _____ be touching your feet.
6. We _____travel by car.

7. It_____be snowing.

8. I _____kill you.

9. All the students _____ have left the classroom.

10. The birds _____be chirping in the morning.

Helping Verbs begin with   **"H"**   letter

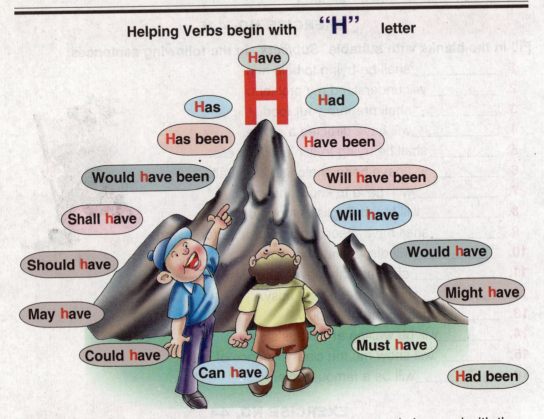

Rule No. 1. Helping Verbs beginning with [H] letter can only be used with the **3rd form of Verb** (or) <u>Past participle</u> .

Example : He must **have seen** you somewhere.
                      3rd form of Verb (Past Participle)

You **had corrected** your mistakes.
           3rd form of Verb (Past Participle)
She will **have accepted** the fact.

Rule No. 2. Helping Verbs beginning with [H] letter can only be used in *Perfect Tenses*.

Example : 1. She <u>has</u> justified her mistakes.   **[Present Perfect Tense]**

         2. You **had** lost your hope.   **[Past Perfect Tense]**

         3. K. Shailja Rao will **have** forgotten me.   **[Future Perfect Tense]**

<u>Important</u> : Perfect means complete so the *Perfect Tense* is the only tense that *completes* the work (or) finishes the action.

Example : She is writing a letter.   [The letter is incomplete]

She <u>has</u> written a letter.   [The letter is complete]

EXERCISE NO. 4-K

Use the correct form of *'Verbs'* given in the brackets :

1. He has _____ [break] all the records in the Asian Games.

2. They had _____[collect] the amount from all the villagers.

3. She will have _____[demand] money from her parents.

4. You would have _____[steal] my books from my drawer.

5. The terrorists must have _____[demolish] the police station.

6. The Principal ought to have _____[follow] all the rules and regulations of the institution.

7. The shopkeepers have_____[close] the shop before the arrival of the procession.

8. Your family members might have _____[decide] to go to Goa.

9. Harry had _____[draw] a beautiful house located in a garden full of flowers.

10. My brother has _____[become] a famous doctor because of his hard work and humble nature.

11. Your daughter must have _____[know] about our plans and programmes.

12. The students will have _____[forget] the questions and answers by next month.

13. Miss Oak should have _____[find] your lost purse.

14. The newspapers will have_____[expose] each and every corruption done by the MLA.

15. The Titanic must have _____[sink] with 2,000 passengers.

EXERCISE NO. 4-L

Use the 'Verbs' given below in your own sentences :

1. Run [will have]   2. Sing [had]   3. Speak [might have]

4. Sink [would have]   5. Shrink [has]   6. Swim [must have]

7. Sit [has]   8. Steal [have]   9. Attack [had]

10. Allow [will have]   11. Arrive [could have]   12. Answer [ought to have]

13. Appoint [should have]   14. Abuse [may have]   15. Accuse [would have].

Verbs begin with "D" Letter

[Do / Does / Did]

The 1st form of Verb is always used with the Verbs beginning with D letter.

Example :

1. She **does not** wait for anybody. [Simple Present]
   Verb 1st form

2. You **do not** continue the job. [Simple Present]
   Verb 1st form

3. They **did not** correct their mistakes. [Simple Past]
   Verb 1st form

EXERCISE NO. 4-M

Choose the correct 'Verbs' and fill in the blanks :

1. Roger does not _____[plays / play / played] well.

2. You do not _____[move / moves / moved] away from the target.

3. They did not _____[remember / remembers / remembered] anything.

4. Your friends do not _____[catches / catch / caught] the thief.

5. Dick does not _____[eats / eat / ate] food in time.

6. The lecturers of our college did not _____[try / tries / tried] to know the result.

7. The captain did not _____[understands /understand / understood] the situation as the ship had collided with an iceberg.

8. The M.H.C.E.T. exam did not _____[starts / start / started] in time.

9. The publisher does not _____[publishes / publish / published] my novel in time.

10. Your family members do not_____[help / helps / helped] you in the time of need.

11. Miss Bell does not _____[study / studies / studied] well for the exam.

12. Richard did not _____[approaches / approach / approached] his boss.

EXERCISE NO. 4-N

Use the 'Verbs' in your own sentences along with the 'Helping verbs' and 'Modal auxiliaries' which are given in the brackets :

1. Remember [do]
2. Post [did]
3. Close [does]
4. Count [do]
5. Catch [does]
6. Watch [did]
7. Prepare [do]
8. Teach [does]
9. Solve [did]
10. Sing [do]
11. Continue [does]
12. Climb [does]
13. Play [did]
14. Study [does]
15. Jump[did]

Helping Verbs & Modal Auxiliaries end with any letter Except S / E

WOULD

SHOULD

CAN

COULD

OUGHT TO

HAD BEEN

HAD TO

USED TO

HAD

MAY

MIGHT

MUST

HAD

SHALL

WILL

SHALL BE

WILL BE

Verbs end with any letter except S / E

SHALL HAVE

Rule No. 1. : These Verbs can be used with all *the Subjects.*

[Exception = Dare]

Example: 1. **You** <u>can</u> win the race.

2. **I** <u>can</u> win the race.

3. **They** <u>can</u> win the race.

4. **He** <u>can</u> win the race.

5. **She** <u>can</u> win the race.

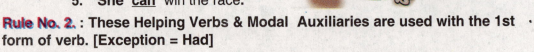

Rule No. 2. : These Helping Verbs & Modal Auxiliaries are used with the 1st form of verb. [Exception = Had]

Example: 1. You **can** write a letter.

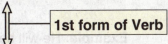

1st form of Verb

2. She **could** write a letter.
3. They **might** write a letter.
4. I **may** write a letter.

Exception = [am]
Note : Have & Be are 1st form of verb .

EXERCISE NO. 4-O

Fill in the blanks with suitable '*Subjects*' in the following sentences:

1. _____can wait for you.
2. _____shall be having suggestions from his parents.
3. _____should know the secrets of her plan and programme.
4. _____had to go to London.
5. _____will have solved all the problems.
6. _____must not stop working.
7. _____ought to marry her.
8. _____had seen the movie directed by K. Ravi Shanker.
9. _____had to look after his parents.
10. _____used to go to the temple daily in the morning.
11. _____should try to win the match.
12. _____would like to meet you in the office.
13. _____had been listening this music for last 5 hours.
14. _____will have been swimming to keep your body fit.
15. _____must arrest the thieves before next Saturday.

EXERCISE NO. 4-P

Use the '*Verbs*' in your own sentences along with the '*Modal Auxiliaries*' given in the brackets :

1. Save [must]   **2.** Know [had to]   **3.** Watch [can]
4. Prepare [could]   **5.** Drink [had]   **6.** Construct [would]
7. Suspect [ought to]   **8.** Wear [should]   **9.** Cut [will]
10. Concentrate [would]   **11.** Direct [used to]   **12.** Insult [would have]
13. Sing [will be]   **14.** Catch [could]   **15.** Advise [must]

Note 1. : '**Be**' is the **First form of verb** so use Ing form of Verb = She will be singing a song. **(Or)** 3rd form of verb (Past Participle)

Ex: This book will be taken away by him.

(2) **'Have'** is also the **First form of verb** so use the 3rd form of Verb.

Example: He will have **gone** to Mumbai.

Verb 1st Form (base form)	Verb 2nd Form (Past form)	Verb 3rd Form (Perfect form)
Go	Went	Gone
Be	Was	Been
Have	Had	Had
Take	Took	Taken

Helping Verbs & Modal Aux. begin with any letter except H / I / A

Should — Shall

Might — May

Could — Can

Would — Will

Shall be — Should be

Must — Dare

Will have — Would have

Should have — Shall have

Would be — Will be

Used to

Rule 1. : These verbs can be used with *any Subject* as needed.

Rule 2. : *Verb 1st form* is always used as a *'Main Verb'*.

Example : She **could catch** the thief easily.

Verb 1st form

Exception : Need & Dare.

Note : Have / Be = Verb 1st form.

Fill in the blanks with suitable *'Subjects'* in the following sentences :

1. _____may help you regarding your plan.
2. _____might feed him, as he was hungry.
3. _____used to go to church every Sunday.
4. _____can act very well.
5. _____ought to meet me at the bus stop.
6. _____must take interest in study as exams are near.
7. _____could lose patience to see her.
8. _____should take care of all the students.
9. _____will abuse him for the mistakes.
10. _____would have cleared the confusion.
11. _____would be dancing on the stage.
12. _____might expose all the secrets.
13. _____will be writing a letter to the boss.
14. _____may pay all the debts in time.

Choose the 'Verbs' given in the brackets and fill in the blanks:

1. His brother may _____you to return all the documents. [promises / promise / promised]
2. She will _____if she works hard. [passes / pass / passed]
3. He would _____his work although it was too late to start it. [completes/complete/completed]
4. They might_____you to give them whatever is needed.[expect/ expects/expected]
5. I will _____forgotten it. [has / have / had]
6. My brother could _____you as he is a kind fellow.[understands/understood/ understand]
7. My mother will _____pleased to see you. [is / be / was / been]
8. Edward might _____to take these gifts from you. [dislike / dislikes / disliked]
9. Everybody should _____the meeting. [attend / attends / attended]
10. Our class teacher would _____to go for a picnic. [decides / decided / decide]
11. It may _____. [rain / rains / rained]
12. No one can _____ a great wrestler as Undertaker. [becomes / became / become]

EXERCISE NO. 4-S

Use the '*Verbs*' in your own sentences along with the '*Helping verbs*' or '*Modal auxiliaries*' given in the brackets :

1. pass [may]
2. pay [might]
3. finish [will]
4. utter [would]
5. punish [can]
6. become [could]
7. require [should]
8. expect [will]
9. remember [shall]
10. ask [might]
11. respect [could]
12. help [may]

Example: 1. You may pass the exam .
2. He might pay his fees in time.

EXERCISE NO. 4-T

Choose 'Verbs' from the brackets and fill in the blanks:

1. _____ I come in, sir? [would / may / will]
2. _____you like to buy some books ? [can / would / need]
3. He_____ [drink / used to drink / can drink] milk before his college life.
4. I wish, she _____never [would / can / used to] do this for me.
5. If she _____[called / calls / would call] me, I shall meet her.
6. You _____[needn't /didn't / mustn't] break the laws. It is a crime.
7. The MLA _____[had to / used to / will] change his party tomorrow.
8. How _____[need / dare / must] you touch me.
9. _____[can / would / may] I help you to clear all the accounts?
10. She _____[will not / could not /did not] pass the exam unless she stops watching TV.

Verbs [Helping / Modal Aux] with   **"O"**   at the end

Has t<u>o</u>   Have t<u>o</u>

Must have t<u>o</u>   Had t<u>o</u>   Will have t<u>o</u>

Shall have t<u>o</u>   Should have t<u>o</u>   Would have t<u>o</u>

Might have t<u>o</u>   Used t<u>o</u>

Ought t<u>o</u>

Rule: Verb 1st form is used after 'O'.

Example :

Verb 1st Form

She **has to** write a letter.
You **will have to** **complete** your work in time.
She **had to** **continue** the job.
I **would have to** **start** my project for my staff.
They **must have to** **write** a story about the modern women.

EXERCISE NO. 4-U

Make sentences by using the *'Main Verbs'* along with the *'Auxiliaries'* given in the brackets :

1. **Construct** (have to)
2. **Present** (shall have to)
3. **Defeat** (must have to)
4. **Wait** (should have to)
5. **Listen** (used to)
6. **Pray** (had to)
7. **Pluck** (could have to)
8. **Believe** (have to)
9. **Catch** (has to)
10. **Cook** (might have to)
11. **Strike** (had to)
12. **Betray** (shall have to)
13. **Oppose** (will have to)
14. **Offer** (should have to)
15. **Cheat** (must have to)
16. **Help** (has to)
17. **Find** (have to)
18. **Learn** (will have to)
19. **Correct** (had to)
20. **Throw** (have to)

BETTER TO DIE IN THE PRIME OF YOUTH FOR A GREAT CAUSE THAN TO LIVE LIKE AN OAK AND DO NOTHING. *–Dr. B.R. Ambedkar*

Persons

Me
My   Mine

First Person

Myself

First Person

M = First Person Singular Number

Exception : I = First Person Singular Number

There are three kinds of 'Persons' .

   (1) First Person.   (2) Second Person.   (3) Third Person.

O = First Person Plural Number

Our Ourself Ours

Ours

Ourselves

Exception : We / Us =. First Person Plural Number

Second Person

Y = **Second Person Singular & Plural Number**

Yourselves   **Y**ourselves

Yourself   **Y**ours

Your   **Y**ou

Third Person

T (or) H = **Third Person Singular Number (1ˢᵗ or 2ⁿᵈ letter)**

His

Himself   **H**erself

Him   **H**er

He   S**h**e

It   **Itself**   **Its**

T + H = **Third Person Plural Number**

They

Them   **T**heir

Theirs   **T**hemselves

Note : All the Nouns are Third Persons.

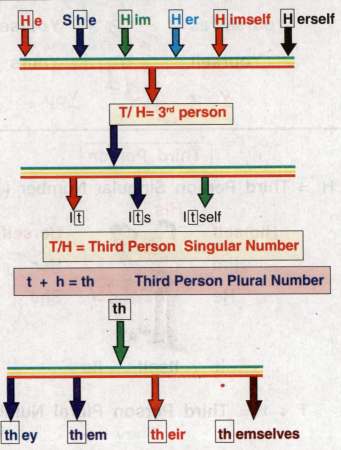

Another Diagram

3 rd PERSON

T/ H **letter** <u>first</u> **or** <u>second letter</u> **of** '<u>Pronoun</u>' **indicates** <u>third person</u>.

He   **S**h**e**   **H**im   **H**er   **H**imself   **H**erself

T/ H= 3rd person

I**t**   I**t**s   I**t**self

T/H = Third Person Singular Number

t + h = th   Third Person Plural Number

th

they   **th**em   **th**eir   **th**emselves

T + H = Third Person Plural = They / them / their / themselves.

All Nouns are 3rd Persons: Rocky / Sam / Paris / Pen etc.

EXERCISE NO. 4-V

Find out the '*Person*' and tell its kind and number :

1. Sam entered into my house like a bull in the china shop.
2. A small leak can sink a great ship.
3. You must work hard to make your dream come true in your life.
4. The great things are done when men and mountain meet, these are not done by jostling in the street.
5. Your silence is your weapon.

6. I do not know the secret of your success.

7. A house full of books is like a garden of flowers.

8. Today's plan decides tomorrow's destiny.

9. As you do not rely on me, I cannot do anything for you.

10. He has to think twice before coming to the final conclusion.

11. Your book is the golden key to open the treasure of success for you.

12. It is true that you will get a red carpet welcome.

13. I know my duty well, please do not try to teach me regarding my project.

14. You open your book once in a blue moon.

15. They cannot understand the pain of a poor man.

16. You will have to accept that he has double eyes.

17. If your finger is itching, you must work hard.

18. This project is a fool's paradise for us.

19. You cannot indulge in a foul play with your friends.

20. You can say that Caesar was a fountain of justice.

**IT IS THE GREATEST OF ALL MISTAKES TO DO NOTHING,
BECAUSE YOU CAN ONLY DO LITTLE.**

SYDNEY SMITH

TENSE

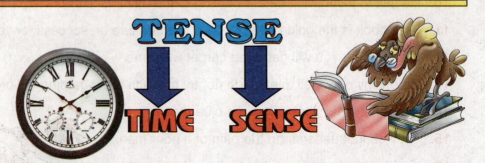

TENSE
↓ ↓
TIME   **SENSE**

What is a Tense ?

Time & **Sense** are the two words that make the word **Tense.**

"Tense" tells us about the sense of time in a sentence.

There are three 'Tenses'.

1. Present Tense.   2. Past Tense.   3. Future Tense.

IDENTIFY THE TENSES		
Verb **1st form**	Verb **2nd form**	
S **E** Present	**D** Past	**L** Future

[S / E / D / L] = Last letter of helping verb or 1ˢᵗ verb

1. Ing = Continuous.

2. H + Verb 3ʳᵈ form = Perfect.

[Has gone/ Had gone/Have gone]

3. H = Has / Have / Had.

4. Was / Were = Past Tense.

5. Am = Present.

NOTE : Been is the 3ʳᵈ form of Verb.

1. Verb 1ˢᵗ form = Go [V-1] be

2. Verb 2ⁿᵈ form = Went [V-2] was

3. Verb 3rd form = Gone [V-3] been

4. Verb 4ᵗʰ form = Going [V-ing] being

5. Verb 5ᵗʰ form = Goes [V-s] is

HOW TO USE THIS TABLE

VERB 1st form	Verb 2nd form	
S / E	D	L
Present	Past	Future

Has **H**ave **H**ad

H + Verb 3rd form = Perfect.

1. **Ing** = **Continuous** Was / Were = Past Tense. Am = Present.

Present = **S / E**   Past = **D**   Future = **L**

Perfect = **H**   Continuous = **ING**

(1) She plays cricket. **[Simple Present Tense]**

S = **Present**

(2) She played cricket. **[Simple Past Tense]**

D = **Past**

(3) She will play cricket. **[Simple Future Tense]**

L = **Future**

(4) She is playing cricket. **[Present Continuous]**

Present = **s**   **ing** = **Continuous**

(5) She was playing cricket. **[Past Continuous]**

Past   ing   = **Continuous**

(6) She will be playing cricket. **[Future Continuous]**

L = **Future**   ing = **Continuous**

(7) She has played cricket. **[Present Perfect]**

Perfect   Present

(8) She had played cricket. **[Past Perfect]**

Perfect   Past

(9) She will have played cricket. **[Future Perfect]**

Future   Perfect

(10) She has been playing cricket.

[Present Perfect Continuous]

Perfect   Present   ing = **Continuous**

(11) She had been playing cricket.

[Past Perfect Continuous]

Perfect   Past   ing = **Continuous**

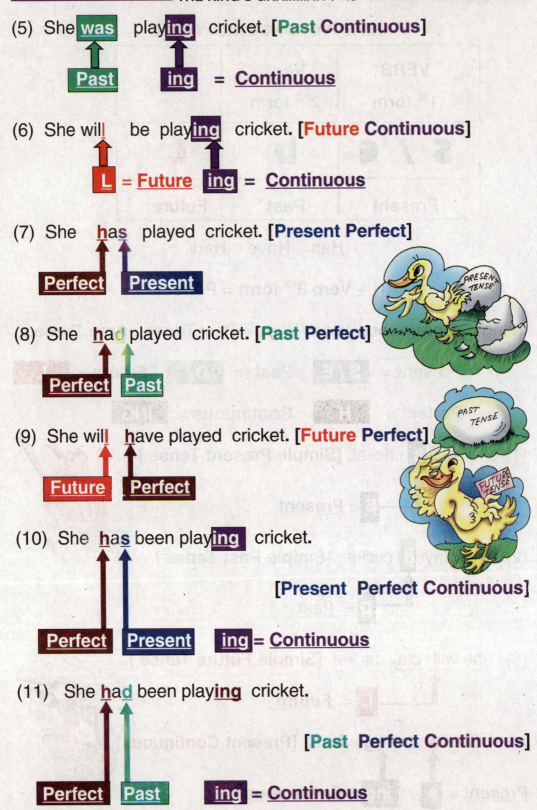

(12) She will have been play**ing** cricket.

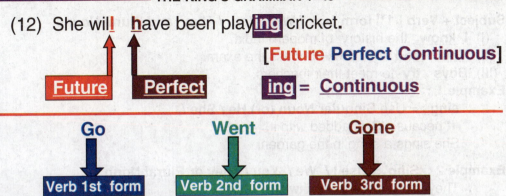

[Future Perfect Continuous]

| Future | Perfect | **ing** = Continuous |

Go — **Verb 1st form**

Went — **Verb 2nd form**

Gone — **Verb 3rd form**

How To Change Into Other Tense
An Easy Approach

TENSE TABLE

	PRESENT	PAST	FUTURE
Simple	She goes	She went	She will go
Continuous	She is going	She was going	She will be going
Perfect	She has gone	She had gone	She will have gone
Perfect Con.	She has been going	She had been going	She will have been going.

EXERCISE NO. 5-A

Change the following sentences into all the *'Tenses'* as shown in examples above:

1. Samuel does his duty.
2. Tom plays football in the garden.
3. She works hard to pass the exam.
4. They try to win the match.
5. Nero sings a song for my friends.

KINDS OF PRESENT TENSE

1. Simple Present Tense
2. Present Continuous Tense
3. Present Perfect Tense
4. Present Perfect Continuous Tense

SIMPLE PRESENT TENSE

Subject + Verb s/es [or] 1st form

A. Singular Subject + Verb S / ES = He / She / It & Singular Noun

  (I) **He** write**s** a letter to his parents.

  (II) **It** rain**s** heavily.

  (III) **Ram** go**es** to the college.

Subject + Verb [1ˢᵗ form] = I / We / You / They and Plural Nouns

 (I) **I** <u>know</u> the history of modern India.

 (II) **You** <u>read</u> the book to pass the exam.

 (III) **Boys** <u>try</u> to meet their teachers.

Example 1 :

 <u>sing**s**</u> = Use **Singular Noun (or) He / She /**
 It because '**S**' is added with it.
 She sing**s** a song in the garden.

Example 2 : 'Sing' = Use I / We / You / They or Plural Noun

 They sing a song very well.

USES OF 'DOES NOT' & 'DO NOT'

A.   **Do not = I / We / You / They & Plural Noun**

B.   **Does Not = He / She / It & Singular Noun**

DOES NOT

 A. She like**s** swimming.

 B. She do**es** not like**s** swimming.

 C. She **does not like** swimming.

 A. He want**s** to discontinue his friendship.

 B. He do**es** not want to discontinue his friendship.

 C. He **does not want** to discontinue his friendship.

  These answers have not been given according to the rules of '**Transformation of sentences**' but these answers have been given according to the rules of the '**Formation of sentences**'.

USES OF 'DO NOT'

 I writ**e** a letter to you .

 I **do** not writ**e** a letter.

 NOTE : There is **no s/es** in write so '**do not**' is used.

Example–A

 1. <u>She</u> **does not** write a story.

 2. <u>He</u> **does not** come here to meet you .

 3. <u>It</u> **does not** rain heavily in Mumbai.

Example – B

1. I do not want to meet her.
2. **You** do not try to get it.
3. **They** do not understand you.
4. **We** do not play football to win the match.

NOTE: Do not / does not = Verb [1st form]

　　e.g. He **does not** go to meet his parents.

　　You **do not** go to collect your books.

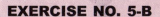

EXERCISE NO. 5-B

Use 'do not' or 'does not' in the following sentences :

1. This black sheep creates so many problems.
2. Your father looks like a true blue blood.
3. She gets a feather in her cap by getting a gold medal.
4. The grey beard man teaches English very nicely.
5. You think about your future.
6. They watch TV at your house.
7. The Sun shines brightly in the sky.
8. John wears different hats to succeed in his life.
9. Birds of same feather have a proper co-ordination.
10. Sam likes fair weather friend only.
11. We eat food in the morning.
12. The beggar sits under the tree.
13. A small bird chirps near the windows.
14. Henry sleeps at night.
15. They talk in the classroom.
16. You add fuel to fire in this hot discussion.
17. He behaves like an ostrich in the office.
18. He meets me once in a bluemoon.
19. John boasts like a paper tiger.
20. You work like a spring chicken.

Simple Present Tense

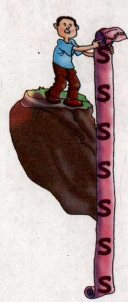

She write **s** a letter to clear the fact.

He work **s** hard to get the goal of his life.

It rain **s** heavily in the morning.

Henry prepare **s** for his final exam.

Sam cook **s** food for his friends.

She doe **s** not know the reality of life.

He doe **s** not eat anything.

He / She / It / singular noun + Verb + s / es

I/ You / We / They / Plural Noun + Verb

You **correct** your mistakes.

We **think** about our projects.

They **know** the real story.

EXERCISE NO. 5-C

Use the words given below in your sentences in 'Simple Present Tense' :

1. beats	**2.** choose	**3.** drives	**4.** wears
5. fight	**6.** fly	**7.** swims	**8.** take
9. works	**10.** wins	**11.** eats	**12.** write
13. rings	**14.** speaks	**15.** strike	

Simple Present Tense shows habit, general truth, universal truth, daily routine, time table, etc.

EXERCISE NO. 5-D

Use the 'Verb' in your own sentences in 'Simple Present Tense' using 'do not' or 'does not'.

1. Collect	**2.** Carry	**3.** Borrow	**4.** Burn
5. Steal	**6.** Take	**7.** Act	**8.** Climb
9. Defeat	**10.** Buy	**11.** Build	**12.** Boil
13. Catch	**14.** Throw	**15.** Write.	

EXERCISE NO. 5-E

Fill in the blanks with suitable 'Verbs' in 'Simple Present Tense' :

1. My brother _____ English very well **[speak]**.

2. You _____ your friend everyday **[abuse]**.

3. I _____ my brother to help you. **[call]**

4. Your father _____ money in the bank. **[deposit]**

5. All the teachers _____ their salary. **[take]**

6. Harry _____ fast to get the gold medal . **[run]**

7. The babies _____ for milk. **[cry]**

8. They _____ well to win the match. **[play]**

9. She _____ a book to pass the exam. **[read]**

10. My brother and your sister _____ to catch the thief. **[try]**

11. The priest _____ the door in the morning. **[open]**

12. All the students _____ the classroom in the evening . **[leave]**

13. The sun _____ in the sky today. **[shine]**

14. My book _____ stolen by her. **[is / are]**

15. You _____ hard to get your aim. **[work]**

EXERCISE NO. 5-F

Fill in the blanks with suitable *'Verbs'* in *'Simple Present Tense'* :

1. My brother _____ so many problems. **[create / creates]**
2. Sita and Ram _____ to forest with Laxman. **[go / goes]**
3. She _____ a good idea. **[have / has]**
4. All the students _____ noise in the class . **[make / makes]**
5. Tina _____ a car on the road. **[drive / drives]**
6. I _____ a letter to my brother. **[write / writes]**
7. You _____ Marathi very fluently. **[speak / speaks]**
8. Sincerity never _____ waste. **[go / goes]**
9. A rolling stone _____ no moss. **[gather / gathers]**
10. Fortune _____ the brave. **[favour / favours]**
11. Knowledge _____ the way to success. **[show / shows]**
12. Good teachers always _____ very hard. **[work / works]**
13. I _____ to succeed in my life. **[try / tries]**
14. God _____ those who love the poor people. **[love / loves]**

Simple Past Tense

I di**d** my duty.

You helpe**d** me in the time of need.

She jumpe**d** off her horse.

They permitte**d** me to address the meeting.

We invite**d** them for dinner.

She di**d** not tell anything.

They poste**d** the letter yesterday.

We should use the second form or past form of verb.

Go [1ˢᵗ form] / Went [2ⁿᵈ form] / Gone [3ʳᵈ form]

Simple Past Tense is used for **story / accident / incident / report** or **any event** occurred in the past.

EXERCISE NO. 5-G

Use the '*Verbs*' given below and frame your sentences in '*Simple Past Tense*' and then use did not in the sentences :

1. Climb	**2.** Confuse	**3.** Cross	**4.** Forget
5. Get	**6.** Choose	**7.** Blow	**8.** Run
9. Polish	**10.** Swim	**11.** Promise	**12.** Praise
13. Laugh	**14.** Kill.		

Ex : She climbed on a tree.   She *did not* climb on a tree. [use did not]

EXERCISE NO. 5-H

Write the correct from of '*Verb*' in the gaps suitable for '*Simple Past Tense*'.

1. She _____ in the temple for you. **(pray)**
2. Rocky _____ me fool on 1st April. **(make)**
3. Swami Vivekanand _____ everywhere to guide the people towards happiness. **(preach)**
4. Undertaker_____himself to be the mightiest wrestler in the world. **(prove)**
5. My mother _____ food for everybody yesterday. **(cook)**
6. Milton _____ a great poet. **(be)**
7. You _____ food to the poor people. **(feed)**
8. I _____ to meet her. **(wish)**
9. Sunanda _____ my brother into the well. **(push)**
10. Bernard Shaw _____ "Arms and the men." **(write)**
11. Sushmita Sen was _____ with the award of Miss Universe. **(crown)**

EXERCISE NO. 5-I

Change the following sentences into '*Simple Past Tense*' and then use 'did not' :

1. Jack gets a wooden spoon after his failure.
2. Tom presents a crystal clear explanation.
3. My brother cracks jokes in the class.
4. Almitra helps her housemaid in household work.
5. Peter knows about the flying saucer.
6. Sam likes icy sugar for a cup of coffee.
7. He buys a magic carpet.
8. I pray to God for your golden future.
9. He pins his hope on his new published book.
10. I receive ill advices for this project.
11. She   gets up at cock's crow time for morning prayer.
12. The cattle graze in the field.

Simple Future Tense

He will do his duty.

She will come here.

They will get success.

Sam will close the door.

I shall complete my work.

We shall create a history.

You will present the project.

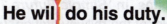

I/We = shall
Rest all subjects = will
In case of determination / threat / command etc. it will reverse.
I/We = will
Rest all subjects = shall

EXERCISE NO. 5-J

Use the 'Verbs' given below and frame your sentences in 'Simple Future Tense'.

1. Punish	**2.** Listen	**3.** Love	**4.** Prepare
5. Prove	**6.** Finish	**7.** Pluck	**8.** Earn
9. Jump	**10.** Compare	**11.** Defeat	**12.** Cook
13. Carry	**14.** Attack	**15.** Close	

EXERCISE NO. 5-K

Fill the 'Verbs' in the gaps in 'Simple Future Tense':

1. She _____ for him at the railway station. **(wait)**
2. I _____ books from the market. **(buy)**
3. Jack _____ you for your help. **(remember)**
4. All the Hindus _____ to temple for prayer in the morning. **(go)**
5. We _____ the match very easily. **(win)**
6. My father _____ me Maths for the final exam. **(teach)**
7. They _____ a story for the new movie. **(write)**
8. You _____ to meet my sister. **(try)**
9. The sailors _____ across the river. **(swim)**
10. I _____ the confusion soon. **(clear)**
11. Sam _____ the sums and come to meet you. **(solve)**
12. The worker _____ the work next week. **(stop)**
13. He _____ your father regarding his confusion. **(meet)**
14. All the staff _____ bonus after 2 weeks. **(get)**

EXERCISE NO. 5-L

Change the following sentences into 'Simple Future Tense'.

1. She wakes up at the dead of night.
2. You prepare breakfast in a willy-nilly manner.
3. I correct all my mistakes very quickly.
4. You change yourself in the time of prosperity.
5. My father suggests me to help her.
6. Mr. Joy talks about the remedy after the loss in business.
7. The birds chirp near my house in the morning.
8. He writes an article with a pen dipped in poison.
9. I accept all the mistakes of mine.
10. Miss Susan has a good idea about it.
11. Macbeth reacts like a man of blood.
12. Kanika guides me regarding my settlement in U.K.
13. His friends encourage him to go abroad.
14. She listens her result with her sinking heart.

Present Continuous

S **Ing**

She **is** coming here to meet you.

Sumo is reading a novel now.

He **is** dreaming to get a prize.

It **is** falling down.

E **Ing**

They are sleeping there.

We are making a plan for your project.

You are cracking jokes in the class.

I **am** mending my shoes.

PRESENT CONTINUOUS
Subject + is / am / are + Verb - ing

EXERCISE NO. 5-M

Use the '*Verbs*' given below and write the sentences in '*Present Continuous Tense*' :

1. Catch	**2.** Cut	**3.** Wash	**4.** Watch
5. Touch	**6.** Talk	**7.** Search	**8.** Tease
9. Teach	**10.** Sell	**11.** Try	**12.** Tell
13. Serve	**14.** Shave	**15.** See.	

EXERCISE NO. 5-N

Fill in the blanks with the correct form of '*Verbs*' suitable for '*Present Continuous Tense*' :

1. All the hunters_____ a tiger in the jungle. **(hunt)**
2. My teacher_____ English very slowly. **(teach)**
3. You _____ a letter to your parents. **(write)**
4. She _____ a house nearby the railway station. **(build)**
5. John _____ well to win the Paramvir Chakra. **(fight)**
6. Your friends _____ at you. **(laugh)**
7. His friend_____very fast to get the gold medal. **(run)**
8. Miss. Bell _____back from Paris. **(return)**
9. Nicky _____ · his mistakes. **(show)**
10. Your brother _____ his pen in the pocket of his red coat. **(put)**
11. Mr. Pandit _____on the Gita, a holy book. **(preach)**

EXERCISE NO. 5-O

Change the following sentences into '*Present Continuous*' and then use 'not' in the same sentence: e.g. She is preparing her breakfast. She is not preparing her breakfast.

1. You ask questions in French only.
2. He throws stones at glass houses.
3. I am collecting money from my clients.
4. She challenges everybody with iron hands.
5. You enjoy TV with your bosom friends.
6. Miss Blair starts her work on firm footing.
7. The men in blue arrested the murderer with blood in his hand.
8. I eat food in the lap of luxury.
9. They try to cheat you.
10. My brother admires his skill.
11. His ears were burning to know about his results.

Past Continuous

PAST **CONTINUOUS**

Was Ing

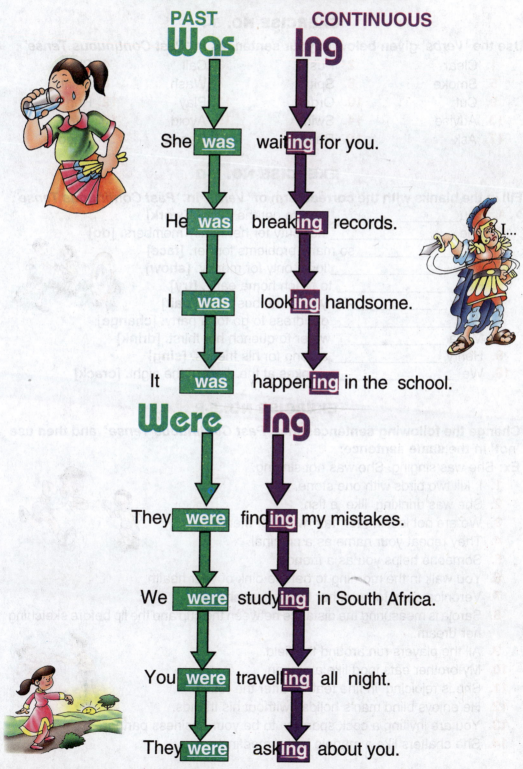

She **was** wait**ing** for you.

He **was** break**ing** records.

I **was** look**ing** handsome.

It **was** happen**ing** in the school.

Were Ing

They **were** find**ing** my mistakes.

We **were** study**ing** in South Africa.

You **were** travell**ing** all night.

They **were** ask**ing** about you.

When a work was continued in past, Past Continuous Tense is used.
Subject + Was / Were + Verb - Ing

EXERCISE NO. 5-P

Use the 'Verbs' given below in your sentences in 'Past Continuous Tense' :

1. Clear	2. Push	3. Call	4. Clean
5. Smoke	6. Spit	7. Wash	8. Paint
9. Cut	10. Order	11. Play	12. Run
13. Advise	14. Swim	15. Avoid	16. Turn
17. Ask	18. Read	19. Repeat	20. Choose.

EXERCISE NO. 5-Q

Fill in the blanks with the correct form of 'Verbs' in 'Past Continuous Tense':

1. You_____ hard to get the target. **[work]**
2. She _____ her duty for her family members. **[do]**
3. I _____ so many problems for her. **[face]**
4. They _____ love, only for money. **[show]**
5. He _____ to reach home early. **[try]**
6. Peter _____ for you at the bus stop. **[wait]**
7. We _____ our dress to go for a party. **[change]**
8. Maria _____ water to quench her thirst. **[drink]**
9. Henry _____ a song for his friends. **[sing]**
10. We _____ jokes at the dead of the night. **[crack]**

EXERCISE NO. 5-R

Change the following sentences into 'Past Continuous Tense' and then use 'not' in the same sentence:

Ex: She was singing. She was not singing.

1. I kill two birds with one stone.
2. She was drinking like a fish.
3. We are not looking for fair weather friends.
4. They repeat your name as a criminal.
5. Someone helps you as a friend.
6. You walk in the morning to get the pink of your health.
7. Veronica goes to meet her English teacher.
8. Saroja is measuring the distance between the cup and the lip before sketching her dream.
9. All the players run around the field.
10. My brother eats food like a pigeon.
11. She is rejoicing in fine feather after the result.
12. He enjoys blind man's holiday without his friends.
13. You are inviting a cock sparrow to be your business partner.
14. She chatters like a magpie in the meeting.

Future Continuous

Generally I / We + shall — Rest all Subjects + will

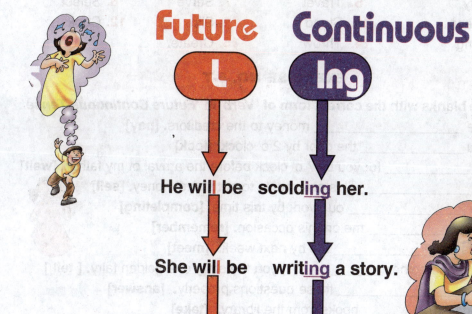

Future
L

Continuous
Ing

He will be scolding her.

She will be writing a story.

They will be preparing for a test.

I shall be solving sums.

Lovina will be playing cricket.

John will be clearing his accounts.

HE WILL DO HIS DUTY.

Sub + shall / will + be + verb- ing

Generally I / We = **shall**

Rest all the Subjects = **will**

In case of command / threat / determination etc., it is reverse .

I / We = **will**

Rest all the Subjects = **shall**

EXERCISE NO. 5-S

Use the '*Verbs*' given below in your sentences in '*Future Continuous Tense*':

1. Give	**2.** Weep	**3.** Walk	**4.** Bet
5. Cry	**6.** Travel	**7.** Serve	**8.** Select
9. Sleep	**10.** Stand	**11.** Slip	**12.** Cook
13. Sing	**14.** Throw	**15.** Create.	

EXERCISE NO. 5-T

Fill in the blanks with the correct form of '*Verb*' in '*Future Continuous Tense*':

1. She _____ money to the creditors. **[pay]**
2. You _____ the door by 2 o' clock. **[lock]**
3. I _____ for you by 7 o' clock before the arrival of my father. **[wait]**
4. He _____ his ornaments to get some money. **[sell]**
5. We _____ our work by this time. **[completing]**
6. Rosy _____ me on this occasion. **[remember]**
7. Miss Oak _____ me by next week. **[meet]**
8. My grandmother _____ you the story of a golden fairy. **[tell]**
9. John _____ these questions properly. **[answer]**
10. Monalisa _____ books from the library. **[take]**

EXERCISE NO. 5-U

Change the following sentences into '*Future Continuous Tense*' and then use not in the same sentence :

e.g. **She will be looking for a better chance.**

She will not be looking for a better chance.

1. She will feel broken hearted after getting the news of her husband's death.
2. I give you a chance to speak the truth.
3. Ricky devoted his body and soul to the nation.
4. Victor finds himself between the devil and the deep sea after his failure.
5. She brushes her teeth in the morning.
6. We continue our work from the bottom of our heart.
7. Kanika feels like butter on both sides after getting her gold medal.
8. Mita guides me to find a bosom friend.
9. Vinod inspires me to achieve the target.
10. I take suggestions from Mr. & Mrs. Devan.
11. Peter is getting a red carpet welcome after the victory.
12. My blood is running cold during the horror show.
13. Miss Bell is trying to step into her uncle's shoes to get his property.
14. Her illness is reducing her to a bag of bones.
15. She was beating a pickpocket in the market.

Present Perfect Tense

Verb 1st form = Go / Verb 2nd t form = Went / Verb 3rd form = Gon

Has / Have + Verb 3rd form = Present Perfect

(A) I / We / You / They / Plural Noun + have

(B) He / She / It / Singular Noun + has

Perfect	Present

H   S

She **has** **caught** a thief.
Verb 3rd form

He **has** **completed** his work.
Verb 3rd form

It **has** **cleared** the fact.
Verb 3rd form

John **has** **taken** my books.
Verb 3rd form

David **has** **examined** it properly.
Verb 3rd form

E = Present

I **have** **lost** my patience.
Verb 3rd form

We **have** **missed** a golden chance.
Verb 3rd form

They **have** **sold** your computer.
Verb 3rd form

Present Perfect Tense is used when the work is completed a few moments before or in near past.

Subject + has / have + Verb 3rd form

He / She / It / Singular Noun + has

I / We / You / They / Plural Noun + have

EXERCISE NO. 5-V

Use the *Verbs* given below in your sentences in '*Present Perfect Tense*' :

1. Lose	**2.** Gain	**3.** Prepare	**4.** Correct	**5.** Come
6. Publish	**7.** Build	**8.** Sell	**9.** Buy	**10.** Cheat
11. Catch	**12.** Teach	**13.** Scratch	**14.** Play	**15.** Watch.

EXERCISE NO. 5-W

Fill in the blanks with the correct form of '*Verb*' in '*Present Perfect Tense*' :

1. I _____ the bell to call you. **(ring)**
2. You _____ for me to get my book. **(wait)**
3. She _____ her work to please her boss. **(complete)**
4. They _____ loudly in order to disturb others. **(cry)**
5. It _____ everywhere. **(snow)**
6. Neha _____ very well in the movie. **(act)**
7. All the students _____ the river. **(cross)**
8. My friend _____ the fact after a long discussion. **(tell)**
9. Sonali _____ my book to study for exam. **(take)**
10. The driver _____ a car to earn some money. **(hired)**

EXERCISE NO. 5-X

Change the following sentences into '*Present Perfect Tense*' and then use not in the same sentence: e.g. You have prepared a plan. You have not prepared a plan.

1. I pray to God for you.
2. She burst into tears after getting a pink slip from her office.
3. You take the bull by the horn to succeed in your life.
4. They call with bad names to the lazy workers.
5. You bought a gold watch from his shop.
6. Robin honoured him with a cap in his hand.
7. Richard builds a house of cards to cheat us.
8. All the robbers rob the bank at the gun-point.
9. The policeman warns the chicken-hearted people regarding riot.
10. My family members help me for my study.

EXERCISE NO. 5-Y

Use the '*Verbs*' given below in your sentences in '*Present Perfect Tense*':

1. Reach	**2.** Leave	**3.** Eat	**4.** Know	**5.** Sleep
6. Show	**7.** Import	**8.** Help	**9.** Pay	**10.** Pass
11. Expose	**12.** Clear	**13.** Take	**14.** Suspect	**15.** Direct
16. Dance	**17.** Attend	**18.** Feed	**19.** Cheat	**20.** Sing
21. Get				

Past Perfect Tense

[Subject + had + Verb 3rd form]

Go/ Went /
Gone = Verb 3rd form = Past Participle]

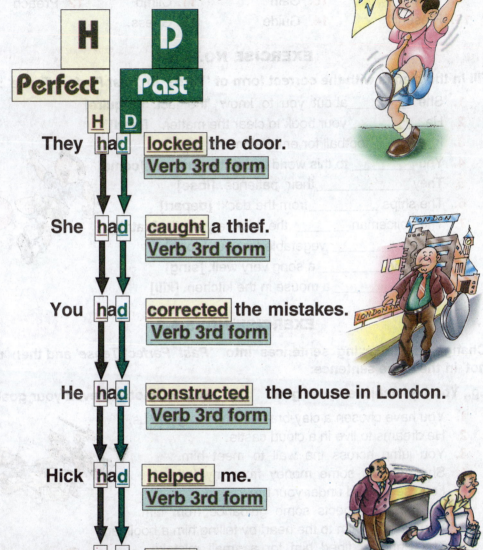

H **D**

Perfect **Past**

H **D**

They **had** **locked** the door.
Verb 3rd form

She **had** **caught** a thief.
Verb 3rd form

You **had** **corrected** the mistakes.
Verb 3rd form

He **had** **constructed** the house in London.
Verb 3rd form

Hick **had** **helped** me.
Verb 3rd form

Miss Dewan **had** **gone** to Delhi.
Verb 3rd form

I **had** **written** a movie script.
Verb 3rd form

EXERCISE NO. 5-Z

Use the 'Verbs' given below in your sentences in 'Past Perfect Tense' :

1. Stop	2. Start	3. Lose	4. Calculate
5. Sell	6. Translate	7. Say	8. Drive
9. Whip	10. Gain	11. Climb	12. Preach
13. Present	14. Guide	15. Guess.	

EXERCISE NO. 5-A-1

Fill in the blanks with the correct form of 'Verbs' in 'Past Perfect Tense' :

1. She _____about you to know the fact. **[enquire]**
2. He _____your book to clear the matter. **[read]**
3. I _____ football for entertainment. **[play]**
4. You _____ to this world to get the success. **[come]**
5. They _____their patience. **[lose]**
6. The ships _____from the dock. **[depart]**
7. The policeman _____ the thief very easily. **[catch]**
8. Mohan _____ vegetable for you. **[cook]**
9. My friend _____ a song very well. **[sing]**
10. Sanjay _____ a mouse in the kitchen. **[kill]**

EXERCISE NO. 5-A-2

Change the following sentences into 'Past Perfect Tense' and then use 'not' in the same sentence:

e.g., You had achieved your goal.   You had not achieved your goal.

1. You have chosen a clay-brained man to guide us.
2. He dreams to live in a cloud castle.
3. You jump across the wall to meet him.
4. She borrows some money from my father.
5. I can see cloud under your brow.
6. My brother expects some guidance from him.
7. You have cut him to the heart by telling him a hooligan.
8. The Principal fined him for a small mistake.
9. The children have left the classroom like flying crows.
10. He was dead drunk in the party.
11. He earns to live life like an ivory tower.
12. My boss has terminated an absent-minded officer.
13. A loudmouth fellow has opened this secret.
14. She has employed a man with rocks on his head to complete this work.
15. Being wet behind his ears, he has not understood this project.

Future Perfect Tense

[Subject + shall / will + have + Verb 3rd form (Past Participle)]

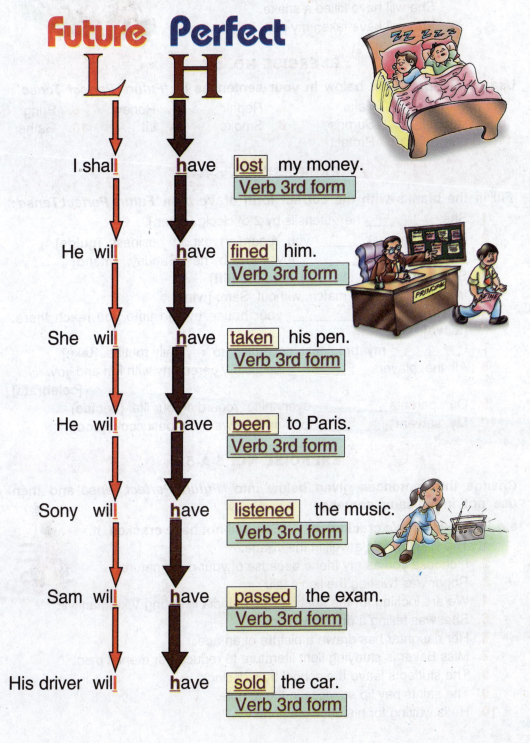

Future L   Perfect H

I shall   have   <u>lost</u> my money.
<u>Verb 3rd form</u>

He will   have   <u>fined</u> him.
<u>Verb 3rd form</u>

She will   have   <u>taken</u> his pen.
<u>Verb 3rd form</u>

He will   have   <u>been</u> to Paris.
<u>Verb 3rd form</u>

Sony will   have   <u>listened</u> the music.
<u>Verb 3rd form</u>

Sam will   have   <u>passed</u> the exam.
<u>Verb 3rd form</u>

His driver will   have   <u>sold</u> the car.
<u>Verb 3rd form</u>

Future Perfect Tense is used when work will be completed in future.

Subject + shall / will + have + Verb [3rd form]

I / We + shall / Rest all Subjects + will

Example : I shall have decorated my house.

She will have killed a snake.

You will have taken my pen.

EXERCISE NO. 5-A-3

Use the 'Verbs' given below in your sentences in 'Future Perfect Tense':

1. Present	2. Take	3. Repair	4. Renew	5. Bring
6. Distribute	7. Surprise	8. Smoke	9. Lit	10. Gather
11. Break	12. Protect			

EXERCISE NO. 5-A-4

Fill in the blanks with the correct form of 'Verb' in 'Future Perfect Tense':

1. She_____ her utensils by 2 o' clock. **[clean]**
2. My brother _____ you regarding export business. **[guide]**
3. The cobbler _____ my shoes by next Sunday. **[mend]**
4. Sachin _____ the ball for a six. **[lift]**
5. India _____ the match without Sam. **[win]**
6. The beggars_____ your house by the time you reach there. **[leave]**
7. I _____ my breakfast according to my daily routine. **[take]**
8. All the players _____ the victory ceremony with fun and joy. **[celebrate]**
9. Our parents _____ everything regarding our life. **[decide]**
10. My servant _____ food as if he were the best cook. **[cook]**

EXERCISE NO. 5-A-5

Change the sentences given below into 'Future Perfect Tense' and then use 'not' in the same sentence:

e.g., **She will have cracked it.** **She will not have cracked it.**

1. The villagers dig a well in the village.
2. I choose you as my friend because of your good nature.
3. Roger was twisting the lion's tail.
4. We are looking for the floating light of India like King Vikramaditya.
5. She was telling a dry story as dust.
6. Her daughter has drawn a picture of an ape.
7. Miss Baker is studying light literature to reduce her mental pain.
8. The students leave the school by 5 o' clock.
9. The saints pay lip services in the temple.
10. He is waiting for his duck diamond.

Present Perfect Continuous Tense

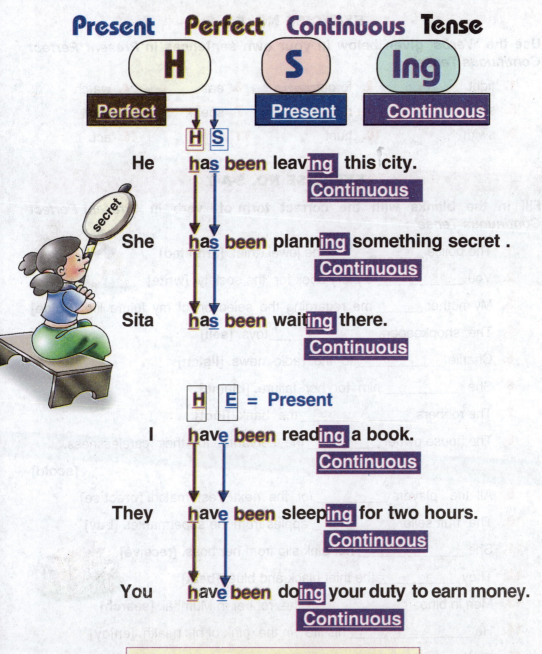

H **S** **Ing**

Perfect — Present — Continuous

H **S**

He **has been** leaving this city.
Continuous

She **has been** planning something secret .
Continuous

Sita **has been** waiting there.
Continuous

H **E** = Present

I **have been** reading a book.
Continuous

They **have been** sleeping for two hours.
Continuous

You **have been** doing your duty to earn money.
Continuous

Present Perfect Continuous Tense

Subject + has / have + been + Verb - ing.
Singular Noun / He / She / It + has.
Plural Noun / I / We / You / They + have.

1. He has been doing his duty.
2. You have been creating so many problems.

EXERCISE NO. 5-A-6

Use the '*Verbs*' given below in your own sentences in '*Present Perfect Continuous Tense*' :

1. fight
2. forget
3. eat
4. watch
5. steal
6. run
7. speak
8. spoil
9. swim
10. hunt
11. sink
12. act.

EXERCISE NO. 5-A-7

Fill in the blanks with the correct form of verb in '*Present Perfect Continuous Tense*' :

1. The police _____ the jewel thief. **[arrested]**
2. You _____ a story book for the society. **[write]**
3. My mother _____ me regarding the selection of my future life. **[guide]**
4. The shopkeepers _____ toys. **[sell]**
5. Charlie _____ to the radio news. **[listen]**
6. She _____ him for her failure. **[blame]**
7. The robbers _____ the bank. **[loot]**
8. The house owner _____ the servants for their carelessness. **[scold]**
9. All the players _____ for the next Test match. **[practise]**
10. The fruit seller_____ apples from the supermarket. **[buy]**
11. She _____her pink slip from her boss. **[receive]**
12. They _____ the thief black and blue. **[beat]**
13. Men in blue _____ the robber in Mumbai. **[search]**
14. He _____his life in the pink of his health. **[enjoy]**
15. This grey beard man _____you regarding your future. **[advise]**

Past Perfect Continuous Tense

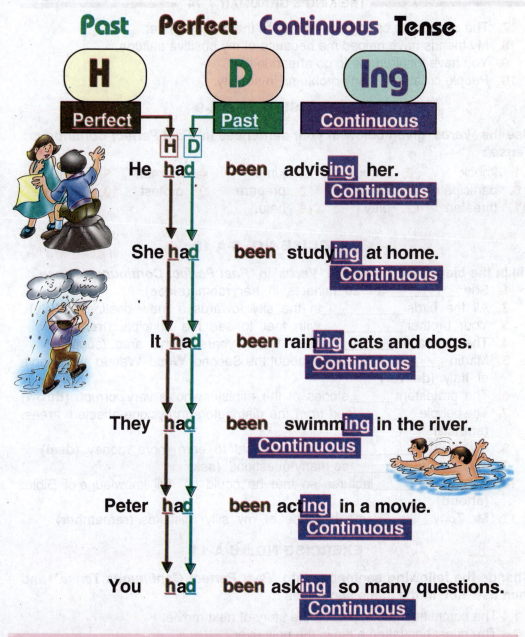

H	D	Ing
Perfect	Past	Continuous

He **had** **been** advis**ing** her.
Continuous

She **had** **been** study**ing** at home.
Continuous

It **had** **been** rain**ing** cats and dogs.
Continuous

They **had** **been** swimm**ing** in the river.
Continuous

Peter **had** **been** act**ing** in a movie.
Continuous

You **had** **been** ask**ing** so many questions.
Continuous

EXERCISE NO. 5-A-8

Change the sentences given below in 'Past Perfect Continuous Tense' and then use 'not' in the same sentences :

1. She was discussing about the lame duck.
2. We are looking for an eagle-eyed detective.
3. They were eating dutch lunch in the canteen.
4. The priest is cursing the people for deceiving him.
5. Allena has broken all the plates.
6. Samuel is trying to throw dust into my eyes.

7. The cheats are calling bad names to the money-lender.
8. My friends have helped me because of my positive attitude.
9. You have inspired me to go ahead in life.
10. People create so many problems in society.

EXERCISE NO. 5-A-9

Use the '*Verbs*' given below in your sentences in '*Past Perfect Continuous Tense*':

1. knock	2. introduce	3. jump	4. murmur	5. listen
6. participate	7. laugh	8. prepare	9. protest	10. struggle
11. threaten	12. play	13. help.		

EXERCISE NO. 5-A-10

Fill in the blanks with suitable '*Verbs*' in '*Past Perfect Continuous Tense*':

1. She _____ for 20 minutes in her room. **(sleep)**
2. All the birds_____in the sky towards a new destination. **(fly)**
3. Your brother_____with fear to see the Principal. **(tremble)**
4. The contractor_____water for 20 years in this area. (supply)
5. Martin _____ a speech about the Second World War to the people of Italy. **(deliver)**
6. The protesters_____stones at the minister who is very corrupt. **(throw)**
7. The people_____food from the distributors in cyclone-affected areas. **(snatch)**
8. My brother_____with the proposal to earn more money. **(deal)**
9. The police_____so many questions. **(ask)**
10. Jesus_____lectures so that he could get full knowledge of Bible. **(attend)**
11. Mr. Tony _____me because of my silly mistakes. **(remember)**

EXERCISE NO. 5-A-11

Change the following sentences into '*Past Perfect Continuous Tense*' and then use 'not' in the same sentences :

1. The committee has approved the story of next movie.
2. The priest has taken a dip in the holy river.
3. She was itching her ears to know the result.
4. Miss G. Oak cooks food for my family members.
5. She decides to keep her promise.
6. They are asking so many questions to know the fact.
7. He was looking for an easy street to achieve the goal.
8. He was eating a humble pie for his fault.
9. The prisoner answered the questions asked to him.
10. Suzy was compelling him to bite the dust.
11. Rocky basks in the glory of success.
12. My mother burst into tears to see me after 20 years.

Future Perfect Continuous

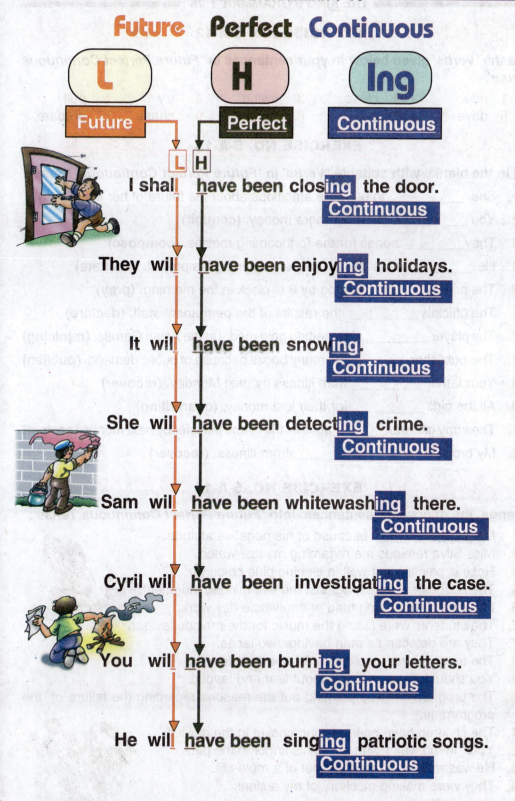

L	**H**	**Ing**
Future	Perfect	Continuous

L H

I shall **h**ave been clos**ing** the door.
Continuous

They wil**l** **h**ave been enjoy**ing** holidays.
Continuous

It wil**l** **h**ave been snow**ing**.
Continuous

She wil**l** **h**ave been detect**ing** crime.
Continuous

Sam wil**l** **h**ave been whitewash**ing** there.
Continuous

Cyril wil**l** **h**ave been investigat**ing** the case.
Continuous

You wil**l** **h**ave been burn**ing** your letters.
Continuous

He wil**l** **h**ave been sing**ing** patriotic songs.
Continuous

EXERCISE NO. 5-A-12

Use the '*Verbs*' given below in your sentences in '*Future Perfect Continuous Tense*':

1. ride	**2.** close	**3.** swing	**4.** try	**5.** pull
6. drive	**7.** cook	**8.** run	**9.** chase	**10.** prepare.

EXERCISE NO. 5-A-13

Fill in the blanks with suitable '*Verbs*' in '*Future Perfect Continuous Tense*' :

1. She _____ to be more ambitious about the future of her life. **(look)**

2. You _____ a crime for more money. **(commit)**

3. They_____ songs for the forthcoming movies. **(compose)**

4. He _____ to talk to his teacher regarding his project. **(hesitate)**

5. The priests _____ to God by 6 o' clock in the morning. **(pray)**

6. The officials _____ the results of the permanent staff. **(declare)**

7. The player _____ after getting gold medal in the Asian Games. **(rejoicing)**

8. The publisher _____ so many books because of public demand. **(publish)**

9. Your father _____ from illness by next Monday. **(recover)**

10. All the girls _____ for their lost money. **(quarrelling)**

11. The army general _____against the Prime Minister by next month. **(protest)**

12. My brother_____ from illness. **(recover)**

EXERCISE NO. 5-A-14

Change the following sentences into '*Future Perfect Continuous Tense*':

1. Mr. Vivian retaliates because of his negative attitude.

2. Miss Silva reminds me regarding my lost watch.

3. Rose is painting the wall in electric blue colour.

4. The advocates protest against the evil-minded judgment.

5. I take bath after being tired of the whole day work.

6. The students were facing the music for their misbehaviour.

7. They are detecting a man having two faces.

8. The teacher was scolding a fat headed student.

9. You should do your duty without fear and favour.

10. The programmer was pointing out the reasons regarding the failure of the programme.

11. The children have been playing cricket in the garden.

12. Your friend was trying to put his finger in the pie.

13. He was making a mountain out of a mole-hill.

14. They were making mockery of my actions.

15. Harry Potter was searching the green-eyed monster.

CHANGE THE VOICE

Voice

ACTIVE VOICE   **PASSIVE VOICE**

VOICE = It is a form of a sentence that tells whether the action is done by the subject or the effect of the action is received by the agent.

ACTIVE VOICE

When a **Subject** acts, the sentence is said to be in **Active Voice**.
He writes a letter.
She is doing her homework.

PASSIVE VOICE

When the effect of action is received by the Agent (Object), the sentence is said to be in **Passive Voice**.

Example : A letter is written by him. **[Passive Voice.]**

letter is not doing anything.

Her homework is being done by her. **[Passive Voice]**

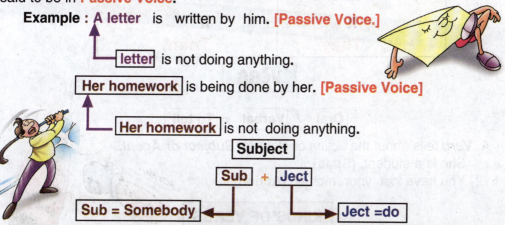

Her homework is not doing anything.

Subject

Sub + Ject

Sub = Somebody ← → **Ject =do**

Somebody who does work is a *Subject* in a sentence.

Object = Ob + Ject

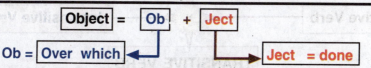

Ob = Over which ← → **Ject = done**

Over which the work is done is called an ***Object.***

He has killed **a tiger** in the jungle.

| Subject | Object |

Object : How to find ?

Object receives effect and it is often found after the '*Main Verb*' [Finite Verb]

He killed a mouse in the kitchen.

| Main Verb | Object | [Mouse receives the effect]

I have smashed the glass.

| Main Verb | Object | [The glass gets effect]

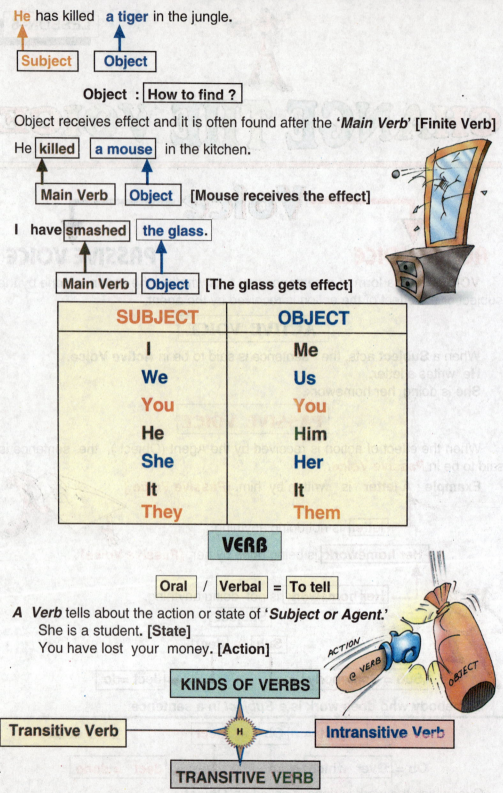

SUBJECT	OBJECT
I	Me
We	Us
You	You
He	Him
She	Her
It	It
They	Them

VERB

Oral / Verbal = To tell

A Verb tells about the action or state of '*Subject or Agent.*'
She is a student. **[State]**
You have lost your money. **[Action]**

KINDS OF VERBS

Transitive Verb   H   **Intransitive Verb**

TRANSITIVE VERB

It is a verb that **transits** its action to the **Object (or) affects** the **Object.**

Transit = Affect.

They **break** **all the plates.**

Transitive Verb **Object** [Plates are affected]

She **hurts** **me** without any reason.

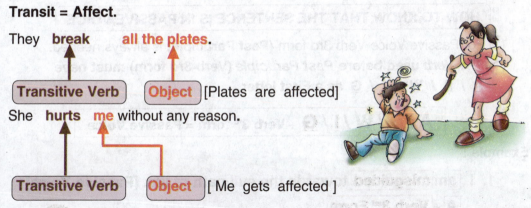

Transitive Verb **Object** [Me gets affected]

INTRANSITIVE VERB

It is a verb that does not transit its action so object is not used with it.
[Intransitive verb = No effect]

He **goes** to school in the morning.

Intransitive Verb

She is **coming** from your house.

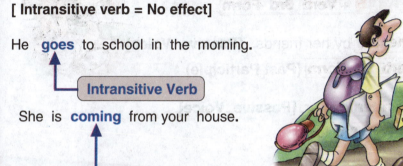

Intransitive Verb

We cannot change the sentence with Intransitive Verb into Passive Voice

Active to Passive Voice

| Verb 1st form = Go |
| Verb 2nd form = Went |
| Verb 3rd form = Gone |

HOW TO KNOW THAT THE SENTENCE IS IN PASSIVE VOICE

(1) For Passive Voice Verb 3rd form **(Past Participle)** is always needed.

(1) *The Verb* used before *Past Participle* (Verb 3rd form) **must have**
A / B / W / I / G as a First letter.

> **A / B / W / I / G** + **Verb 3rd form = Passive Voice**

Example :

1. I **am misguided** towards the evil path of life. **[Passive Voice]**
   A + **Verb 3rd Form**

2. The book has **been stolen**. **[Passive Voice]**
   B + **Verb 3rd Form**

3. She **was cheated** by her friends. **[Passive Voice]**
   W + **Verb 3rd Form** (Past Participle)

4. A letter **is written** by her. **[Passive Voice]**
   I + **Verb 3rd form**

5. My routine **got disturbed** because of your foolishness **[Passive]**
   G + **Verb 3rd form**

EXERCISE NO. 6-A

Tell whether the sentences are in *'Active Voice'* or *'Passive Voice'* :

1. I **h**ave helped you.
2. A poem is **b**eing written by her.
3. She **c**rosses the river.
4. A river **i**s crossed by her.
5. He **p**lays football in the garden.
6. He **h**as done his duty in time.
7. They **a**re remembered for their help.
8. You **s**hould forgive him for his mistakes.
9. You **a**re being taught English very well.
10. My brother **r**eads a book in the class.
11. Sam has **b**een punished by her brother.
12. Miss Tiffy **d**rove a car last night.
13. A kite **w**as stolen from his shop.
14. A story has **b**een written by her.
15. He **d**ives into the swimming pool.

Transformation : Active Voice to Passive Voice

Three rules are applied in all the sentences.

1 Subject and Object will be replaced by each other.

2 In Passive Voice Verb 3ʳᵈ form (past participle) is always used.

3 By is used in Passive Voice.

Example :

She writes a letter . [Active voice]

A letter is written by her . [Passive Voice]
1 2 3 1

You will often get two types of sentences.

FIRST TYPE

(1) You will get One Verb (Only Main Verb) in the sentence.

Example: I dived into the pool.

SECOND TYPE

(2) You will get Two Verbs = Helping & Main Verb in the sentence.

I have done a mistake.

First types of sentences	Second types of sentences
Only Main Verb (One Verb)	**Helping and Main Verb** (Two or More Verbs)
Is / Am / Are [Present Tense]	**Be = [Verb 1ˢᵗ form] (GO)**
Was / Were [Past Tense]	**Being = [Verb + Ing] (Going)**
	Been = H + Verb 3ʳᵈ form (Gone)

1st type of sentences

Example : Verb ends with S / E = Present

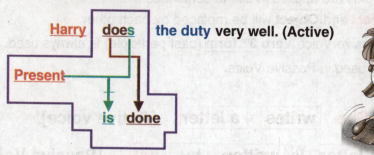

Harry **does** the duty very well. (Active)

Present

is done

The duty **is done** by Harry very well. (Passive)

Example :

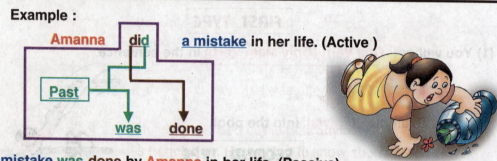

Amanna **did** a mistake in her life. (Active)

Past

was done

A mistake **was done** by Amanna in her life. (Passive)

Example :

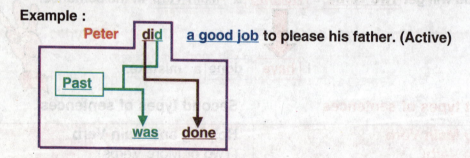

Peter **did** a good job to please his father. (Active)

Past

was done

A good job **was done** by Peter to please his father. (Passive)

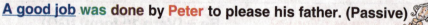

In Case of One Verb (Main Verb)

S = Is

She write**s** <u>a letter</u> to her friend. [Active Voice]

written (Verb 3rd form)

Present = is

<u>A letter</u> **is** <u>written</u> **by** <u>her</u> to her friend. [Passive Voice]

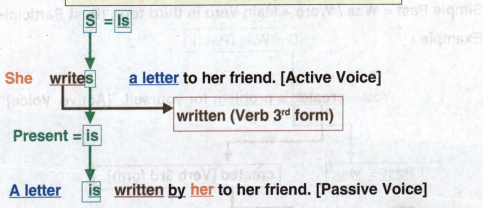

Example :

S = Is

He cracks <u>a joke</u> during a free period. [Active Voice]

cracked (Verb 3rd form)

Present = is

<u>A joke</u> **is** <u>cracked</u> **by** <u>him</u> during a free period. [Passive Voice]

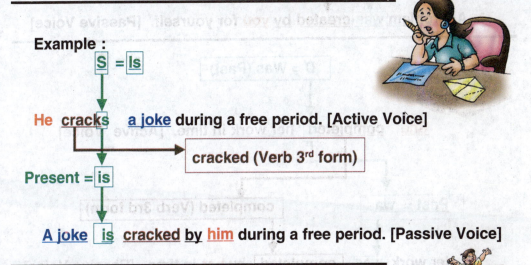

Example :

S = Is

Henry doe**s** <u>a job</u> for his family members. [Active Voice]

Done (Verb 3rd form)

Present = is

<u>A job</u> **is** <u>done</u> by <u>Henry</u> for his family members.

[Passive Voice]

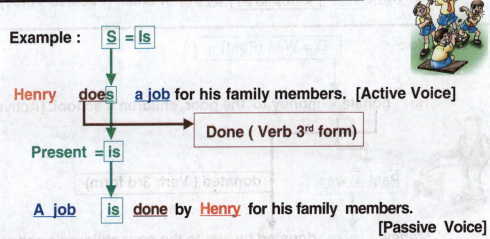

ONLY ONE MAIN VERB

Simple Past = Was / Were + Main Verb in third form (Past Participle)

Example :

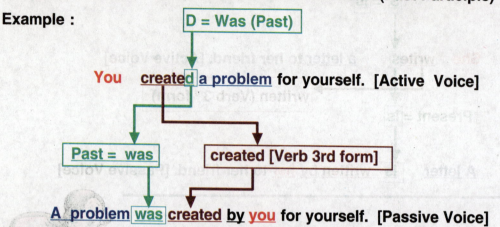

D = Was (Past)

You created a problem for yourself. [Active Voice]

Past = was

created [Verb 3rd form]

A problem was created by you for yourself. [Passive Voice]

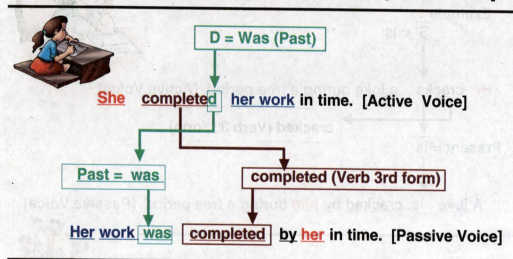

D = Was (Past)

She completed her work in time. [Active Voice]

Past = was

completed (Verb 3rd form)

Her work was completed by her in time. [Passive Voice]

Example :

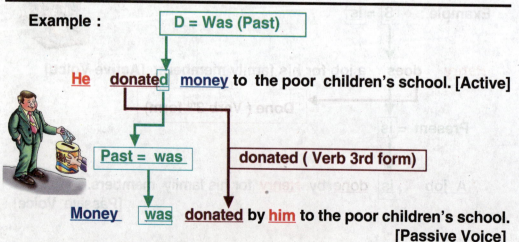

D = Was (Past)

He donated money to the poor children's school. [Active]

Past = was

donated (Verb 3rd form)

Money was donated by him to the poor children's school.
[Passive Voice]

Use is / am / are in Present tense.
Use was / were in Past tense.

Rule :

(1) If there is only one main verb , we should use Is / Am /Are in Present Tense and was / were in the past tense before **Past Participle** or the **3rd form of Verb** .

(2) When **Helping** and **Main verb** both are used in the sentence, **"be"** will always be used in **Passive Voice.**

A song was being sung by him. (Passive) [Continuous Tense]

A song has been sung by him. (Passive) [Perfect Tense]

A song will be sung by him.(Passive) [Simple Future & Modal Aux.]

Rule : When '**Helping and Main verb**' both are used in the sentence, **be / being / been** is used before the **third form of verb (Past Participle)**

Verb + Ing = Being

Verb 1st Form = Be

H + Verb 3rd Form = Been

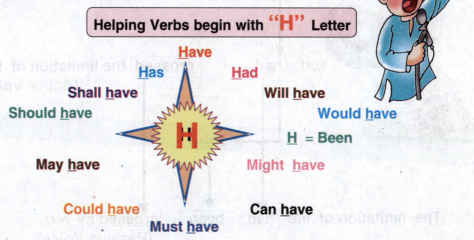

Helping Verbs begin with "H" Letter

Have
Has   Had
Shall have   Will have
Should have   Would have
H = Been
May have   Might have
Could have   Can have
Must have

HELPING VERBS BEGIN WITH "H"

HAS HAVE HAD

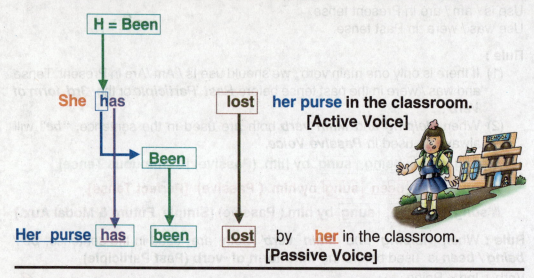

H = Been

She **has**   **lost**   her purse in the classroom.
[Active Voice]

Been

Her purse **has** **been**   **lost**   by   **her** in the classroom.
[Passive Voice]

Ex.

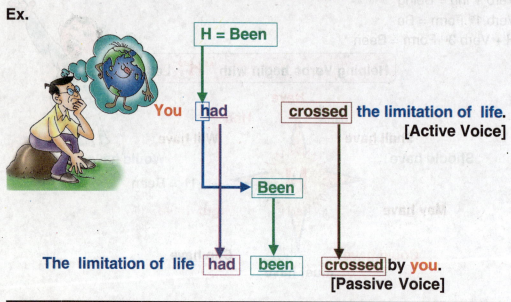

H = Been

You **had**   **crossed** the limitation of life.
[Active Voice]

Been

The limitation of life **had** **been**   **crossed** by you.
[Passive Voice]

Ex. **The army** **would** **have**   **conquered** **the fort**.
[Active Voice]

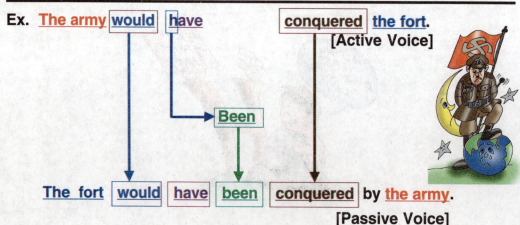

Been

The fort **would** **have** **been** **conquered** by **the army**.
[Passive Voice]

Example :

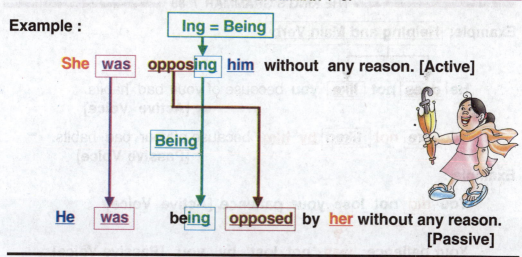

Ing = Being

She **was** oppos**ing** **him** without any reason. **[Active]**

Being

He **was** be**ing** **opposed** by **her** without any reason.
[Passive]

Example :

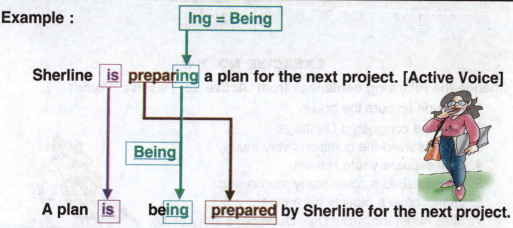

Ing = Being

Sherline **is** prepar**ing** a plan for the next project. **[Active Voice]**

Being

A plan **is** be**ing** **prepared** by Sherline for the next project.

Example :

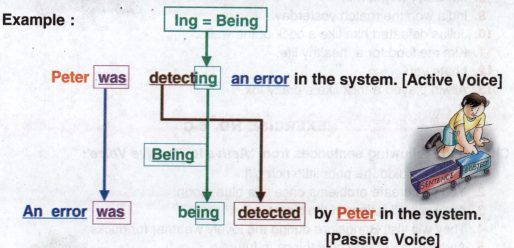

Ing = Being

Peter **was** detect**ing** **an error** in the system. **[Active Voice]**

Being

An error **was** be**ing** **detected** by **Peter** in the system.
[Passive Voice]

Exception to the above rule :
[Do not / Does not / Did not]
Do / Does = Is / Am / Are.   Did = Was / Were.

Example: **Helping and Main Verb**

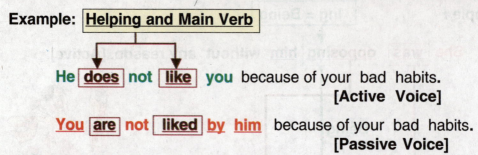

He does not like you because of your bad habits.
[Active Voice]

You are not liked by him because of your bad habits.
[Passive Voice]

Example :

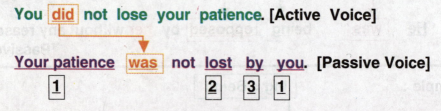

You did not lose your patience. [Active Voice]

Your patience was not lost by you. [Passive Voice]
1   2   3   1

EXERCISE NO. 6-B

Change the following sentences from '*Active* to *Passive Voice*':

1. Fortune favours the brave.
2. Romans conquered Carthage.
3. Jacob solved the questions very easily.
4. Shakespeare wrote Hamlet.
5. He published a novel many moons ago.
6. James gave a blow to his brother.
7. Miss Anderson wrote Ugly Duckling, a story of life.
8. Mr. Barry forgot me.
9. India won the match yesterday.
10. Julius defeated him like a cock of the walk.
11. Kim ate food for a healthy life.
12. I hate you.
13. Allwin played a trick like a crazy fox.

EXERCISE NO. 6-C

Change the following sentences from '*Active* to *Passive Voice*':

1. She will guide the poor little rich girl.
2. You can create problems once in a blue moon.
3. Andy will kill a tiger in the forest.
4. They will visit Bangalore during the lovely weather for ducks.
5. Andrew can create new things in future.
6. Tulip will build a house of cards tonight.
7. Mr. Chaplin will destroy the apple's cart.
8. You might eat food after my arrival.

9. Dick will help the baby born with a silver spoon in the mouth.
10. Students would misguide you regarding the capital errors.

NO PASSIVE VOICE

Future Continuous Tense and All Perfect Continuous Tenses.

EXERCISE NO. 6-D

Change the following sentences from *'Active to Passive Voice'*:

1. Mr. Brian was watching the project like a hawk.
2. Miss Clara was collecting money from the bank.
3. Jack is earning almighty dollar in U. S. A.
4. Chaplin was preparing a plan to get the brass ring.
5. They are refusing him to do the work.
6. Boys in blue are arresting the criminals.
7. David is explaining the fact.
8. Miss Eden is reading a book based on alpha and omega of life.
9. Jolly was learning the black art.
10. They are preparing a Trojan horse.
11. Your friends were stealing money.
12. James is earning money in Paris.

EXERCISE NO. 6-E

Change the following sentences from *'Active to Passive Voice'* :

1. Miss Gloria has lost her patience just now.
2. Greg has dropped him from the team like a hot potato.
3. I have identified the dark horse.
4. Harry Potter has found Aladdin's cave.
5. Miss Grace has closed the door.
6. Jack has played cricket to win the match.
7. My brother has met you before my arrival.
8. Miss Hansel has kept him dangling regarding his selection.
9. I had taken medicine for good health.
10. Gladiator had killed the blue monster.
11. My parents have taken my book from the table .
12. Your son had snatched my pen.
13. You will have cheated him.
14. She had lost her purse.

EXERCISE NO. 6-F

Change the following sentences from *'Active to Passive Voice'* :

1. He helped your brother because of his good nature.
2. She rewarded him for his active nature.
3. The French always adored, admired and appreciated Napoleon.
4. One should do one's duty.
5. A handicapped beggar has picked my pocket.
6. He enjoys playing cricket.
7. India expected a great victory.
8. A foolish fellow cheated me.
9. He loves his daughter like a sugar dad.
10. I have appointed a guard to look after you.
11. They elected Mr. Fabion, the chairman.

PASSIVE VOICE TO ACTIVE VOICE

1. FIRST TYPE	2. SECOND TYPE
Be / Being / Been + Verb 3rd form	**Is / Am / Are / Was / Were + Verb 3rd form**
1. They have been exposed there.	1. Your parents were advised well.
2. He was being misguided by me.	2. Your novels were published.
3. These books will be taken away.	3. My pocket is picked because of rush.

Pen is mightier than sword.

How To Solve the First Types of Sentences.

1. Cut be been by & exchange the place of *Subject* and *Object*.

Cut = X

Being = Verb + Ing

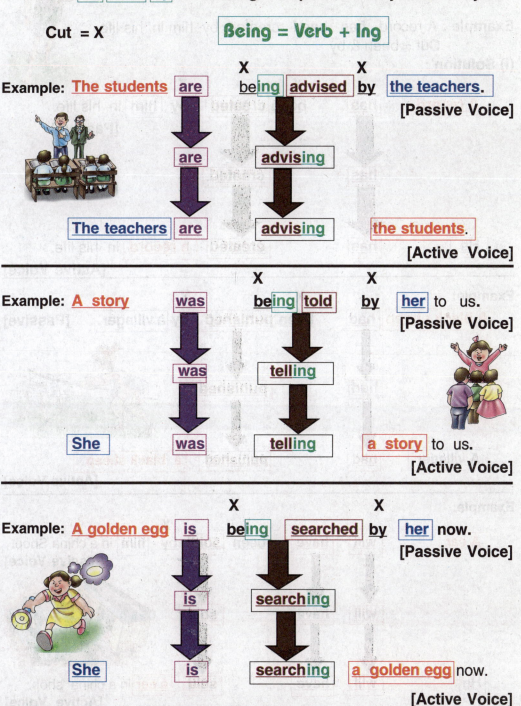

Example: The students | are | be<del>ing</del> | advised | by | the teachers.

[Passive Voice]

are | advising

The teachers | are | advising | the students.

[Active Voice]

Example: A story | was | be<del>ing</del> | told | by | her | to us.

[Passive Voice]

was | telling

She | was | telling | a story | to us.

[Active Voice]

Example: A golden egg | is | be<del>ing</del> | searched | by | her | now.

[Passive Voice]

is | searching

She | is | searching | a golden egg | now.

[Active Voice]

Note : No Passive Voice in Future Continuous.

Been

Example : A record has been created by him in his life.

　　　　Cut = been & by

(i) Solution :

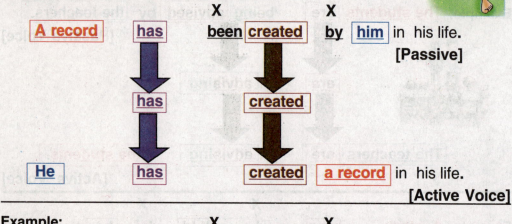

| A record | has | X been created | by | him in his life. | **[Passive]** |

| | has | | created | |

| He | has | | created | a record in his life. | **[Active Voice]** |

Example:

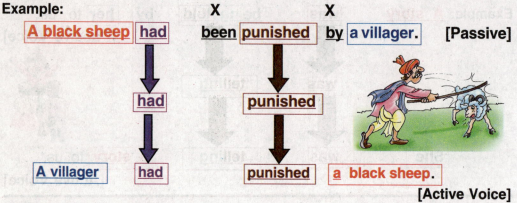

| A black sheep | had | X been punished | by | a villager. | **[Passive]** |

| | had | | punished | |

| A villager | had | | punished | a black sheep. | **[Active Voice]** |

Example:

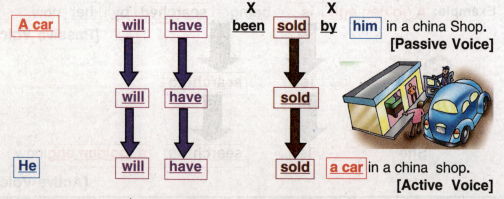

| A car | will | have | X been sold | by | him in a china Shop. | **[Passive Voice]** |

| | will | have | | sold | |

| He | will | have | | sold | a car in a china shop. | **[Active Voice]** |

Be = 1st form of Verb

<u>Cut = be & by</u>

Example : The novel will be sold by her in the market.

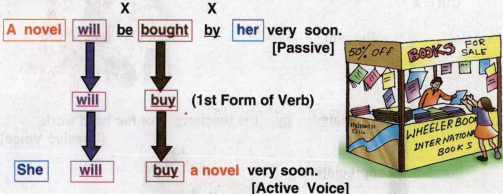

A novel	will	be	bought	by	her	very soon.
X   X

[Passive]

will ... buy   (1st Form of Verb)

She   will   buy a novel very soon.
[Active Voice]

Ex:

Ugly ducklings | have | to | be | found | by | you .   [Passive]
                             X   X

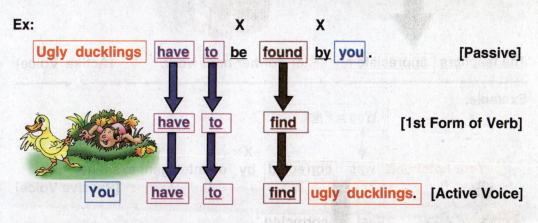

have to   find   [1st Form of Verb]

You   have to   find ugly ducklings. [Active Voice]

Ex:

The big bug | can | be | killed | by | him very easily.   [Passive]
                   X   X

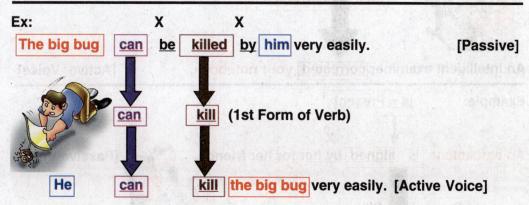

can   kill   (1st Form of Verb)

He   can   kill the big bug very easily. [Active Voice]

How to Solve the Second Types of Sentences.

You will get : is / am / are / was / were & 3rd form of verb (Past Participle)

Cut : |Is|/|Am|/|Are|/|Was|/|Were| & by

Cut = X

Example:

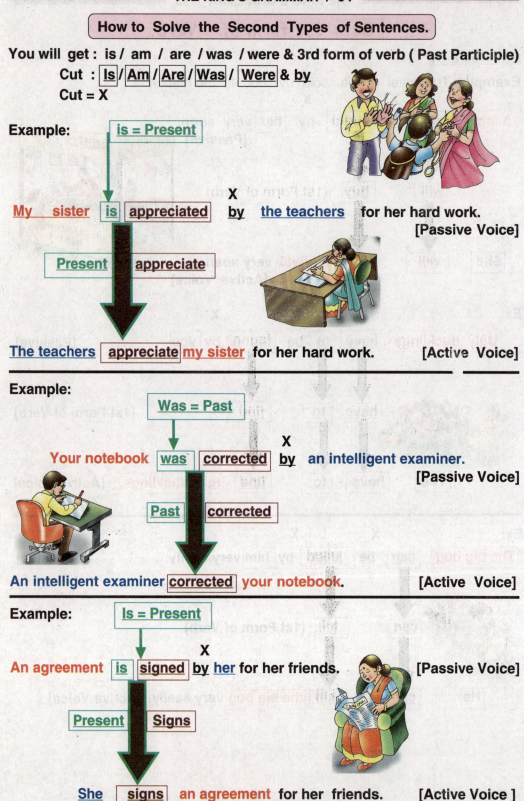

is = Present

X

My   sister |is| |appreciated| by the teachers for her hard work.
                                                    [Passive Voice]

|Present| |appreciate|

The teachers |appreciate| my sister for her hard work.   [Active Voice]

Example:

Was = Past

X

Your notebook |was| |corrected| by an intelligent examiner.
                                                    [Passive Voice]

|Past| |corrected|

An intelligent examiner |corrected| your notebook.   [Active Voice]

Example:

Is = Present

X

An agreement |is| |signed| by her for her friends.   [Passive Voice]

|Present| |Signs|

She |signs| an agreement for her friends.   [Active Voice]

EXERCISE NO. 6-G

Change the following sentences into *'Active Voice'* :

1. The programme was being prepared by the members of the committee.
2. She is being taken to hospital by his family members.
3. You are being cheated by your friends.
4. An essay was being written by Miss Lucy in the class.
5. Clothes were being washed by the washerwoman.
6. The building is being built by a rich merchant.
7. The newspaper was being read by your mother.
8. Smoking is being controlled by him according to my mother.
9. I was being remembered by my family members.
10. A patient is being operated in the hospital.
11. The letters were being burnt by him.
12. The river was being crossed by her.
13. A car is being driven by you.
14. TV was being watched by my friends.
15. Your brother is being advised by your parents.

EXERCISE NO. 6-H

Change the following sentences into '*Active Voice*':

1. The book has been taken by your friends to study.
2. The illegal houses have been demolished by the Municipal Commissioner.
3. Mr. Joy will have been misguided by me by next Monday.
4. Your TV might have been repaired by the mechanic.
5. My mother will have been helped by you.
6. Her pen has been thrown away by her friend.
7. The fort must have been conquered by Napoleon.
8. An award has been received by Miss Jolie.
9. This parliamentary seat had been won by an honest man.
10. Your letters have been received by your parents.
11. The movie will have been seen by all the family members.
12. Macbeth had been killed by Macduff.
13. The newspaper could have been sold earlier this morning.
14. The stories had been copied by the film producer.
15. Her ornaments will have been snatched by a thief.

EXERCISE NO. 6-I

Change the following sentences into 'Active Voice':

1. She could be recognised by anybody in the party.
2. The treasure must be guarded by the policeman.
3. You must be obeyed by the students.
4. All the rules should be followed by your staff.
5. This computer has to be operated by the experts.
6. The book would be prescribed by the Principal.
7. Shailja might be punished by her tutor.
8. Almitra will be confused by me at this matter.
9. Your confusion will be cleared by my brother.
10. I shall be blamed for my laziness.

EXERCISE NO. 6-J

Change the following sentences into 'Active Voice':

1. The thief was caught by a Black Watch near the railway platform.
2. The players were loudly cheered by the audience.
3. The cheat was taken to prison by the men in blue.
4. A bowl of cherry was gifted to me by Sam.
5. The door is opened by your mother with beautiful blossoms.
6. The award was given by the President to him.
7. My money is robbed by a robber with a dagger in his hand.
8. My boss was offered a red carpet welcome by the committee members.
9. A castle of dream was built by Sam in open air.
10. A heart of gold is appreciated by the honest people.
11. A bunch of keys was lost by him.
12. A golden hello was given to me by her.
13. A lion cannot be killed in his den.
14. This piece of land is acquired by him.
15. The story book was read by your daughter carefully.

> **Some Important Points**

We cannot use 'by' with the words given below when you change from Active to Passive. We should use 'with' instead of 'by' :

Pleased, satisfied, disgusted, charmed, enthroned, etc. + with

I pleased him. **(Active)**

He was pleased by me. **(Incorrect Passive)**

He was pleased with me. **(Correct Passive)**

We cannot change the voice of :

1. Future Continuous

2. Present Perfect Continuous

3. Past Perfect Continuous

4. Future Perfect Continuous

5. Sentences having Intransitive verbs **[Except order & request]**

Order and Request

(a) Go there and sit down. **(Active Voice)**

You are ordered to go and sit down. **(Passive Voice)**

(b) Please come here. **(Active Voice)**

You are requested to come here. **(Passive Voice)**

ACTIVE TO PASSIVE VOICE

Order & Request

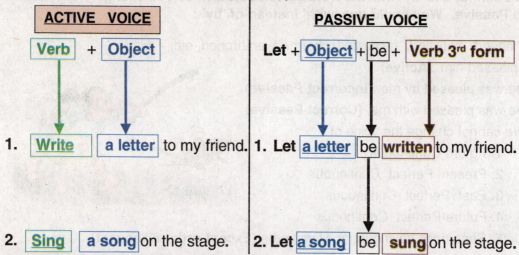

ACTIVE VOICE	PASSIVE VOICE
Verb + Object	Let + Object + be + Verb 3rd form

1. **Write** | **a letter** to my friend. 　　1. Let **a letter** **be** **written** to my friend.

2. **Sing** **a song** on the stage. 　　2. Let **a song** **be** **sung** on the stage.

Play football in the garden.
Let football be played in the garden.

PASSIVE TO ACTIVE VOICE

Passive = Let + Object + Be + Verb 3rd form + by us.

Active = Let + us + Verb 1st form + Object.

(A) Let the door be closed by us. **[Passive Voice]**

　　Ans : Let us close the door. **[Active Voice]**

(B) Let the mouse be killed by her. **[Passive Voice]**

　　Let her kill the mouse. **[Active Voice]**

EXERCISE NO. 6-K

Transform the following sentences into 'Passive Voice' :

1. Bring a pencil for drawing.
2. Try to get your money back.
3. Keep it with you for your safety.
4. Mend your shoes yourself.
5. Catch the fish to sell it.
6. Continue the job for your family members.
7. Think thousand times at this project before you come to any conclusion.
8. Cross the road very carefully.
9. Kill me.
10. Complete your work in time.

PASSIVE TO ACTIVE VOICE

Passive = Let + Object + Be + Verb 3rd form + by us.

Active = let + us + Verb 1st form + Object.

(a) Let the door be closed by us. **[Passive Voice]**

    Ans: Let us close the door. [Active Voice]

(b) Let the mouse be killed by her. **[Passive Voice]**

    Ans: Let her kill the mouse. [Active Voice]

EXERCISE NO. 6-L

Change the following sentences into 'Active Voice' :

1. Let the windows be opened by us.
2. Let my brother be scolded by my parents.
3. Let the vegetables be bought by us.
4. Let the boys be trained by him.
5. Let the problems be solved by her.
6. Let the situation be cleared by you.
7. Let the rent be paid by you.
8. Let the movie be seen by us.
9. Let a song be sung by us.
10. Let this question be asked by you.

EXERCISE NO. 6-M

Change the Voice :

1. Dream sketches the destiny of life.
2. You are demanding a lurking wish.
3. She headed a group of courageous students.
4. She was awarded for her lifetime hard work.
5. You must hold your killing tongue.
6. New challenges are accepted by the Prince of Darkness.
7. He spent each moment with the Prince of Peace.
8. Your life has been left unsupported.
9. Our institution has guided a number of great scientists.
10. They richly deserve the prestigious award.
11. She transformed sorrow into joy.
12. The villagers have caught a wolf in lamb's clothing.
13. My friends awakened my sleeping conscience.
14. Milton's poems touch the human soul even today.
15. Both the Indian as well as English movies show this variety.

16. The earliest works of Sir William Shakespeare were appreciated.
17. He was burning the candle of ill flame.
18. The troops of France were often commanded by Napoleon.
19. Dances are especially composed according to the need of the show.
20. They have shared our sorrows.
21. These thoughts must have been presented by Plato.
22. He had been introduced to my foolish friend.
23. She is studying English, a living language.
24. They replaced her for the same reason.
25. Modern movies are usually edited in studios.
26. Edward had met and threatened all the teachers.
27. This project provides a golden opportunity to the people.
28. He can be handled by you easily.
29. You will have forgotten the old flame.
30. The neem tree provides precious natural medicines.
31. A washerman informed me about the accident of my brother.
32. Those instructions had not been followed by the Commander-in-Chief.
33. They were much delighted by my soul-touching thoughts.
34. The magic of prosperity turns sand into gold.
35. Beauty in action makes the heart a golden temple.
36. Your accent can provide soul to your life style.
37. Honesty would gift happiness to your life.
38. Strong reasons create strong actions.
39. He has named his daughter "Pearl."
40. Prosperity is gifted to hardworking people by God.
41. Adversity tests friendship.
42. You should not trust the advice of a man in difficulty.
43. Ambition inspires the life to battle for success.
44. Authority forgets a dying king.
45. This beautiful rose will leave you unfolded.
46. Beggars cannot choose anything of their choice.
47. A fool can stumble a stone twice.
48. This suggestion instantly deflated my desire.
49. You can pour oil on troubled water.
50. Try that again.

DIRECT & INDIRECT SPEECH

DIRECT SPEECH : When anything, which is spoken or written by somebody, is written or presented as it is (same), it is called 'Direct Speech'.

Example : She said, "I am very happy." [Direct Speech]

INDIRECT SPEECH : When anything, which is spoken or written by somebody, is written or presented by you in your own words, it will be *Indirect Speech*.

Example : She said that she was very happy. [Indirect Speech]

FROM DIRECT TO INDIRECT SPEECH

A Direct Speech can have : Question mark [**?**] Mark of Exclamation [**!**] or Full Stop [**.**] at the end of a sentence.

The **Indirect Speech** has only **Full stop [.]** at the end of all the sentences.

Ex. He said, "Is he unhappy **?**" [Direct Speech]

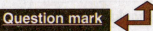 Question mark

He asked if he was unhappy. [Indirect Speech]

 Full Stop

Ex. He said, " What a beautiful flower **!**" [Direct Speech]

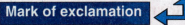 Mark of exclamation

He exclaimed that it was a very beautiful flower. [Indirect Speech]

 Full Stop

Ex. My brother said, "They had been waiting for the bus." [Direct Speech]

 Full Stop

 Full Stop

My brother said that they had been waiting for the bus.

[Indirect Speech]

Full Stop

CHANGE IN TENSES

Present Tense = Past tense

Is / Am / Are = Was / Were / May = might / Ought = ought

Ex.   You said, " She   does some work properly." [Direct]

D

You said that she   did some work properly. [Indirect]

Ex.   We said, "She clears the fact in the court." [Direct]

D

We said that she   cleared the fact in the court. [Indirect]

Ex.   My teacher said, "It has to be solved." [Direct]

D

My teacher said that it had to be solved. [Indirect]

FUTURE TENSE

Shall / Will = should / would

Ex. He said, "He   will protect the wild life any way." [Direct]

D

He said that he   would protect   the wild life any way. [Indirect]

Ex. You said , "She will be trying to fill a bottomless pit." [Direct]

D

You said that she would be trying to fill a bottomless pit. [Indirect]

Ex. They said, "He will have eaten his lunch like a bird." [Direct]

D

They said that   he   would have eaten his lunch like a bird."

[Indirect]

Ex. My teacher said, " She   will   have been writing a novel."

D

[Direct]

My teacher said that she would have been writing a novel. [Indirect]

Past Tense = had

Rule 1. In all Past tenses **had** will be used. Only – **was / were** = **had been**

Past

Ex.   She said, "He **continue**d his job well." [Direct Speech]

HAD

She said that he **had** **continued** his job well. [Indirect Speech]

Past

Ex. They said, " She **distribute**d some sweets." [Direct Speech]

HAD

They said that she **had** **distributed** some sweets.
[Indirect Speech]

Was / Were = Had been

Ex. You said, "He **was** trying to understand the fact." [Direct Speech]

had been

You said that he **had been** trying to understand the fact.
[Indirect Speech]

Ex.   I said, "They **were** preparing for the final exam."
[Direct Speech]

had been

I said that they **had been** preparing for the final exam.
[Indirect Speech]

Ex.   She said, "He **was** a very good doctor." [Direct Speech]

had been

She said, that he **had been** a very good doctor."
[Indirect Speech]

EXERCISE NO. 7-A

Change the following sentences into *'Indirect Speech'* **:**

1. You said, "He is dull like a dish water while working in the office."
2. She said, "Nobody is appreciating the dog's dinner."
3. He said, "Peter is composing a patriotic song for the college function."
4. I said, "Krishna is telling the truth as he is at the death's door."

5. They said, "A poor fellow has been looking for a dead man's diamond shoes to get rid of his poverty."
6. Miss Taylor said, "Tulip is telling his coach where his shoe pinches."
7. You said, "Soloman works hard in order to achieve the goal."
8. Miss Donwalker said, "Titanic is dead in the sea."
9. David said, "He is behaving like a dog with two tails after getting the gold medal."
10. I said, "All the students are waiting for the arrival of their teachers."
11. Miss Susane said, "Mr. Oak is drinking Coca-Cola with his friends."
12. Richard said, "Edward has crossed the road before the arrival of bus."
13. Sam said, "There is an open door for the hardworking people in this institute."
14. Robin said, "The soldier is dead as a door nail in the story."

EXERCISE NO. 7-B

Change the following sentences into *'Indirect Speech'* **:**

1. She said, "He will have to choose between devil and deep blue sea."
2. You said, "She will have to help the blue-eyed boys during the office time."
3. I said, "They will have been trying to rock the boat in order to upset the project."
4. My brother said, "Bhavna will have been looking for a better chance to know the fact."
5. Henry said, "She will have to keep the pot boiling in order to please everybody."
6. Simon said, "Her students will be trying to read me like a book."
7. He said, "Miss Naurah will be borrowing a trouble without any reason."
8. I said, "He will have been enjoying milk and honey after getting his uncle's property."

9. The commander said, "His army will have achieved all the targets planned by them."

10. The driver said, "They will have been to Norman Point before 5 o' clock."

11. Your father said, "His daughter will never attend a dog and a pony show."

12. The gardener said, "She will be treating with me like mud under the Lotus."

EXERCISE NO. 7-C

Change the following sentences into *'Indirect Speech'* :

1. She said, "He gave a dog, a bad name."

2. They said, "She was selling her soul to the devil."

3. I said, "It was raining cats and dogs."

4. Edwin said, "Sam was dreaming about a beggar riding on a horseback."

5. Her father said, "His books had been taken by Tulip."

6. Mr. Bruce said, "David ate like a horse after his recovery from illness."

7. Miss Barry said, "He got the award because of his talent."

8. Andy said, "She prayed for her brother's better health."

9. Albert said, "The beggars near the temple were not choosing between a dollar and a pound."

10. The Army General said, "The troop won the war ultimately."

11. The news reporter said, "The fire broke out after 12 o' clock before the arrival of minister."

12. Franklin said, "Jemina acted well in order to get the best acting award."

13. I said, "After 80 years, Mr. Lawrence was living on borrowed time."

14. I said, "Geoffrey was blowing his own trumpet."

15. Kim said, "He guided his daughter towards a better and brighter future."

Change the Person
1st Person

Subject of Reporting Verb

A. **She** said, "**I** had done **my** duty for **my** family and **my** self." [Direct]

She said that **she** had done **her** duty for **her** family and **her** self. [Indirect]

Subject of Reporting Verb

He said, "**I** had been working for **my** future, **my** friends and **my** self." [Direct]

He said that **he** had been working for **his** future, **his** friends and **him** self. [Indirect Speech]

Jill said, "**I** had bought **my** money bag from **my** friend's shop." [Direct]

Jill = Girl

Ans: **Jill** said that **she** had bought **her** money bag from **her** friend's shop. [Indirect Speech]

Subject

You said, "**I** **will** have completed **my** homework in **my** class." [Direct]

You said that **You** **would** have completed **your** homework in **your** class. [Indirect]

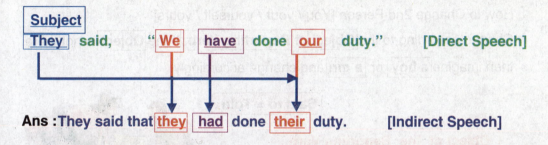

Subject

They said, "**We** **have** done **our** duty." [Direct Speech]

Ans : They said that **they** **had** done **their** duty. [Indirect Speech]

EXERCISE NO. 7-D

Change the following sentences into '*Indirect Speech*':

1. Kim said, "I will have been sleeping as I am dead to the world after completing my work."

2. Kate and Rose said, "We have completed our project in time."

3. Vivian said, "I want to leave my office as my father is at the death's door."

4. They said, "We have to come out from deep water and behave normally."

5. Hick said, "My brother has created a history in the field of sports."

6. She said, "Our family life style has not been changed according to our modern society."

7. Your sister said, "We calculate the account to know the profit."

8. Susan said, "My enemy is arguing like a devil's advocate."

9. Silvia said, "I shall have been waiting for my better chance."

10. My doctor said, "My profession is to try for better health."

11. I said, "I am thinking to dice with death in order to get the golden crown of success."

12. Mr. Paul said, "I have been defeated like a done dinner in the election."

13. Philip said, "I have done my job with responsibility."

14. Miss Percy said, "Our teachers are trying different strokes for different folks."

15. Andy said, "My parents will meet my class teacher regarding my mischievous behaviour."

How to Change 2nd Person [You / your / yourself / yours]

Change according to the **Object** of **Reporting Verb.** If the **Object** is not there then imagine **a boy** or **a girl** and change accordingly.

Said to = Told

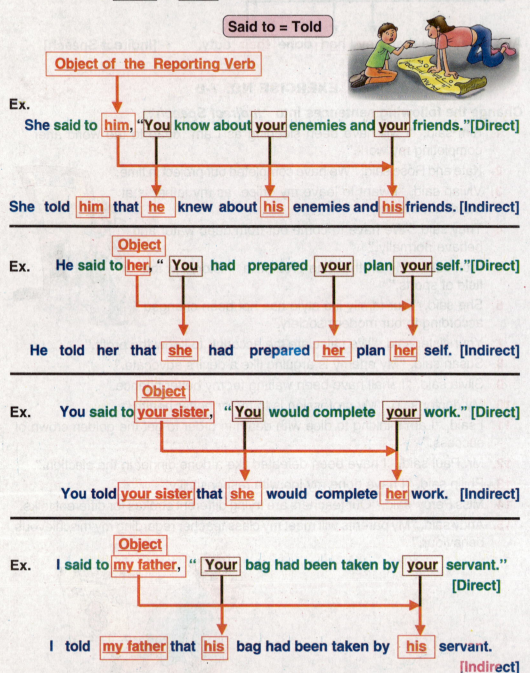

Object of the Reporting Verb

Ex.

She said to **him**, "**You** know about **your** enemies and **your** friends."[Direct]

She told **him** that **he** knew about **his** enemies and **his** friends. [Indirect]

Object

Ex. He said to **her**, " **You** had prepared **your** plan **your** self."[Direct]

He told her that **she** had prepared **her** plan **her** self. [Indirect]

Object

Ex. You said to **your sister**, "**You** would complete **your** work." [Direct]

You told **your sister** that **she** would complete **her** work. [Indirect]

Object

Ex. I said to **my father**, " **Your** bag had been taken by **your** servant."
[Direct]

I told **my father** that **his** bag had been taken by **his** servant.
[Indirect]

NO OBJECT

In case of **no object,** imagine **a boy** or **girl** and change accordingly.

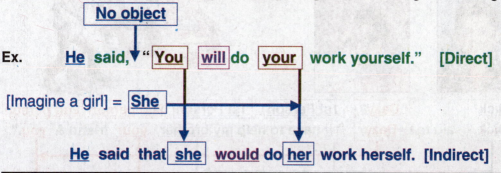

Ex.　　He said, "**You** **will** do **your** work yourself." **[Direct]**

[Imagine a girl] = **She**

He said that **she** **would** do **her** work herself. **[Indirect]**

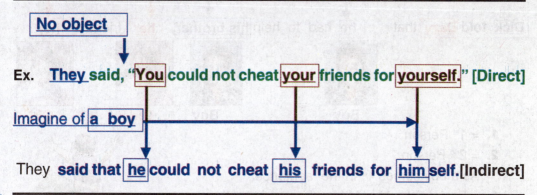

Ex.　**They** said, "**You** could not cheat **your** friends for **yourself.**" **[Direct]**

Imagine of **a boy**

They **said that he** could not cheat **his** friends for **him** self.**[Indirect]**

EXERCISE NO. 7-E

Change the following sentences into '*Indirect Speech*' :

1. He said to her, "You have dressed up in a funny manner like a dog's dinner."
2. You said to him, "You have to create a history."
3. She said to him, "You will have to act like a sick cat."
4. Sheena said to them, "Your programs are failed because of your foolish habits."
5. Miss Vincent said, "You have to react like a dose of salt immediately."
6. I said, "You have to be very careful as you are using double-edged sword."
7. We said, "You will be taking medicine for your better health."
8. Raymond said to Dick, "You do your work according to your pre-decided programs."
9. Miss Ray said, "You cannot survive for a long time after chasing a dragon."
10. She said, "Your parents will have to know the fact of your life."
11. Shailja said to Hick," You have to spend money on the cheap and cheerful things."
12. I said, "You are preparing for the next election campaign."
13. Mr. Neil said to me, "You are as important as a cherry in the cake for this institute."

1st & 2nd Person Both

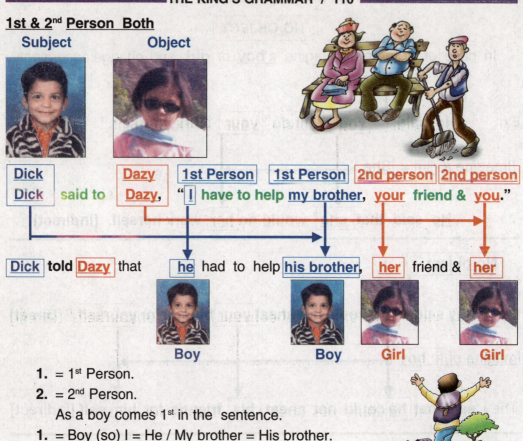

Subject   **Object**

Dick   Dazy   1st Person   1st Person   2nd person   2nd person

Dick **said to** Dazy, "I **have to help** my brother, your **friend &** you."

Dick **told** Dazy that he had to help his brother, her friend & her

Boy   **Boy**   **Girl**   **Girl**

1. = 1st Person.
2. = 2nd Person.
   As a boy comes 1st in the sentence.
1. = Boy (so) I = He / My brother = His brother.
   As a girl comes 2nd in the sentence.
2. = Girl (so) Your = Her / You = Her.

3rd PERSON

T/ H letters **first** or **second** letter of **Pronoun** indicates **third person.**

He	She	Him	Her	Himself	Herself	It	Its	Itself

T/H = Third person singular number

T + H Third person plural number

they	them	their	themselves

All <u>Nouns</u> are 3rd <u>Persons</u> : <u>Ram / Shyam / Tokyo / Pen etc.</u>

No Change in 3rd <u>person</u>

Only change <u>helping Verb</u> or <u>main verb</u> (without helping verb)

She said, "He will be helping his brother and his parents." [Direct]

She said that he would be helping his brother and his parents. [Indirect]

I. In case of Reporting verb (says / will say) in <u>Present</u> or <u>Future tense</u>.

II. No change in helping Verb or Tense of Reported Speech.

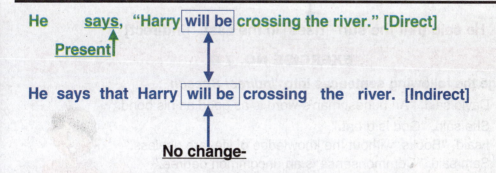

She will say, "Sam is staying with his family members." [Direct]

Future

She will say that Sam is staying with his family members. [Indirect]

No change-

He says, "Harry will be crossing the river." [Direct]

Present

He says that Harry will be crossing the river. [Indirect]

No change-

EXERCISE NO. 7-F

Change the following sentences into 'Indirect Speech' :

1. She said, "He has to tighten his belt after losing his job."
2. He said to me, "She waited for her friends at her home."
3. You said, "She has to accept the beginning of the end of her career."
4. I said, "They went to Kolkata in order to get a job."
5. They said, "He will not buy anything cheap and nasty as the birthday present."
6. Sammy said, "He has a habit of chopping and changing his decisions at the eleventh hour."
7. Sarah said to me, "He has begged money for his friends."
8. Serena said, "She has to complete her task to get promotion."
9. He said, "Sandra has a chance to bite the cherry soon."
10. Mr. Oscar said, "He solemnly assured her to help at any cost."
11. Phillips said to my father, "These books are neither published for a chick nor for a child ."
12. My teacher said to me, "He has locked the big bickies in the jewelry box."
13. I said, "We have not seen big cheese yet in this party."
14. Miss Sibby said, "She will have to reveal the hidden truth."
15. Shubha said, "They had a good idea to solve this problem."

II. In case of <u>universal</u> <u>truth</u>, <u>general</u> <u>truth</u> and <u>habitual action</u>, tense should not be changed. So the Verb will be same.

The teacher said, "Man is mortal." [Direct]

The teacher said that man is mortal. [Indirect]

He said, "The sun rises in the east." [Direct]

He said that the sun rises in the east. [Indirect]

EXERCISE NO. 7-G

Change the following sentences into *'Indirect Speech'* :

1. David said, "An honest man's word is as good as his bond."
2. She said, "God is great."
3. I said, "Books, without the knowledge of life, are useless."
4. Sam said, "Commonsense is an uncommon degree."
5. You said, "The earth moves round the sun."
6. He said, "Love makes life live better and happier."
7. They said, "Diamond cuts diamonds."
8. Olive said, "Two and two makes four."
9. Confucius said, "Everything has its beauty but everyone cannot see it."
10. St. Vincent said, "The soul is immortal ."
11. Heraclitus said, "Eyes are more accurate witness than ears."

DIRECT SPEECH	INDIRECT SPEECH
Ago	Before
Last night	The previous night
Yesterday	The previous day
Tomorrow	The next day
Today	That day
Thus	So
Hence	Thence
Here	There
Hither	Thither
These	Those
This	That
Now	Then

QUESTIONS ?

In place of **said** = **asked**.

1. In case of **wh** word = **asked** + **wh word**.   [Wh = **What / When / Who** etc.]
2. In case of **Helping Verb** = **asked if**

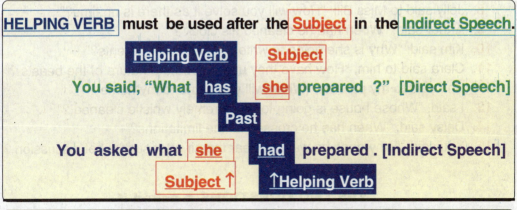

HELPING VERB must be used after the **Subject** in the **Indirect Speech**.

Helping Verb Subject

You said, "What **has** **she** prepared ?" [Direct Speech]

Past

You asked what **she** **had** prepared . [Indirect Speech]

Subject ↑ ↑Helping Verb

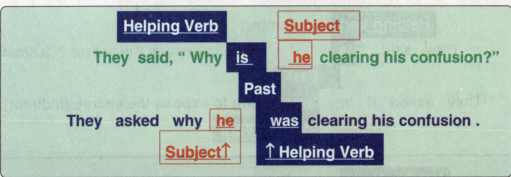

Helping Verb Subject

They said, " Why **is** **he** clearing his confusion?"

Past

They asked why **he** **was** clearing his confusion .

Subject↑ ↑ Helping Verb

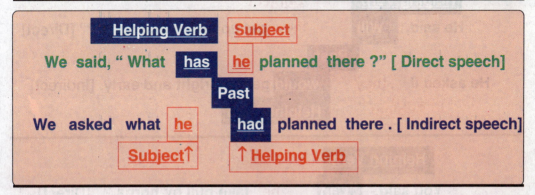

Helping Verb Subject

We said, " What **has** **he** planned there ?" [Direct speech]

Past

We asked what **he** **had** planned there . [Indirect speech]

Subject↑ ↑ Helping Verb

EXERCISE NO. 7-H

Change the following sentences into 'Indirect Speech' :

1. Mr. Bruke said, "When will you keep your chin up to get success?"
2. You said, "How has she stopped her chop logic during the meeting ?"
3. Bruno said, "Where have they exposed the naked truth?"

4. Miss Charlie said, "Which bungalow would you like to buy ?"
5. Ruby said to him, "How much money do you want to keep yourself happy as a sand boy ?"
6. Miss Cherry said, "Whom will he help for that purpose ?"
7. I said to her, "Where is your elder brother now ?"
8. Jolly said to Miss Bill, "How will you solve it as there is no time?"
9. Arthur said, "When had he cleaned his clock ?"
10. Kim said, "Why is she going to write a letter to her parents?"
11. Clara said to him, "How have they understood the nature of the beasts ?"
12. She said to my parents, "When will you come to my home ?"
13. I said, "Whose house is going to be extremely whistle cleaned ?"
14. Daisy said, "When has he crossed all the limitations?"
15. You said, "Why does he want to clear the air after such a hot discussion ?"

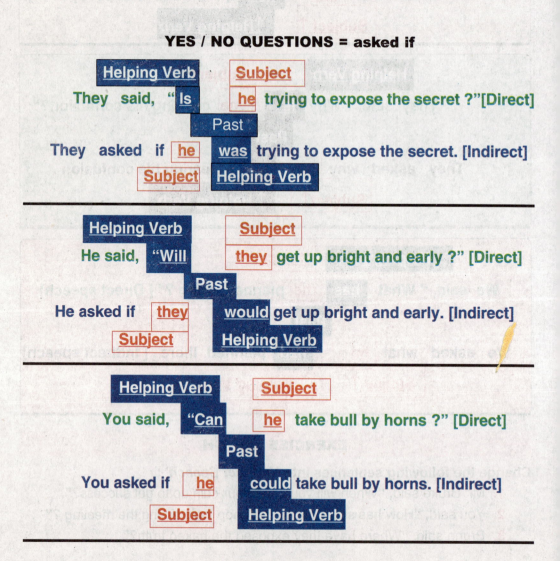

YES / NO QUESTIONS = asked if

Helping Verb   Subject

They said, "Is   he trying to expose the secret ?"[Direct]

Past

They asked if he was trying to expose the secret. [Indirect]

Subject   Helping Verb

Helping Verb   Subject

He said, "Will   they get up bright and early ?" [Direct]

Past

He asked if they would get up bright and early. [Indirect]

Subject   Helping Verb

Helping Verb   Subject

You said, "Can   he take bull by horns ?" [Direct]

Past

You asked if he could take bull by horns. [Indirect]

Subject   Helping Verb

EXERCISE NO. 7-I

Change the following sentences into _'Indirect Speech'_:

1. She said, "Are they willing to continue the discussion under the cloud ?"
2. You said, "Has he become a cold turkey after the medical treatment ?"
3. They said to her, "Was she clearing her confusion ?"
4. He said, "Have you corrected all the mistakes ?"
5. I said, "Will the teachers perform well in their classes ?"
6. Kanika said, "Could the parents complain against the teachers ?"
7. Flavian said, "Are you willing to meet him in a cold light day ?"
8. Fleming said to me, "Will her student pass the exam ?"
9. Mili said, "Can you help me to solve this problem ?"
10. Clara said to Rosy, "Have the judge sentenced him for life imprisonment in cold blood ?"
11. Monica said, "Can he cook your goose secretly in order to upset you ?"
12. Hick said, "Will she call you to get some help ?"
13. Jack said, "Has she been in common touch after getting a gold medal in the Asian Games ?"
14. Mr. Donwalker said, "Have too many cooks spoiled my dinner ?"
15. I said, "Will the green-grocer sell vegetables at reasonable rates ?"

YES / NO QUESTIONS [Do / Does / Did]

Cut = Do / Does / Did. Use asked if

1. Does/do = Verb **2ⁿᵈ form** [Past form]   **2. Did** = **had** + Verb **3ʳᵈ form.**

Ex.   I said, " Does she meet him for discussion ?" [Direct speech]
      asked if↑   ↑cut   Past

      I asked if   she met him for discussion. [Indirect Speech]

Ex.   X
    You said to me, " Do they remember him because of his good nature?"
       asked if ↑ ↑cut   Past   [Direct Speech]

    You asked me if they remembered him because of his good nature.
                                              [Indirect Speech]

Ex.   X
    Rinkey said , " Does Sakshi accept the gift ?" [Direct Speech]
     asked if ↑   ↑cut   Past

    Rinkey asked if Sakshi accepted the gift. [Indirect Speech]

Ex.   Nelson said, "Does he appreciate her diplomatically?"
       asked if↑   ↑cut   Past   [Direct Speech]

    Nelson asked if he appreciated her diplomatically.
                                              [Indirect Speech]

Ex. My brother said, "Did she help her sister during assessment ?"

Solution: [Direct Speech]

Did = Had

My brother <u>said</u>, "Did she <u>help</u> her sister during assessment ?"
<u>asked if</u> ↑ Did [Direct Speech]
Had

My brother <u>asked if</u> she had helped her sister during assessment.

[Indirect Speech]

Did = Had

Ex. Hick <u>said</u>, "Did he <u>provide</u> such facilities to them ?" [Direct]
<u>asked if</u> ↑ Did
Had

Hick <u>asked if</u> he had provided such facilities to them.

[Indirect Speech]

Did = Had

Ex. John <u>said</u>, "Did Jack advise so ridiculously for the project ?"
<u>asked if</u> ↑ Did [Direct Speech]
Had

John <u>asked if</u> Jack had advised so ridiculously for the project.

[Indirect Speech]

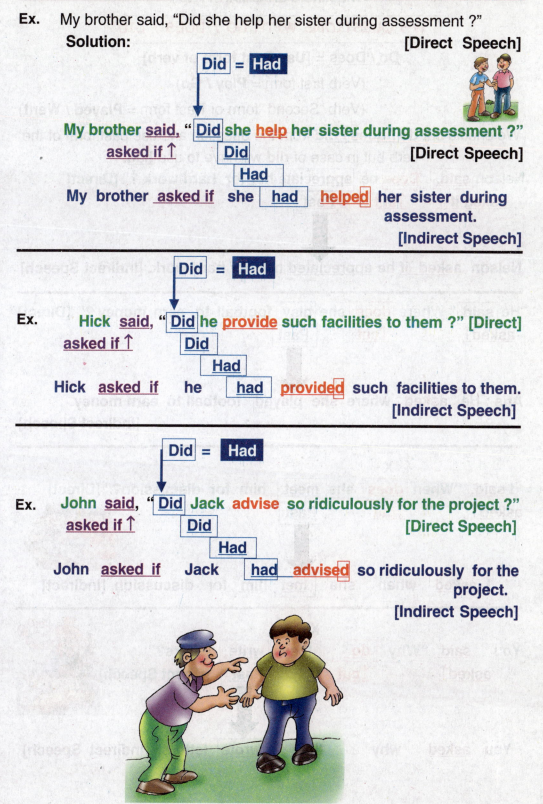

"WH QUESTIONS WITH DO / DOES / DID"

Do / Does = [Use Past form of verb]

(Verb first form = **Play / Go**)

(Verb Second form or Past form = **Played / Went**)

We should cut **do / does / did** from the question and use past form of the verb but in case of **did** we have to use **had.**

Nelson said, "Does he appreciate her for hard work ?" [Direct]
asked if ↑   ↑cut   Past

Nelson asked if he appreciated her for hard work. [Indirect Speech]

He said, " Where does she play football to earn money ?" [Direct]
asked↑   ↑cut   Past

Ans : He asked where she played football to earn money.
[Indirect Speech]

X

I said, "When does she meet him for discussion?" [Direct]
asked↑   ↑cut   Past

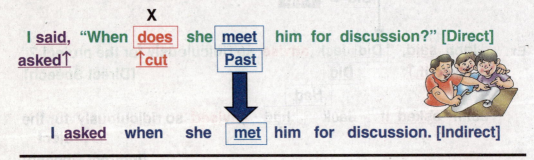

I asked when she met him for discussion. [Indirect]

X

You said, "Why do they write letters?"
asked↑   ↑cut   Past   [Direct Speech]

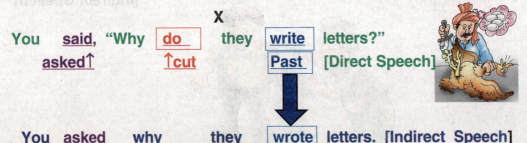

You asked why they wrote letters. [Indirect Speech]

Cut **did** and use **had + Verb 3rd form** (Past Participle)

X

My brother <u>said</u>, "How ~~did~~ she ~~confess~~ her crime in the court?"
<u>asked</u>↑ **Had**   [Direct Speech]

My brother <u>asked</u> how she had confessed her crime in the court.
[Indirect Speech]

X

She <u>said</u>, "When ~~did~~ he ~~provide~~ them instructions without any
<u>asked</u>↑ **Had** permission?"
                                    [Direct Speech]

She <u>asked</u> when he had provided them instructions without
any permission.

[Indirect Speech]

X

You <u>said</u>, "Where ~~did~~ they ~~collect~~ the information for their project?"
<u>asked</u>↑ **Had**   [Direct Speech]

You <u>asked</u> where they had collected the information for their project.
[Indirect Speech]

EXERCISE NO. 7-J

Change the following sentences into 'Indirect Speech' :

1. I said, "When does he sing a song in his empty apartment?"
2. She said, "Where do they spend their high days and holidays?
3. You said, "Why do you feel so ashamed after supporting the devil of terror?"
4. They said, "When did he kill the goose laying golden eggs?"
5. He said, "Where does he have to collect his money from?"
6. The President said to the members, "Why do you want the election?"
7. My brother said, "How does she know the high and mighty personalities?"
8. Sanjay said, "When did they vote against that corrupt minister?"
9. Yukta said, "Where do all the people wait for me with open arms?"
10. Your friend said, "Which news do you think can hit the headlines?"
11. Ashok said to Rishi, "Why did she not pass the exam?"
12. David said, "Who does his work irresponsibly?"

COMMAND / ORDER

ORDER

These sentences begin with the **first form of Verb,**

1. **Bring** me a glass of water. [Order]

      Verb 1ˢᵗ form

2. **Sing** a song for us. [Order]

      Verb 1ˢᵗ form

3. **Do** your duty properly. [Order]

      Verb 1ˢᵗ form

4. **Write** a letter to your parents. [Order]

      Verb 1ˢᵗ form

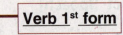

Said to = Ordered

to

She **said to** Henry, "Sing a song for him." [Direct]

ordered

She **ordered** Henry **to** sing a song for him. [Indirect]

PLEASE = REQUESTED TO

You **said**, " **Please** help him immediately." [Direct]

requested to

You **requested** to help him immediately. [Indirect]

EXERCISE NO. 7-K

Change the following sentences into *'Indirect Speech'* **:**

1. I said, "Please try to understand his poor condition."
2. You said, "Get out from my room."
3. They said, "Continue your work."
4. He said, "Please help me."
5. My brother said, "Do your duty properly."
6. She said, "Please write a letter to my parents."
7. You said, "Work hard otherwise you may fail."
8. I said, "Tell him to meet me."
9. The teacher said, "Write neatly and correctly."
10. Rick said, "Please give me your books."

LET SENTENCES

EXAMPLES :

1. Akshata said to Angel, "Let us go to school." **[Direct]**
   Akshata proposed Angel that they should go to school. **[Indirect]**
2. Hick said, "Let us have dinner." **[Direct]**
   Hick proposed that they should have dinner. **[Indirect]**
3. I said, "Let us do some work." **[Direct]**
   I suggested that we should do some work. **[Indirect]**
4. She said to my friends, "Let me work." **[Direct]**
   She requested my friends to let her work. **[Indirect]**
5. My father said, "Let your homework be completed before 6 o' clock." **[Direct]**
   My father ordered him to complete his home work before 6 o'clock. **[Indirect]**
6. He shouted, "Let me go." **[Direct]**
   He shouted to let him go. **[Indirect]**
7. The beggar said, "Let me have a cup of tea." **[Direct]**
   The beggar desired that he might have a cup of tea. **[Indirect]**

EXCLAMATION AND WISHES

Change the 'Exclamatory Sentence' into 'Assertive Sentence' and write again.

Hari said, "What a beautiful girl she is !" [Exclamatory Sentence]
[Direct]

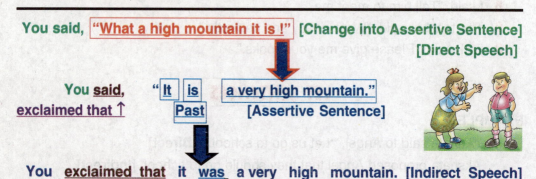

Hari said, " She is a very beautiful girl."
exclaimed that ↑   Past   [Assertive Sentence]

Hari exclaimed that she was a very beautiful girl. [Indirect Speech]

You said, "What a high mountain it is !" [Change into Assertive Sentence]
[Direct Speech]

You said,   "It is   a very high mountain."
exclaimed that ↑   Past   [Assertive Sentence]

You exclaimed that it was a very high mountain. [Indirect Speech]

Rules : Alas – exclaimed with sorrow.
Hurrah – exclaimed with joy.

Examples :

1. The tall man said, "Alas ! I cannot talk." **[Direct]**
   The tall man exclaimed with sorrow that he could not talk. **[Indirect]**

2. The writer said, "Hurrah! I have got the Nobel Prize." **[Direct]**
   The writer exclaimed with joy that he had got the Nobel Prize. **[Indirect]**

3. The commander said, "Soldiers, may God bless you!" **[Direct]**
   Addressing the soldiers the commander prayed that God might bless them.
   [Indirect]

4. She said to us, "Good luck, my friends!" **[Direct]**
   She bade good luck to his friends. **[Indirect]**

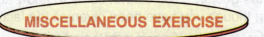

MISCELLANEOUS EXERCISE

EXERCISE NO. 7-L

Change the following sentences into 'Indirect Speech' :

1. My father said, "Money will burn a hole in your pocket very soon."

2. She said, "They are working hard so they will find roses, roses all the way."

3. The Prime Minister said, "All the food should be distributed among the poor people only."

4. The traveller said, "I want to know about the way to the temple built by Ashoka, the great king."

5. The Commander said, "Before the enemies will be alert, attack and kill them, one minute before the midnight."

6. The teacher said, "Birbal was famous for his quick-witted judgments and accurate decisions."

7. The young lady said, "Please leave him. The fellow whom you are beating is my husband not a pick-pocket."

8. She said, "I hope that he will even do a necessary evil to get a good result of his hard work."

9. " What a foolish idea !" said the lecturer, "You are crying for a full moon in a dark sky without stars."

10. "Wilson College is located near the sea side," said the guide, "You will have to hire a taxi as it is 100 miles away from here."

11. "If anyone has to rely on you, he will have to sacrifice his life," said the traitor.

12. "According to the Kerala State Beverages Corporation, the state has lost the first position to Tamil Nadu in the percapita consumption of liquor in the country," the MLA said.

13. The General Manager said, "Colgate gets another seal of approval from the Indian Dental Association."

14. She said, "The award was judged by a panel of eminent business tycoons."

15. The Jail Superintendent said, "Twenty-one women inmates of Lucknow Jail have been selected for the eight-month dress designing course."

16. The doctor said, "The next stage is to change the pattern of your breathing."

17. They said, "We must try to look after the court's decision in order to get proper relief."

18. "I am Prof. Sinha," he said, "The most unfortunate person who is not eligible to acquire any achievement in life..."

19. She said, "Curse him. He is now feeling like a lamb in a slaughter house."

20. She said to the doctor, " You cannot come to know about the real cause of disease even though you have been given all the facilities."

21. Listen Minister, "said the King, "Open the royal treasure and distribute everything to the poor people."

22. The saint said, "Remember, if you do a crime, you will go to hell and God will never accept you as His son."

23. They said, "Let us continue our hard work with zeal and honesty."

24. The teacher admired, "He got a golden hand-shake after the retirement from his job."

25. "How silly you are !" she said, "You should know very well about her life style as you are his friend."

26. "I am sorry," he said, " We all are sinners."

27. The pilot said, " There is no hope to land, pray to God for safety."

28. The teacher said, "Your forked tongue will only insult you without any reason."

29. "Ah !" the old woman said, "Don't kill me."

30. "Your itching palm is the main cause of your failure," the Manager said.

31. The customer said, "The products are not as remarkable as they are expected to be."

32. "Oh !" my sister said, "I am hungry but I cannot see a greasy spoon near by."

33. Madonna said, "You must speak French and Tamil if you want to improve your accent."

34. The student said, "Why are you watching me like a hawk during the exam time ?"

35. "After his failure in the test, he is crazy like a cut snake," my friend said.

| **A Final Concept to Indirect Speech : two or more than two sentences** |

Example :

She said, "I want to work hard. I will surely achieve the target. Why is he trying to cheat me ? **Am** I looking to be a foolish girl? Please tell me the truth."

(1) Use Verb after the Subject

She said, "I want to work hard. I will surely achieve the target. Why

is he trying to cheat me ? Am I looking to be a foolish girl ? Please tell me the truth."

She said, "I want to work hard. I will surely achieve the target. Why he is trying to cheat me ? I am looking to be a foolish girl ? Please tell me the truth."

(2) Use Reporting Verb

She said that I want to work hard. She added that I will surely achieve the target.

She asked why he is trying to cheat me ? She further asked if I am looking to be a foolish girl ? She requested to tell me the truth.

(3) Use only Full Stop

She said that I want to work hard. She added that I will surely achieve the target.

She asked why he is trying to cheat me. She further asked if I am looking to be a foolish girl. She requested to tell me the truth.

(4) Mark the 1ˢᵗ Verb and change them in Past tense.

She said that I want to work hard. She added that I will surely achieve the target.

She asked why he is trying to cheat me. She further asked if I am looking to be a foolish girl. She requested to tell me the truth.

Verbs into Past Tense

She said that I wanted to work hard. She added that I would surely achieve the target.

She asked why he was trying to cheat me. She further asked if I was looking to be a foolish girl. She requested to tell me the truth.

(5) Mark and change the 1ˢᵗ & 2ⁿᵈ person.

She said that I wanted to work hard. She added that I would surely achieve the target.

She asked why he was trying to cheat me. She further asked if I was looking to be a foolish girl. She requested to tell me the truth.

Ans : She said that she wanted to work hard. She added that she would surely achieve the target.

She asked why he was trying to cheat her. She further asked if she was looking to be a foolish girl. She requested to tell her the truth. **(Indirect Speech)**

EXERCISE NO. 7-M

Change the following sentences from 'Direct to Indirect Speech' :

1. "Sana, I have a surprise for you," I said.

   "I'll take off my coat and hat and show you a magic."

   She said, "No, wait. I do't want to see any magic as I am getting late for my school."

2. One afternoon, I said to my mother, "I won a gold medal and a golden pen."

   "You have worked hard for many weeks," she sighed, "I'm proud of you, my son."

3. "You do not understand," she said, "I want to become a teacher."

   "Will you tell me something about your academic plans?" my mother asked.

4. Andy said, "The matter has gone far away from your grip because of your foolishness. You seem to be totally senseless."

   She replied, "I shall go ahead with my unchanged program. Victory needs patience and courage."

5. Donna said," I feel that I'll succeed in my next attempt." "Why Donna, don't you agree that you have just made a silly attempt, the most unsuccessfully ever in your life ?" her mother asked her.

   "I have discovered the facts. I do not need your suggestion," replied Donna.

6. He suggested foolishly, "Oh Peter Palace ! Walk straight for about twenty minutes, then turn towards the right direction, walk for about two hours then you can ask to the shopkeeper.

   He will tell you about the location of Peter Palace."

   The traveller said, "Thank you for your kind suggestion."

7. "You can tell me about the weather forecast," the farmer said,

   "I'm anxious to continue my farming."

   The astrologer predicted, "No, I am sorry to say that it may not rain."

   "I think that it is going to rain", being disappointed, the farmer said.

8. He said, "I have left my home without closing the door."

   She said, "Do not think of all the trouble as God is with us".

   "You are a foolish lady if you think that God will guard your house," Clara suggested.

9. "I'm hungry and I am waiting for a piece of bread now," said the beggar.

   They said, "We do not have any money so we cannot give you."

   The beggar jumped to his feet and said, "I know what to do !" He picked one of the packets and ran away.

10. "The key is somewhere," she said. "Can't you find it ?"

    "We'll go back and try to find it as soon as possible."

    "You are too angry to understand us. Aren't we too tired to walk any further ?" said the children.

11. "God is also not with us as we're in a pickle now," she cried, "How are you going to get into the house ?"

    He said," That's what I'd like to know."

    The children said, "What'll you do ? We're hungry and want food.

    We must get into the house."

12. Jeffery asked, "Can these books change my fortune ?"

    "Nothing is lucky if you do not work hard. If you want success, set your target and stick to the goal", Grandmother suggested.

13. "There are so many flower plants in the garden," said Rocky, "What is so special about it ?" "We have planted and cared it well," replied Miss Kate.

14. Grandfather said, "You like looking at the waves and floating boats."

    "Yes," said Ram, "But the beach is away from here and I cannot see any taxi. How can we reach there ?" "I am waiting for my friend who will be soon here with his cab so you should have patience," he replied.

15. Sanjay said, "You should respect him with your heart and soul."

    Tamanna ran indoors and came back with tears in her eyes and said, "I am so sorry about my behaviour. Please beg me pardon."

16. "Look ! She is coming towards me. Let's make our sad faces to win her sympathy," Hick suggested. Nancy said, "Yes, while she will be scolding you,

    I shall start weeping along with my friends. It will help you to win her sympathy more easily."

17. "I'm sure, he was not in the classroom. Where has he appeared from ?" asked Tony. "We were saved this morning," said Shailja, "But now we may have punishment." "What a bad luck !" commented Malchom.

18. "Where the hell are you ? He is coming here," said Rick.

    "Only I can answer as I am the worst enemy of yours", replied Sana watching at my sorrowful face.

19. "It shows how foolish you are ! I have made a silly mistake to rely on you," Rambo said. I said, "What a joke ! You have been too cruel to me. You cannot make such comments while I am in need of your guidance."

20. "Are you a wise guy or a fool ? When you have come out of your house without a pen, you cannot appear in the exam," my friend said to me. I said, "Thank you for your kind suggestion. You did a superb job but I have a pencil and a rubber as there is my drawing exam."

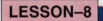

Punctuation Marks

Those marks, which are used to restrict a sentence in a correct order according to the uses, are called '*Punctuation Marks*'.

[.] is needed at the end of each sentence.

Signs to end the sentence

Full Stop → [.]

Question Mark → [?] → [.]

Mark of Exclamation → [!]

What is the difference among these 3 marks?

The placement of Verb **makes all the differences.**

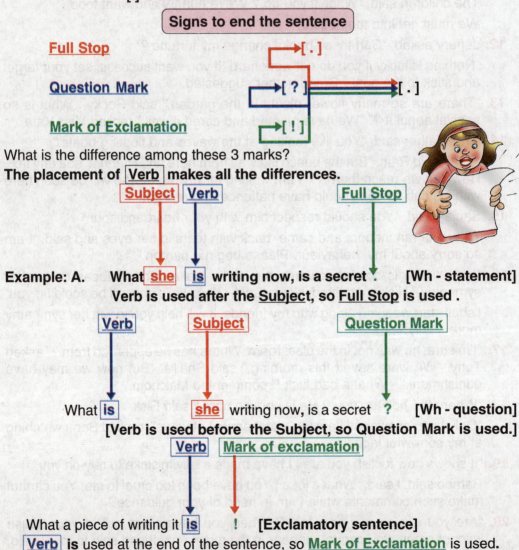

Subject Verb   Full Stop

Example: A.   What she is writing now, is a secret .   [Wh - statement]

Verb is used after the Subject, so Full Stop is used .

Verb   Subject   Question Mark

What is   she writing now, is a secret ?   [Wh - question]

[Verb is used before the Subject, so Question Mark is used.]

Verb Mark of exclamation

What a piece of writing it is   !   [Exclamatory sentence]

Verb **is used at the end of the sentence, so Mark of Exclamation is used.**

Example: B.

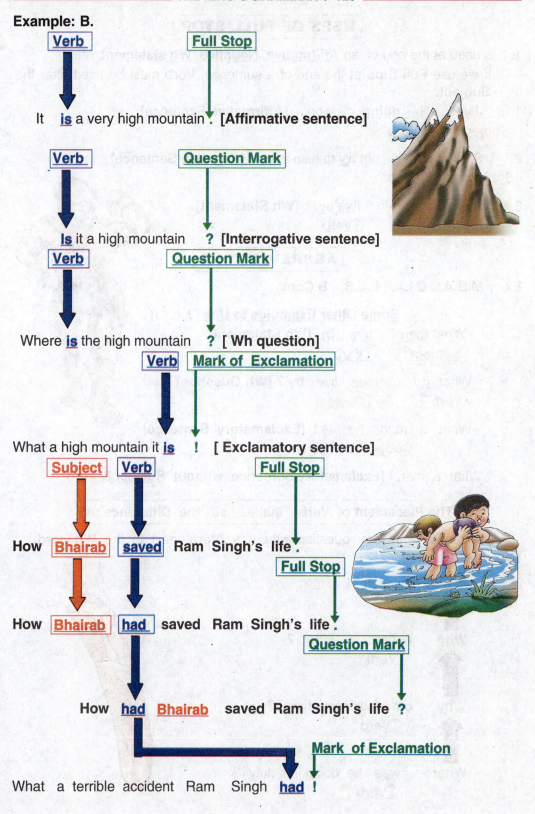

Verb   Full Stop

It **is** a very high mountain **.** [Affirmative sentence]

Verb   Question Mark

Is it a high mountain **?** [Interrogative sentence]

Verb   Question Mark

Where **is** the high mountain **?** [Wh question]

Verb   Mark of Exclamation

What a high mountain it **is** **!** [Exclamatory sentence]

Subject   Verb   Full Stop

How **Bhairab** **saved** Ram Singh's life **.**

Full Stop

How **Bhairab** **had** saved Ram Singh's life **.**

Question Mark

How **had** **Bhairab** saved Ram Singh's life **?**

Mark of Exclamation

What a terrible accident Ram Singh **had** **!**

USES OF FULL STOP

1. It is used at the end of an <u>**Affirmative**</u>, <u>**Negative**</u>, <u>**Wh statement**</u>, etc.

If we use **Full Stop** at the end of a sentence, **Verb** must be used after the **Subject**.

1. <u>**Jack**</u>   <u>**is doing**</u> his work. **[Affirmative Sentence]**
    <u>Subject</u>↑   ↑<u>Verb</u>

2. <u>**She**</u>   <u>**does**</u> not <u>**try**</u> to help you.   **[Negative Sentence]**
    <u>Subject</u>↑   ↑<u>Verb</u>

3. What   <u>**women**</u>   <u>**live**</u> by. **[Wh Statement]**
    <u>Subject</u>↑   ↑<u>Verb</u>

ABBREVIATIONS

Ex.   **M.B.A. , C.I.A. , L.L.B. , B.Com.**

<u>**Some Other Examples to Use**</u> **[? . !]**

What <u>**men**</u>   <u>**live**</u>_ by. **[Wh Statement]**
<u>Subject</u>↑   ↑<u>Verb</u>

What <u>**do**</u>   <u>**men**</u> live by **?** **[Wh Question]**
<u>Verb</u> ↑   ↑<u>Subject</u>

What a man <u>**he**</u> <u>**is**</u> **!** **[Exclamatory Sentence]**
<u>Subject</u>↑   ↑<u>Verb</u>

What a man **!** **[Exclamatory Sentence without <u>Subject & Verb</u>]**

The Placement of Verb   Makes   all   the Difference :

We cannot write any question without a **'<u>Verb</u>'** next to the **<u>Wh word</u>**.
Ex.

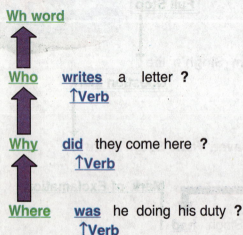

<u>Wh word</u>

<u>Who</u>   <u>writes</u> a letter **?**
    ↑<u>Verb</u>

<u>Why</u>   <u>did</u> they come here **?**
    ↑<u>Verb</u>

<u>Where</u>   <u>was</u> he doing his duty **?**
    ↑<u>Verb</u>

[OR]

<u>Helping Verb</u> must be used before the <u>**Subject**</u> :

Ex.

1. Which   book   **is**   **she**   reading **?**
                ↑Verb   ↑**Subject**

2. Whose   pen   **has**   **he**   stolen **?**
                ↑Verb   ↑ **Subject**

3. **Does**   **she**   play   chess **?**
       ↑Verb   ↑ **Subject**

4. **Are**   **they**   swimming   now **?**
      ↑Verb   ↑ **Subject**

Mark of Exclamation !

There are three types of '<u>**Exclamatory Sentences**</u>'.

Ex.

1. <u>Alas !</u> he is dead. [<u>**Interjection**</u> & Simple Sentence]

2. What a wonderful idea **!** [Exclamatory sentence <u>**without a Verb**</u>]

3. What a wonderful idea it **is !** [Exclamatory sentence <u>**with a Verb**</u> at the end]
                    ↑Verb

EXERCISE NO. 8-A

Punctuate the sentences given below using *'Full stop'*, *'Question mark'* and *'Mark of exclamation'* [**.** / **?** / **!**].

1. Where she is trying to get a job, is unknown

2. How is he playing without any guidance

3. What a man he is

4. What a joke

5. Does she have a good idea

6. Why has he taken your book

7. What a lovely drive

8. They must be happy to know about it

9. Where she is going now, is a secret

10. May I help you

11. Do you know the hidden truth

12. They might have exposed your secret

13. Alas her father has passed away
14. Should she be angry to see you
15. How wonderful you are
16. What do people know about it
17. What a fantastic performance
18. You will have to fight your own battle
19. Why will you discontinue it
20. It is a remarkable victory

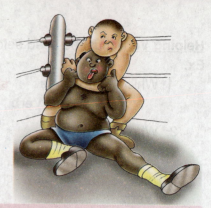

EXERCISE NO. 8-B

Use '*Capital letters*' and '*Punctuate*' the paragraph given below using '*Full stop*', '*Question mark*' and '*Mark of exclamation*' [. / ? / !]

Gandhiji is our father of nation once he had been to South Africa he was travelling in a first class compartment after some time a white person came and requested him to leave the compartment and go to the 3rd class compartment where coloured people used to travel he had a first class ticket so he refused to leave the compartment the T.T.E. was called he asked where is your ticket Gandhi showed it but again he asked, will you leave this compartment "Gandhiji exclaimed what a joke why should I leave the compartment" he further asked when he refused to do so he was thrown out with his luggage from the compartment Gandhiji was shocked Ah what a humanity he could not get justice this insulting incident lit the fire of freedom in Gandhiji's heart.

USES OF COMMA [,]

(*i*) Same '**Parts of speech**' in a sentence.

Noun

Ram , **Sita** , **Hari** , **Radha** , **Mohan** , **Gita** , **Rakesh** and **Ravina** are waiting for you.

(*ii*) **Pairs** in a sentence.

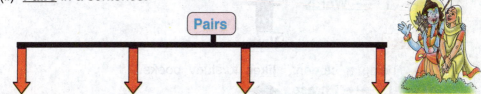

Pairs

Ram and Sita , **Hari and Radha** , **Mohan and Geeta** , **Rakesh and Ravina** , are waiting for you.

(*iii*) **Same Tenses** in a sentence.

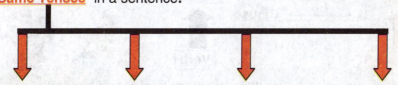

Ram is reading, **Sita is singing**, **Hari is playing** but **I am studying**.
↑**Present Continuous** ↑**Present Con**. ↑ **Present Con**. ↑**Present Con**.

(*iv*) A Set of **Phrases:**

Being late, **having mistakes in his work**, he was scolded by the boss.

(*v*) A set of **Clauses**

Because he is laughing, **as she is smiling**, **I am happy**.

Usually 'Subject' and 'Verb' are used together in a sentence.

When **Subject** and **Verb** are far away from each other, commas will be used after '**Subject**' and before '**Verb**' in the sentence.

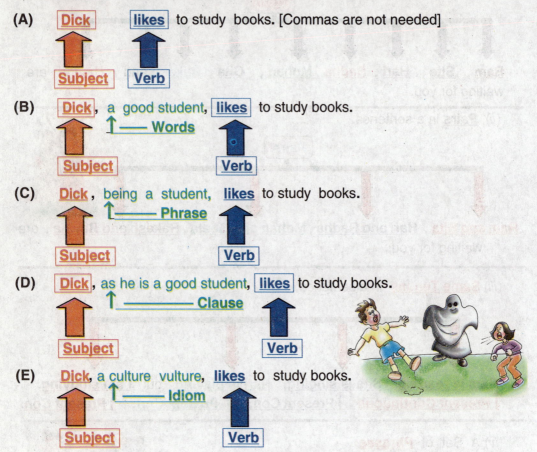

(A) Dick likes to study books. [Commas are not needed]

Subject Verb

(B) Dick, a good student, likes to study books.
↑ —— **Words**
Subject Verb

(C) Dick, being a student, likes to study books.
↑ ——— **Phrase**
Subject Verb

(D) Dick, as he is a good student, likes to study books.
↑ ——————— **Clause**
Subject Verb

(E) Dick, a culture vulture, likes to study books.
↑ ——— **Idiom**
Subject Verb

Usually 'Helping verb' and 'Main verb' are used together.

When '**Helping Verb**' and '**Main Verb**' are far away from each other, commas will be used after '**Helping verb**' and before '**Main verb**' in the sentence.

She **is trying** to cheat us.

[Commas are not needed as **helping verb** and **main verb** are used together]

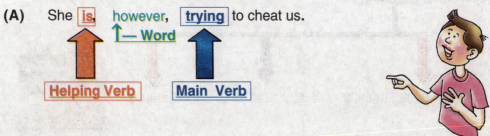

(A) She is however, trying to cheat us.
↑— **Word**
Helping Verb **Main Verb**

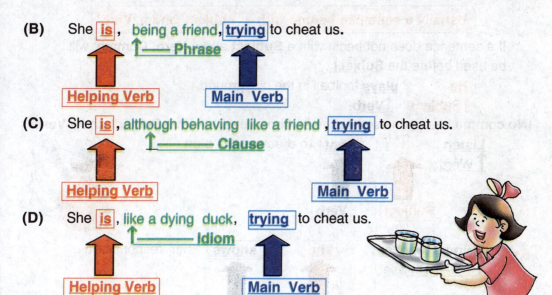

(B) She is , being a friend, trying to cheat us.

↑—— Phrase

Helping Verb   Main Verb

(C) She is , although behaving like a friend , trying to cheat us.

↑———— Clause

Helping Verb   Main Verb

(D) She is , like a dying duck, trying to cheat us.

↑———— Idiom

Helping Verb   Main Verb

Usually a sentence begins with a 'Subject' and a 'Verb'

If a sentence does not begin with a **Subject** and a **Verb**, **Comma** will be used before the **Subject** .

He   plays football in the playground.
↑Subject   ↑Verb.

[**No comma** has been used as the sentence begins with a **Subject** and a **Verb**]

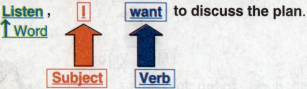

Listen ,   **I**   **want** to discuss the plan.
↑Word

Subject   Verb

Being a teacher ,   **she**   **knows** her responsibility.
↑———— Phrase

Subject   Verb

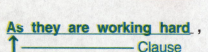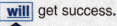

As they are working hard ,   **they**   **will** get success.
↑————————— Clause

Subject   Verb

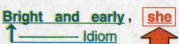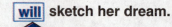

Bright and early ,   **she**   **will** sketch her dream.
↑———— Idiom

Subject   Verb

(*vi*) When a sentence begins with **a joining word** [Subordinating Conjunction], [,] **Comma** will be used between the two **Clauses** [or] **Sentences**

As she came, he had gone.
↑Joining word [Subordinator]

Whenever you call me, I shall come to meet you.
↑Joining word [Subordinator]

Because she is my friend, I shall help him.
↑Joining word [Subordinator]

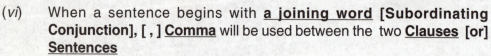

Usually a sentence begins with a 'Subject' and a 'Verb'.

(*vii*) **Comma** can be used when an extra word **(Noun / Pronoun)** is added at the end of a sentence or in the beginning of a sentence. **[Vocative Case]**

(1) Come here, <u>**Hick**</u>.
　　　　　　↑**Noun**

(2) She is writing a letter, <u>**Rick**</u>.
　　　　　　　　　　　↑**Noun**

[This statement is told to <u>**Rick**</u>]

(3) <u>**Silvia**</u> , why are you sad ?
　　-Noun

(4) <u>**Mack**</u> , you are not doing your home work.
　　-Noun

(viii) <u>**Comma**</u> is used in <u>**Direct Speech.**</u>
She said, "I am waiting for you."
"Why are you making so many mistakes?," the teacher asked.

(ix) **Numbers: 2,00,00,00,00,000.**

(x) When after an exclamatory expression, mark of exclamation is not used ;
but it is used at the end of the sentence, comma will be used after the
exclamatory expression .

E.g. **O God ! I am helpless. / O God , I am helpless!**

(xi) **INVERTED COMMAS**　 " "

Used in <u>**Direct Speech** .</u>

(i) She said, "I want to meet you."

(ii) You asked, "Why have they gone?"

EXERCISE NO. 8-C

Use *'Commas', 'Full Stops'* **and** *'Capital letters'* **in the following sentences:**

1. Whatever she decides does it at any cost
nothing is impossible for her as being an iron
lady her determination is her motto hard work
is her routine and dedication is her life

2. Watch me I have to go ahead in my life nobody
is here to accompany me except you please
be my inspiration empower me with words and
help me to achieve the culmination of life

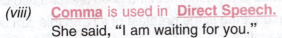

3. Perhaps they would like to create problems even though
they are your friends they have no sympathy regarding
the loss you have had in your business

4. Some days ago sleeping in the garden I found myself
lost in the dream world everything seemed to be beautiful

5. Milton being a great poet had no eyes to see anything in the world but his soul could feel the beauty of nature it inspired him and thus he could write his poetic feelings

6. She therefore returned back to her home after being cheated insulted and scolded after all she did not reply anything I think she will definitely take her revenge

7. Opportunity never knocks the door if you do not work hard you cannot get success in your life try to understand the critical stages of your life

8. One has to be a low brow a bit to a politician ready and willing to see people sacrificed slaughtered for the sake of an idea whether a good one or a bad one

9. The only real dignified human doctrine is the greatest of all and this can only be achieved by utmost self-sacrifice

10. The roots of education can be bitter but the fruits are sweet

11. Where might is a master justice is a servant

12. Miss Bell being a busy lady must return back early or her parents would be worried

13. Willing to see a cave in the forest I saw some old saints with their followers having bath in a lake praying to God and preaching for peace

EXERCISE NO. 8-D

Use 'Commas' and 'Full Stops' and 'Capital letters' in the following sentences:

1. Having insulted me he because of his rubbish behaviour would be losing so many friends would avoid repeating the same in the future to anybody

2. Get out I do not want to see your face Meghna

3. I will work hard continue my attempts stick to the goal achieve the target or die

4. My boss being overloaded with work consequently he will not be able to find these mistakes

5. As I had desired to become an actor I came to Mumbai after facing a horrible struggle my golden dreams shattered into pieces

6. Consult the doctor take care of the patient or her disease will be fatal

7. Meet this fellow you will come to know more about that cheat who has picked my pocket snatched my gold watch made in Japan at the bus stop when I was waiting for the bus to Nasik

8. She was shocked she fell unconscious after the medical treatment she lost her memory power

9. The fox being hungry looking for a piece of bread saw a foolish crow sitting at a branch of a tree he praised the crow for the golden voice and took the bread away the crow could not do anything except opening his beak watching the wicked fox eating his share

10. He after winning the race got the gold medal in Asian Games and never turned back all through his life

11. Sam being a rich merchant people know him as the greatest miser of the city who has no money for the poor and helpless people

12. I am trying to bring dream come true in my real life Sana it is not possible

13. Miss Thatcher may not be very beautiful her nature is very good but her parents are too rude

Capital Letter

1. <u>A Sentence</u> always begins with a **Capital letter.**
2. <u>Capital letters</u> are used for writing **topics or titles.**
3. <u>Capital letters</u> are used in abbreviations. **(I. A. S., M.Com., C.A. etc.)**
4. <u>A Proper Noun</u> always begins with a **Capital letter.(Bangalore,Delhi,etc,)**
5. <u>I</u> and <u>O</u> are always **Capital**. (When they are not used in **words**)
   Example:
   - A. <u>I</u> am trying to solve the problem.
   - B. As she is my friend, '<u>**Oh God**</u> help him !
   - C. He knows that <u>I</u> am unhappy.
6. **Capital letter** is used within <u>**Inverted Commas**</u> ["   "].
   Example: A. You said, " It is your duty now. "
   B. I said, "You will have lost every thing."
7. **Capital letter** is used to provide importance to the word.

Apostrophe

- A. <u>**Possessives**</u> : Girls' hostel , my father's book, your friend's dress etc.
- B. <u>**Omission of letters**</u> : She'll not continue the job.

Hyphen

Compound Word

1. A man-of-words
2. walking-stick
3. dining-table

Compound Adjective

1. <u>kind-hearted</u> man
2. <u>soft-spoken</u> doll
3. <u>dull-minded</u> fellow.

Compound Noun

1. Sister-in-law
2. Commander-in-chief
3. Step-son.

Compound Number

1. Three-fourth land
2. One-third area.

Compound Sentence (without conjunction)

He worked hard-he did not have proper planning.

Prefix & Suffix

Hyphen is used with some Prefixes and Suffixes
Anti-terrorism, Anti-nationalism, etc.

Same Vowel or Consonant Sound

Same Vowel or **Consonant sound :**

Pre-examination.

6-8-2000

EXERCISE NO. 8-E

Use 'Commas', 'Full Stops', 'Capital letters' 'Apostrophe' and 'Hyphen' etc. in the following sentences:

1. Tell me the fact if you have faith on me

2. Miss I would like to help you regarding your academic problems

3. Taj Mahal which was built by Shahjahan is said to be a great wonder in the world

4. i want to help you come and meet me if you are helpless

5. a few of them are sub-normal some of them are and many of these fellows are devils

6. peter however tried to achieve the goal rest of them even didn t attempt

7. as i met him he who had been a good friend of mine refused to talk

8. when she went to meet her friends she saw that it was <u>raining cats and dogs</u> she returned back she saw that a dog was chasing a cat

9. long long ago king vikramaditya who was a well known king had been loved by all the citizens of his kingdom even he is honoured today the stories based on his life are retold everywhere in india

10. life as a housewife is not a bed of roses her hard work has proved her importance in the family life

11. once a young man went to Buddha s ashram in order to have his blessing as he honoured buddha and he desired to have wisdom then buddha asked what is your caste the young man replied I dont know even then he preached and accepted him as his disciple as the man spoke the truth

12. while sitting under the tree she tried to collect all the fruits fallen from the branches some fruits were fresh some rotten and some half eaten

13. as children love nehruji he is called as chacha nehru a symbol of love and devotional feeling

14. bombay which is said to be the bollywood is facing the problem of film piracy as the movies are pirated and shown on cable it is very difficult for the producers to get more profit

15. a good character is made up of faith truthfulness and devotional life

16. A home is a temple of joy a classroom of honesty an institution of amusement an academy of happiness a home is where you get love not where you live

17. There are two types of fools a rich merchant who feels money is the only power to conquer the world the second one is the reformer who feels he can cure the world by snatching money form rich people distributing it to the people who are lazy careless poor and powerless

18. Never lose courage indignation patience perseverance these are the most precious gifts you being a man of words must preserve them in the treasure of life

19. My dream my beautiful world is visible while closing my eyes in a calm cool peaceful and painless environment only unfortunately my real life is a world without dream ambition hope and desire

Semi colon ;

(A) When there are many sentences or pieces of sentences telling or explaining about **the first Subject**, semi colon will be used.

first subject

Ram is an intelligent boy; he has got highest marks; for that reason he may get a gold medal.

(B) When two sentences are closely related or it affects the other one, semi colon will be used.

1. Bob was a slow swimmer. She put a shark in the pool; **that speeded him up.**

2. She was waiting for a better chance **; and she grabbed it.**

(C) When different thoughts or ideas are approaching the same concept.

Reading makes a full·man; **speaking an active man;** writing an accurate man.

(D) 'And' joins two similar types of sentences.

┌── I like swimming <u>and</u> she also likes swimming.

But when two sentences with opposite ideas or attitudes are joined by and, Semi colon can be used.

└→ I <u>like</u> swimming ; <u>and</u> she <u>hates</u> swimming.

(E) When a comma is used in a co-ordinating clause of a compound sentence, we can use semi colon.

Example: **She is courageous**, **iron-hearted lady; and she is the Prime Minister of U. K.**

Colon :

1) List of anything

It is used for the list of : objects, thoughts, ideas, etc.

(i) The name of states are : Punjab, Kerala, Rajasthan, etc.

(ii) She likes : swimming, singing and dancing.

(iii) He should be loving, having a respective nature and morality : as these are the qualities of a good husband.

2) Quotation

1. Nehruji said : Work is worship.
2. Napoleon said : Nothing is impossible in the world.
3. Plato said : Life is a battle, conquer it .

3) Two Balancing Statements

1. This is right : that is wrong.
2. You are a cheat : he is foolish.
3. It is cold : that is hot.

4) Dialogue

1. John : Will you continue your journey towards Paris ?
2. Thomas : I wish, I could follow you.

5) Two opposite thoughts closely related to each other

Exercise is good for health : no exercise can cure you.

Life is a journey : no one can travel easily.

Dash -

Interruption in a statement

1. Your son ----- I do not know anything about him.
2. I have ------------ nothing to say

Join a group of anything

Lahore bus, Delhi bus, Kathmandu bus, Kabul bus are impossible dreams.

Lahore — Delhi — Kathmandu — Kabul buses are impossible dreams.

EXERCISE NO. 8-F

Supply all the necessary 'Punctuation marks' and 'Capital letters' in the following sentences :

1. the olympic torch which had completed its 100 days odyssey to sydney on thursday was brought into the stadium in a relay by 8 of the greatest woman athletes including swimming sensation shane gould dawn fraser shirley strickland and debbie flintoffking

2. who is the angel asked the child who brings such beautiful presents for the children his name is santa claus replied mother in the night before christmas when everybody is asleep he comes down from the heaven with presents for the good children only

3. if a man is kind he cannot be killed even you kill him he will remain in the heart of people fortune favours the brave who fight for the humanity if you are brave and you fight for the humanity god will bless you

4. god said see the light and follow the path of honesty and truth you will find a heaven on the earth.

5. If you sacrifice your life for the humanity you may be honoured with the crown of honesty in the temple of lord

6. If you leap in the dark you will meet the princess of darkness miss black beauty with sword of damocles

7. peter said you should not play with <u>black diamond</u> if you are <u>clay brained</u> you should work like <u>a clock</u>

8. his bad habits are smoking drinking gossiping roaming outside till the dead of night

9. john being double faced cannot get his <u>duck diamond</u> any more

10. kindly be careful here <u>walls have ears</u> <u>roads have feet</u> <u>words have wings</u> air <u>has feelings</u>

11. although you have itching ears being a man of words you have to lend your ears to those who are <u>apple of your eyes</u> even though you are however not telling a <u>cock and bull</u> story you have to face the music

12. he as a soldier will never show <u>white feather</u> to his enemies while fighting his battle of life he always avoids dry facts if you play <u>ducks and drakes</u> with his sentiments you will have to face the horrible consequences

13. I whenever try to help her always find her busy in the <u>devil's book</u> it is amazing what a foolish idea to use the time if she behaves like this she will never get a single friend till her last enemy

14. diet being a very complicated factor of life plays a very important role in common life even you have healthy body you cannot guide anyone

15. thinking about life i think more about water and soil which help the trees grow green and environment clear cool calm & clean

16. Extremely hot in the desert the <u>henhearted</u> cannot survive in such environment it is however very difficult to adjust

17. A letter can even clear your confusion if you are not confident you should e-mail me i as soon as possible would try to win your confidence

18. phillip being vice chancellor was generally high and mighty you <u>hollowhearted</u> cannot work under him what a comment said he

19. He is quite surprised a little dismayed very much shocked however no one could predict it

20. Adult education if you implement you can educate and develop your nation even though tree plantation campaign would be implemented soon no one knows the future of nation

21. How fortunate you are your hard work patience perseverance would decide it soon I feel work is worship rest is rust sleep is sorrow

22. Please however reconsider your decision if you want everybody to support you being a member of jury you should remain attentive.

Degree of Comparison

When two or more **'Nouns or Pronouns'** are compared with the scale of degree, the comparison is called the **'Degree of Comparison'**.

It has 3 kinds:

1. Positive Degree.
2. Comparative Degree.
3. Superlative Degree.

Positive Degree

When two or more **Nouns** or **Pronouns** are compared to one another, and they have the similar degree of quality, it is called **Positive Degree.**

1. She is as white as snow.
2. He is as foolish as an owl.
3. You are as cunning as a fox.

Comparative Degree

When two or more **Nouns** or **Pronouns** are compared to one another and they have different degree of quality, it is called **Comparative Degree of Comparison.**

1. They are better than you.
2. She is more beautiful than you.
3. He is lazier than you.

Superlative Degree

When one **Noun** or **Pronoun** is compared to more than one **Nouns, Pronouns,** (or) a group, class etc of its own kind having different degrees of quality, it is called **Superlative Degree of Comparison.**

1. He is the best student of this college.
2. She is the most intelligent lady in our society.
3. This is the nearest building to the station.

Degree of Comparison

Singular Number

Positive	Comparative	Superlative	Changes

Ex:

Singular ↓

Ganga is the <u>longest</u> <u>river</u> in India. [Superlative]

Singular ↓

Ganga is <u>longer than any other</u> <u>river</u> in India. [Comparative]

Singular ↓

<u>No other</u> <u>river</u> is <u>as long as</u> Ganga in India . [Positive]

Ex:

Singular ↓

Bible is <u>holier than any other</u> <u>book</u> in theworld. [Comparative]

Singular ↓

Bible is <u>the holiest</u> <u>book</u> in the world. [Superlative]

<u>No other</u> <u>book</u> is <u>as holy as</u> Bible in the world. [Positive]

↑ Singular

Ex:

Singular ↓

<u>No other</u> <u>comedian</u> was <u>as popular as</u> Charlie Chaplin.
[Positive]

Singular ↓

Charlie Chaplin was <u>more popular than any other</u> comedian.
[Comparative]

Singular ↓

Charlie Chaplin was <u>the most popular</u> <u>comedian</u>. [Superlative]

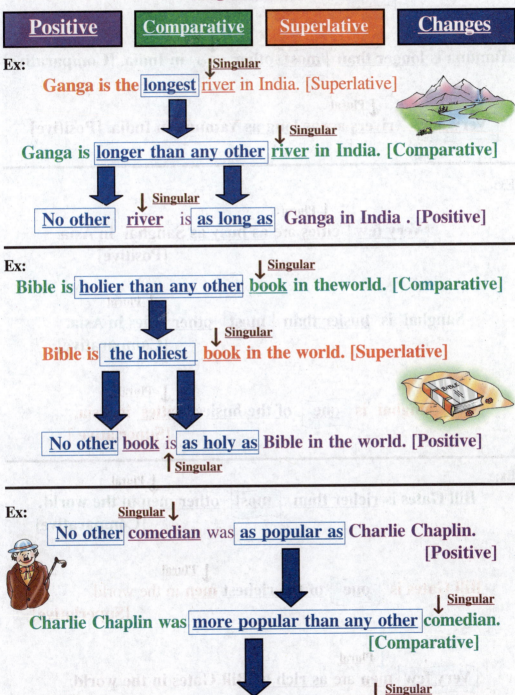

Ex:

Plural Number

Yamuna is [**one**] of the longest ↓ **Plural** **rivers** in India. [Superlative]

Yamuna is <u>longer than</u> [**most**] other ↓ **Plural** **rivers** in India. [Comparative]

[**Very few**] ↓ **Plural** **rivers** are <u>as long as</u> Yamuna in India. [Positive]

Ex:

[**Very few**] ↓ **Plural** **cities** are <u>as busy as</u> Sanghai in Asia.
[Positive]

Sanghai is <u>busier than</u> [**most**] other **cities** ↓ **Plural** in Asia.
[Comparative]

Sanghai is [**one**] of the busiest **cities** ↓ **Plural** in Asia.
[Superlative]

Ex:

Bill Gates is <u>richer than</u> [**most**] <u>other</u> **men** ↓ **Plural** in the world.
[Comparative]

Bill Gates is [**one**] of the richest **men** ↓ **Plural** in the world.
[Superlative]

[**Very few**] ↓ **Plural** **men** are <u>as rich as</u> Bill Gates in the world.
[Positive]

<u>Two Individuals (or) Groups</u>

You cannot transform such sentences into superlative degree.
Ex:

The Atlantic Ocean is deeper than the Arabian Sea anyway.
[Comparative]

↓

The Arabian Sea is not as deep as the Atlantic Ocean anyway.
[Positive]

Ex:

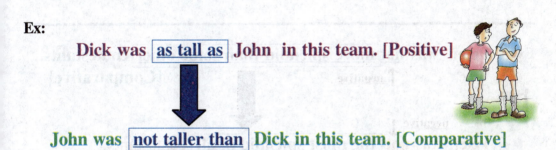

Dick was as tall as John in this team. [Positive]

↓

John was not taller than Dick in this team. [Comparative]

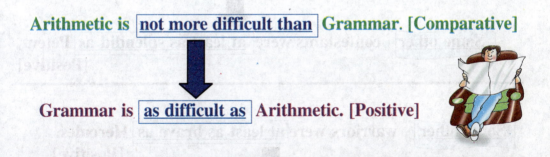

Arithmetic is not more difficult than Grammar. [Comparative]

↓

Grammar is as difficult as Arithmetic. [Positive]

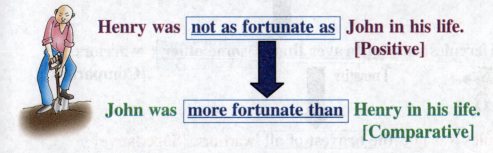

Henry was not as fortunate as John in his life.
[Positive]

↓

John was more fortunate than Henry in his life.
[Comparative]

Negative and Plural

Ex: Big Bazaar is **not** the largest of all Super Markets.
[Superlative]

Big Bazaar is **not** larger than some other Super Markets.
[Comparative]

Some other Super Markets are at least as large as Big Bazaar.
[Positive]

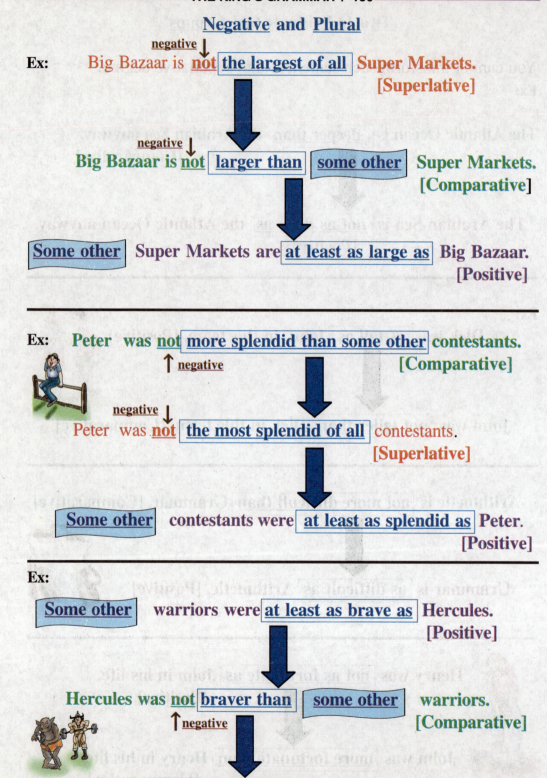

Ex: Peter was **not** more splendid than some other contestants.
[Comparative]

Peter was **not** the most splendid of all contestants.
[Superlative]

Some other contestants were at least as splendid as Peter.
[Positive]

Ex:

Some other warriors were at least as brave as Hercules.
[Positive]

Hercules was **not** braver than some other warriors.
[Comparative]

Hercules was **not** the bravest of all warriors. [Superlative]

Negative and Plural

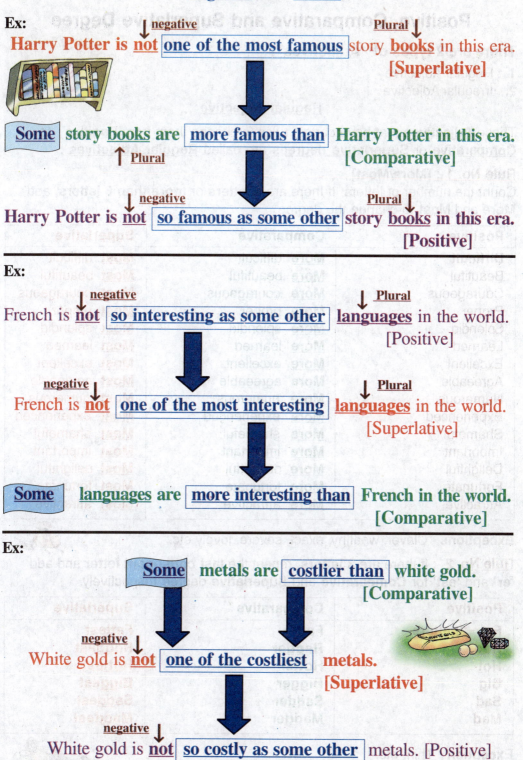

Ex:

negative | Plural

Harry Potter is **not** | **one of the most famous** | story **books** in this era.
[Superlative]

Some | story **books** are | **more famous than** | Harry Potter in this era.
↑ Plural | [Comparative]

negative | Plural

Harry Potter is **not** | **so famous as some other** | story **books** in this era.
[Positive]

Ex:

negative | Plural

French is **not** | **so interesting as some other** | **languages** in the world.
[Positive]

negative | Plural

French is **not** | **one of the most interesting** | **languages** in the world.
[Superlative]

Some | **languages** are | **more interesting than** | French in the world.
[Comparative]

Ex:

Some | metals are | **costlier than** | white gold.
[Comparative]

negative

White gold is **not** | **one of the costliest** | metals.
[Superlative]

negative

White gold is **not** | **so costly as some other** | metals. [Positive]

Table
Positive, Comparative and Superlative Degree

There are 2 types of 'Adjectives' :

1. Regular Adjective
2. Irregular Adjective

Regular Adjective

Those **Adjectives** that have certain rules to change them from **Positive** to **Comparative** or **Superlative degrees** are called **Regular Adjectives** .

Rule No. 1 : [More/Most]
Count the number of letters. If there are **6 letters** or **more than 6 letters,** add **More** and **Most** to change the degree.

Positive	Comparative	Superlative
Difficult	**More** difficult	**Most** difficult
Beautiful	**More** beautiful	**Most** beautiful
Courageous	**More** courageous	**Most** courageous
Proper	**More** proper	**Most** proper
Splendid	**More** splendid	**Most** splendid
Learned	**More** learned	**Most** learned
Excellent	**More** excellent	**Most** excellent
Agreeable	**More** agreeable	**Most** agreeable
Numerous	**More** numerous	**Most** numerous
Experienced	**More** experienced	**Most** experienced
Shameful	**More** shameful	**Most** shameful
Important	**More** important	**Most** important
Delightful	**More** delightful	**Most** delightful
Fortunate	**More** fortunate	**Most** fortunate
Attractive	**More** attractive	**Most** attractive

Exceptions - Clever, wealthy, exact, severe, lovely etc.

Rule No. 2 : If there are **3 letters,** repeat the **last consonant letter** and add 'er' and 'est' for **Comparative** and **Superlative** degree respectively.

Positive	Comparative	Superlative
Fat =3Letters	**Fatter**	**Fattest**
Red	**Redder**	**Reddest**
Hot	**Hotter**	**Hottest**
Big	**Bigger**	**Biggest**
Sad	**Sadder**	**Saddest**
Mad	**Madder**	**Maddest**

Exception - Thin, etc.

Rule No. 3 : If consonant **'y'** is used at the end of the word, **'ier' & 'iest'** are used to change the degree.

Positive	Comparative	Superlative
Wealthy	Wealthier	Wealthiest
Heavy	Heavier	Heaviest
Merry	Merrier	Merriest
Easy	Easier	Easiest
Happy	Happier	Happiest
Dry	Drier	Driest
Ugly	Uglier	Ugliest
Pretty	Prettier	Prettiest
Lovely	Lovelier	Loveliest

Rule No. 4 : **The Adjectives ending with 'e' take 'r' and 'st' to change the degree.**

Positive	Comparative	Superlative
Able	Abler	Ablest
Wise	Wiser	Wisest
Noble	Nobler	Noblest
White	Whiter	Whitest
Fine	Finer	Finest
Brave	Braver	Bravest
Large	Larger	Largest

Rule No. 5 : **Generally Adjectives take 'er' or 'est' to change degree.**

Positive	Comparative	Superlative
Great	Greater	Greatest
Kind	Kinder	Kindest
Bold	Bolder	Boldest
Small	Smaller	Smallest
Young	Younger	Youngest
Sweet	Sweeter	Sweetest
Small	Smaller	Smallest
Tall	Taller	Tallest
Clever	Cleverer	Cleverest

No use of 'er' and 'est' in Regular Adjectives :

In case, there is one person and his own two qualities are compared :
e.g. She is more kind than clever.

Irregular Adjectives

Irregular Adjectives have no rules. Only you have to learn by heart.

Positive	Comparative	Superlative
Far	Farther	Farthest
Fore	Former	Foremost
Many	More	Most
Much	More	Most
Good / well	Better	Best
Little	Less / Lesser	Least
Bad / evil / ill	Worse	Worst
Late	Later	Latest
Old	Older / Elder	Oldest / Eldest
(In)	Inner	Innermost / in most
(Up)	Upper	Uppermost / up most
(Out)	Outer	Utmost / Outer most
(Fore)	Further	Furthest

In, Up, Out, Fore are Adverb forms.

EXERCISE NO. 9-A

Change the '*Degree of Comparison*' :

1. Difficulty is sweeter than victory.
2. My son was the best performer in Air Force Academy, Bangalore.
3. Ironically, education is the most painful aspect of life.
4. Malabar Hill is cooler than Ontophill.
5. You're as intelligent as a man of words.
6. J.R.D. is one of the most popular personalities.
7. Grammar is more difficult than literature.
8. The dancing in India is as varied as the land of India itself.
9. Indian dancers are not as impressive as Western dancers.
10. Shiva is one of greatest classical dancers in the universe.
11. 'Hamlet' is one of the best tragedies in English literature.
12. Hollywood is one of the most important acting centres.
13. The puppet theatre is one of the oldest forms of theatre in India.
14. 'King Lear' is more famous than most other English plays.
15. 'Mayor of Casterbridge' is the most famous novel.
16. Dr.Tony was not as popular as Mr. Bush.
17. Mrs. Thatcher is one of the greatest women in the world.

18. She was one of the greatest orators in her days.
19. My birthplace is better than any other capital city in the world.

20. My mother tongue is the greatest language.
21. Chalk is more important than cheese in our life.
22. The fight for justice is the noblest quality.
23. Terrorism is bigger danger than any other outside threat.
24. The Moon is not as large as the Jupiter.
25. Green Park is as green as the <u>glory of Green Heaven</u>.
26. Some story books are more interesting than Black Night.
27. Water is the greatest boon of the century.
28. Neem is one of the most suitable medicines in hot arid areas.
29. He is more knowledgeable than you.
30. Europeans have the healthiest teeth.
31. This joke book is more famous than most other story books.

32. After your failure, your life is as difficult as a cat on a hot tin roof.
33. His issue is more complicated than a <u>devil's advocacy</u>.
34. She hurried still faster than him.
35. He knows that reading is better than thinking.
36. Mowgli ran as fast as Superman.
37. The <u>West wall</u> was longer than most other walls in the city.
38. He was taller than his grandfather.
39. Sam is not one of the best coaches in the world.
40. Qutub Minar is older than most other historical buildings.
41. Cricket is not one of the most famous sports.
42. Robby has grown taller than his friends.

43. He was thinner than most other contestants.
44. Very few continents are as overpopulated as Asia.
45. Very few plays are as inspiring as Midsummer Night's Dream.
46. Mr. Shaw was the wisest man in U. K.
47. Some story books are more famous than the Fable of Aesop.
48. Mr. Barry is not one of the most experienced scientists.
49. Miss Sana is not more important than some other participants.
50. This is the heaviest metal in this laboratory.
51. Very few factors are as important as the system of life.
52. Bible is the holiest book on the Earth.

53. No other capital city is as busy as London.
54. New York is richer city than Washington D. C.
55. Titanic was larger than any other ship.
56. You are not more intelligent than your sister.
57. Almas is not taller than some other contestants.
58. Very few footballers are as laborious as Ronaldo.
59. Jupiter is not the largest of all planets in the universe.
60. Gladiators were not the bravest of all fighters in Rome.
61. Macbeth was not more intelligent than Macduff.
62. Diana was more beautiful than most other Princesses.
63. Aryans were more creative than any other social reformers.
64. Armstrong's space journey was more adventurous than Gulliver's travel.
65. My knowledge is not more than a drop in the ocean.
66. Making a mountain out of a mole-hill is as easy as telling a cock and bull story.
67. The last hope is as important as last opportunity.
68. Crying for the spilt milk is as foolish as weeping for a moon.
69. Pen is mightier than sword.
70. A fair weather friend is as useless as a gem without gold ring.
71. A feather in your cap is more important than a diamond in your ring.
72. Walls have the more sensitive ears than any other element in this office.

Question Tag

A question which is asked at the tail of a sentence **in order to get confirmation** is called a '**Question Tag.**' **Mostly there are three types of sentences :**

1. Sentences with a '**Helping and a Main Verb.**'
2. Sentences with only one '**Main Verb.**'
3. **Order, Request & Let Sentences .**

 Note : Affirmative sentences = Negative Question Tag
       Negative sentences = Affirmative Question Tag

Helping and Main Verb   **Affirmative Sentences**

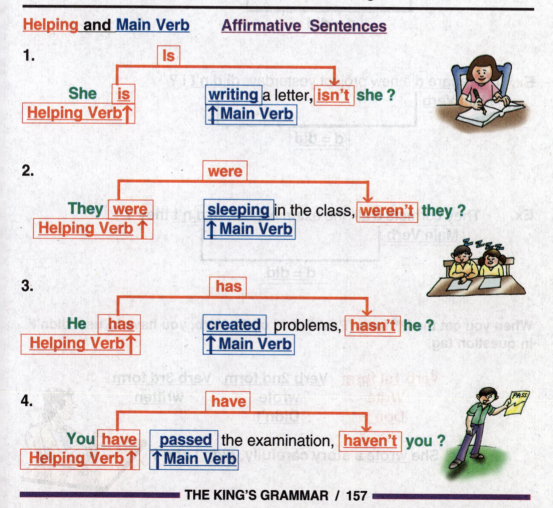

1.
Is

She **is**   **writing** a letter, **isn't** she ?
Helping Verb↑   ↑**Main Verb**

2.
were

They **were**   **sleeping** in the class, **weren't** they ?
Helping Verb ↑   ↑**Main Verb**

3.
has

He **has**   **created** problems, **hasn't** he ?
Helping Verb↑   ↑**Main Verb**

4.
have

You **have**   **passed** the examination, **haven't** you ?
Helping Verb↑   ↑**Main Verb**

THE KING'S GRAMMAR / 157

5. I <u>could</u> solve it, couldn't I ?

Exception : I <u>am</u> very happy, aren't I ? I <u>am</u> very happy, ain't I ?

Only Main Verb

Ex. They <u>cooke</u>d food for me, <u>di d n't</u> they ?
      Main Verb

d = did

Ex. You <u>create</u> d so many problems, <u>di d n't</u> you ?
      Main Verb

d = did

Ex. I <u>prepare</u> d a new project yesterday, <u>di d n't</u> I ?
      Main Verb

d = did

Ex. They <u>correcte</u> d all the exam papers, <u>di d n't</u> they ?
      Main Verb

d = did

When you get the 2ⁿᵈ form [Past Form] of the Verb, you have to use 'didn't' in question tag.

Verb 1st form	Verb 2nd form	Verb 3rd form
Write	wrote	written
Don't	Didn't	

She <u>wrote</u> a story carefully, <u>didn't</u> she ?

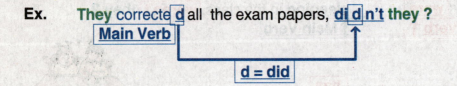

Ex.

She <u>collect</u> <u>s</u> her money to buy a gift, <u>doe</u> <u>s</u> <u>n't</u> she ?
Main Verb

S = does

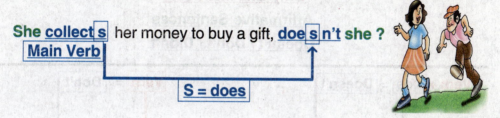

Ex.

He <u>work</u> <u>s</u> hard to achieve his goal, <u>doe</u> <u>s</u> n't he ?
Main Verb

S = does

Ex.

It <u>snow</u> <u>s</u> heavily in Nepal, <u>doe</u> <u>s</u> n't it ?
Main Verb

S = does

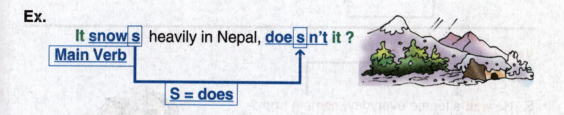

Ex.

Peter <u>know</u> <u>s</u> the fact of life, <u>doe</u> <u>s</u> n't he ?
Main Verb

S = does

1. You have to use <u>doesn't</u> when "S" is used at the end of the '<u>Verb</u>'.

2. When you get 1st form [Base form / Present Form] of the '<u>Verb</u>', you have to use <u>don't</u> in question tag.

Verb 1st form	Verb 2nd form	Verb 3rd form
Write	wrote	written
Don't	Didn't	

They <u>write</u> a poem every day, <u>don't</u> they ?

Only One Main Verb
Affirmative Sentences
Doesn't / Don't / Didn't

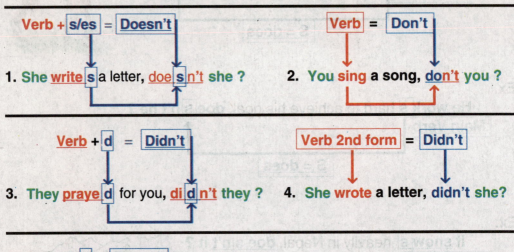

Verb + s/es = Doesn't   Verb = Don't

1. She write s a letter, doe s n't she ?   2. You sing a song, don't you ?

Verb + d = Didn't   Verb 2nd form = Didn't

3. They praye d for you, di d n't they ?   4. She wrote a letter, didn't she?

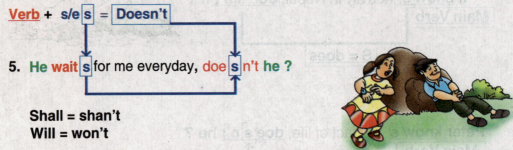

Verb + s/e s = Doesn't

5. He wait s for me everyday, doe s n't he ?

Shall = shan't
Will = won't

EXERCISE NO. 10-A

Rewrite the following sentences adding appropriate 'Question tags':

1. I like to eat food once in a blue moon.
2. Life is a bitter sweet.
3. You have been waiting for her.
4. I shall clear alpha and omega of this fact.
5. My brother is doing his duty for almighty dollar.
6. All the teachers could continue the lectures.
7. I am going to give a lecture on A. I. D. S., an angel of death.
8. Your friends will have to complete the work in time.
9. The policeman arrested the thief.
10. Rick is as old as Adam.
11. You throw stones at your friends.
12. Miss Dolly used to add fuel to fire.

Negative Sentences

Negative Sentences = **Affirmative Question Tags**

We should use helping verbs in **Question tags**.

1. They **did** not catch the thief, **did** they ?
Helping verb↑ ↑negative

2. You **can** not solve it, **can** you ?
Helping verb↑ ↑ negative

3. Sam **could** not approach me, **could** he ?
Helping verb↑ ↑ negative

4. Jack **does** not help you, **does** he ?
Helping verb↑ ↑negative

5. She **could** not cross the river, **could** she ?
Helping verb↑ ↑negative

6. I **shall** not continue this project, **shall** I ?
Helping verb↑ ↑negative

Some Important Question Tags

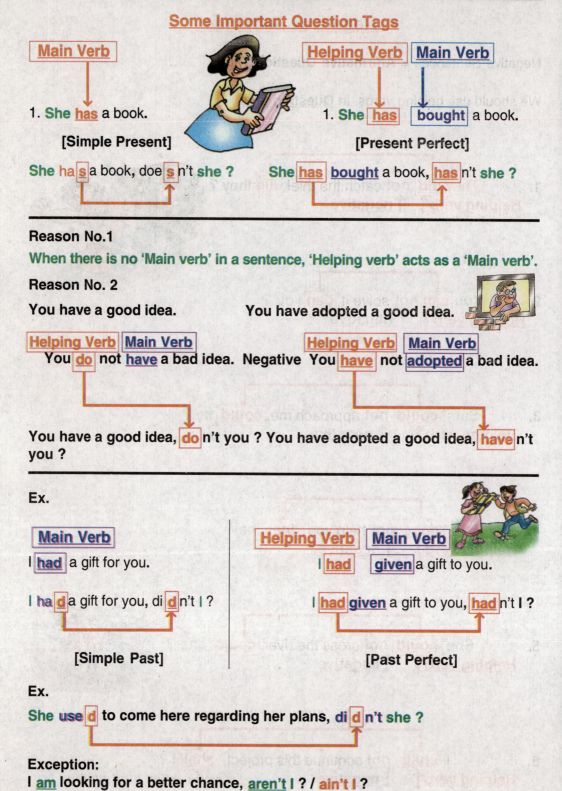

Main Verb

1. She has a book.

[Simple Present]

She has a book, doesn't she ?

Helping Verb | Main Verb

1. She has bought a book.

[Present Perfect]

She has bought a book, hasn't she ?

Reason No.1

When there is no 'Main verb' in a sentence, 'Helping verb' acts as a 'Main verb'.

Reason No. 2

You have a good idea.

You have adopted a good idea.

Helping Verb | Main Verb

You do not have a bad idea.   Negative

Helping Verb | Main Verb

You have not adopted a bad idea.

You have a good idea, don't you ? You have adopted a good idea, haven't you ?

Ex.

Main Verb

I had a gift for you.

I had a gift for you, didn't I ?

[Simple Past]

Helping Verb | Main Verb

I had given a gift to you.

I had given a gift to you, hadn't I ?

[Past Perfect]

Ex.

She used to come here regarding her plans, didn't she ?

Exception:

I am looking for a better chance, aren't I ? / ain't I ?

EXERCISE NO. 10-B

Rewrite the following sentences adding appropriate 'Question tags' :

1. I am not looking for the Street-Arab.
2. You will not be going to meet him.
3. She had not recommended you.
4. He would not come here.
5. They should not do it.
6. My parents have not been helping me.
7. You had not discussed from A to Z about the plan.
8. It does not rain heavily.
9. Your father will not be happy to see me.
10. Barking is worse than biting.
11. Robby did not do any mistake.
12. You will not dismiss the bird-eyed staff.

EXERCISE NO. 10-C

Rewrite the following statements adding appropriate 'Question tags' :

1. Snigdha had a sparkling sense of wit.
2. Jack blows his own trumpet only.
3. You can see that <u>chitty faced</u> girl.
4. Raja Ram Mohan Roy richly deserved the title of "The Father of Modern Society."
5. I shall buy it for my bosom friend.
6. Bhavna does not understand the meaning of 'kick the bucket.'
7. Wordsworth's poems have magnetic touch.
8. Textile Industry is being an important part of our occupational life.
9. The English established 13 colonies in North America.
10. Today is a red letter day of my life.
11. The <u>black diamond</u> is cheap.
12. She belongs to my native place.
13. It stopped once and for all because of capital errors.
14. The extreme cold of Greenland compelled the Eskimos to use reindeer skin.
15. He acted cheap and nasty.
16. They surely did the work.
17. People flocked to cities in search of jobs.
18. She deserves the title of Miss India.

19. Ayurveda ascribes amazing curative powers to the neem.
20. Art is equally important.
21. Accidents like this do occur occasionally.
22. The dirty smell came from inside the house.
23. They'll scratch your eyes out.
24. The key wasn't found by the chicken-hearted fellow.
25. She was trying to cook chop-chop.
26. We cannot live in a cloud castle.
27. The workers' remarks were crystal clear.
28. I must try to get my money.
29. Being dead drunk, he was unable to stand anymore.
30. Give me a bunch of flowers.
31. You are unable to save your friend from the jaw of death.
32. They took the bag from the bus.
33. Anne has taught me how to face an enemy.
34. The mind works like a machine.
35. My goal is to become an actor.
36. My wretched condition made my father unhappy.
37. It is a destination moon to become a Guinness record holder.
38. Ronit went down to bring the book.
39. He is discussing like a devil's advocate.
40. Shut the door.
41. They must be very proud of their achievement.
42. It's the only option that can save the people from cholera.
43. It's an unforgettable dream with neither head nor tail.
44. The driver was stunned for a moment.
45. Nobody can support a lame duck.
46. I am trying to settle the dispute.
47. I'm not a caring fellow.
48. It sounds bad.
49. The police eyed the shopkeeper like an eagle.
50. They're not cheating the public.
51. Jonty is watching you carefully.
52. Miss Lall wasn't in her normal sense yesterday.
53. You didn't come to the office.

54. I am waiting for my duck diamond.

55. It isn't raining now.

Command, Request & Let sentences

Example :

1. Let's go ahead, shall we ?
2. Get out from here, will you ?
3. Catch him immediately, will you ?
4. Please help me, will you ?
5. Please give me your pen, will you ?

EXERCISE NO. 10-D

Rewrite the following statements adding appropriate 'Question tags' :

1. Let's work hard now.
2. Please sing a song for us.
3. Macduff killed Macbeth.
4. Students have <u>itching ears</u> to know their results.
5. Napoleon invaded Austria.
6. Sir Thomas Hardy wrote 'Mayor of Casterbridge'.
7. I am not trying to approach him.
8. They have enclosed the bio-data with the application.
9. You can approach your friend for help.
10. He prepares his breakfast in the morning.

11. Your sister will not be ready to face the problems.
12. She does not try to co-operate with you.
13. They could not meet their parents.
14. My father will have reached London.
15. Caesar was a great king.
16. Empty vessels make much noise.
17. Diamond cuts diamond.
18. She used to speak in tongue during prayer.

19. I start working with my father.
20. He sticks to his idea.
21. His suggestion is just like a bee in the bonnet for this event.
22. The policeman was <u>smelling a rat at</u> the murder spot.

23. Time and tide wait for none.
24. Napoleon used to command his army like ruling the roost.
25. After meeting you, I feel myself standing between a rock and a mountain.

Article

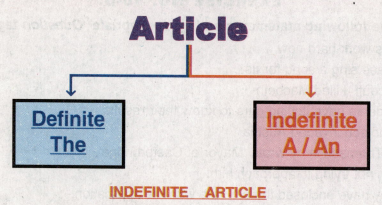

An Article is an <u>Adjective</u> which is used to indicate whether the <u>Noun</u> is definite or indefinite.

There are 2 types of **Articles**.

Article

| Definite
The | Indefinite
A / An |

INDEFINITE ARTICLE

'**A**' and '**An**' are **Indefinite Articles.**

They indicate that the noun which is used in a sentence is neither particular nor definite.

This is <u>a</u> boy. [Any boy —— not definite —— who is he?]

Difference between '**A**' and '**An**'

A = Consonant sound.

An = Vowel sound.

Both are used for singular number but

Vowel = a/e/i/o/u+an.

Example: 1. She had taken <u>an</u> <u>apple</u>.

2. I want to eat <u>an</u> <u>o</u>range.

3. There is <u>an</u> <u>u</u>mbrella for you.

[When a student does not know anything about the symbols of '<u>Sound</u> <u>system</u>', we should follow the methods given on the next page.]

Now see the following examples :

a / e / i / o / u / + 'a'

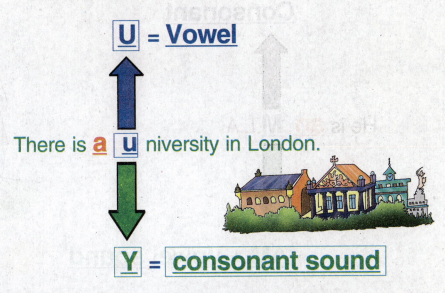

U = **Vowel**

There is **a** **u** niversity in London.

Y = **consonant sound**

[When we pronounce university "U" has a consonant sound in the beginning. Now pronounce **U**mbrella & **U**niversity and listen the sound carefully and feel the difference.]

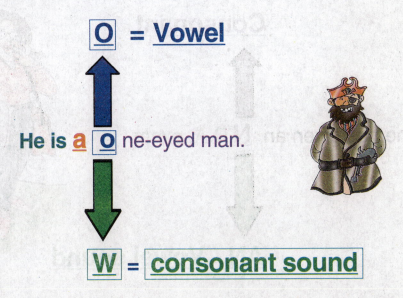

O = **Vowel**

He is **a** **o** ne-eyed man.

W = **consonant sound**

[When we pronounce 'One', it has a consonant sound in the beginning. Now pronounce **O**range, **O**ffice & **O**ne, listen the sound carefully and feel the difference.]

"An" is used with Vowel sound and "A"is used with Consonant sound.

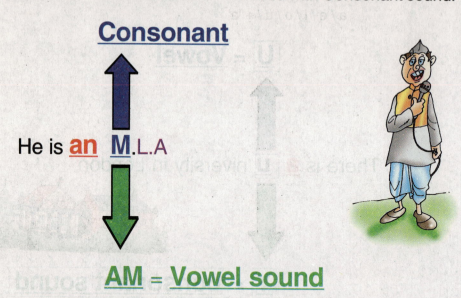

Consonant

He is **an** **M**.L.A

AM = **Vowel sound**

[When we pronounce **M**.L.A, it has a "Vowel" sound in the beginning. Now pronounce **M**ango, **M**oney & **M**.L.A., listen the sound carefully and feel the difference.]

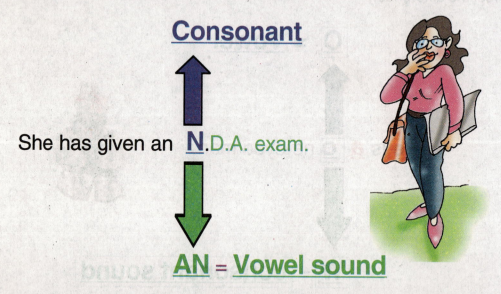

Consonant

She has given an **N**.D.A. exam.

AN = **Vowel sound**

[When we pronounce **N**.D.A, it has a "Vowel" sound in the beginning. Now pronounce **N**umber, **N**eedle & **N**.D.A., listen the sound carefully and feel the difference.]

Uses of Article "The" [One and Only One]

1. One and Only one – Part of your body : the head, the neck, the backbone, the forehead, the tongue etc.

2. One and Only one – In your home : the ceiling, the floor, the main gate, the kitchen, the boundary wall etc.

3. One and Only one – In your classroom : the blackboard, the duster, the 1st boy, the last boy, the monitor, the tallest student, the weakest student etc.

4. One and Only one – In your school : the Head master, the Prefect, the Head boy or girl, the head of department, the school bell, the maingate, etc.

5. One and Only one – In your playground : the last batsman, the 3rd umpire, the goal post [each part of playground], the first half of game, the match point, man of the match , man of the series etc.

6. One and Only one – In a university : the Vice Chancellor, the head office, the library, the D.E.N. etc.

7. One and Only one – In your city : the District Magistrate, the M.L.A., the Police Commissioner etc.

8. One and Only one – In your state : the Chief Minister, the Governor, the Capital of state, the State education minister etc.

9. One and Only one – In a court : the High Court, the Supreme Court, the Judge, the Public prosecutor, the Capital punishment [once in a life], the Life imprisonment [once in a life] etc.

10. Once in a life – The date of birth, the date of death, the 1st marriage anniversary, the golden jubilee celebration, the lifetime achievement award etc.

11. One and Only one – In your office : the boss, the head clerk, the staff incharge, the date of salary [in a month], the General Manager, the Director, the Personnel Manager etc.

12. One and Only one – In your country : the President, the Prime Minister, the Ruling party, the Home Minister, the Capital city, the boundary line, the Chief Justice, the Foreign Minister, the Defence Minister etc.

13. One and Only one – Buildings & Monuments : the Taj Mahal, the Qutub Minar, the Buland Darwaja, the Gateway of India, the Red Fort, the Elephanta Cave, the Minakshi Temple etc.

14. <u>One and Only one</u> – Rivers and Oceans: the Ganga, the Yamuna, the Kaveri, the Saraswati, the Brahmaputra, the Indian Ocean, the Arabian Sea, the Bay of Bengal, the Pacific Ocean, the Red Sea etc.

15. <u>One and Only one</u> – In the World: the World Bank, the U.N.O., the SAARC, the Asia, the Europe, the British Airways, the Indian Air Force etc.

16. <u>One and Only one</u> – In the Universe: the Sun, the Moon, the Jupiter, the Earth, the Sky, the Heaven, the Hell etc.

17. <u>One and Only one</u> – Direction/Caste/Religion: the North, the South, the East, the West, the Hindu, the Sikh, the Muslim, the Koran, the Gita, the Guru Granth Sahib, the Parsi, the Brahmin etc.

18. <u>One and Only one</u> – Historical events: the Independence Day, the Republic Day, the Gulf War, the World War etc.

19. <u>One and Only one</u> – Ordinal: the 1st boy, the last girl, the next episode etc.

20. <u>One and Only one</u> – Proper noun (names) Qualified by Adjective: the great king, Samudra Gupta / the brave man, Hercules etc.

21. <u>One and Only one</u> – Book: the Bible, the Quran, the Gita etc.

22. <u>One and Only one</u> – Train / Ship etc.: the Rajdhani Express, the Vaishali Express, the Punjab Mail, the Titanic etc.

Articles cannot be used with <u>Material Noun</u>, <u>Abstract Noun</u>, <u>Name of a person</u> etc.

Example :

1. <u>Ram</u> works hard to pass the examination. **[Name of a person]**

2. <u>White gold</u> is a precious metal. **[Material Noun]**

3. <u>Honesty</u> is the best policy. **[Abstract Noun]**

4. <u>Man</u> is mortal. **[Common Noun]**

Articles can be used with Material Noun, Abstract Noun, Common Noun, Name of a person **etc., if some words or phrases have been used after it.**

1. <u>The man,</u> whom you know, is a teacher. [Common Noun]

   ↑————— Clause

2. <u>The woman,</u> in trouble, is a beggar. [Common Noun]

   ↑— Phrase

3. <u>The gold,</u> which I bought from America, has been robbed. [Material Noun]

   ↑————————Clause

4. **The honesty,** of my brother, is well known. [Abstract Noun]
↑ —— Phrase

EXERCISE NO. 11-A

Fill in the blanks with suitable 'Articles' :

1. He is __an__ Indian by birth, not __an__ American.
2. __The__ Red Fort is __a__ historical building in Delhi.
3. __The__ sun sets in __the__ west.
4. You are __the__ most honourable man in this town.
5. __An__ idle man's mind is __a__ devil's workshop.
6. Iron is __an__ useful metal.
7. He is __the__ most intelligent boy in our school.
8. This is __the__ sewing machine you had given me to sell in the market.
9. Tamil Nadu is in __the__ southern part of India.
10. She had __a__ stupid idea for this project.
11. __The__ Ganga is __the__ sacred river.
12. Benaras is __the__ holy place.
13. Have you read __the__ 'Mahabharata'.
14. It was half __an__ hour past ten when you had met __a__ university Registrar.
15. __An__ Indian can easily be recognized in __the__ foreign countries.
16. English is __a__ global language.
17. __The__ Indian Ocean lies to __the__ south of India.
18. They struck him on __the__ face.
19. Chinese is __an__ easy language for __the__ Chinese only.
20. Please sketch __the__ map of Indonesia.
21. Mount Everest is __the__ highest peak in all over the world.
22. They have __an__ orange, __an__ apple and __a__ banana for their breakfast.
23. __The__ Times of India is __a__ popular newspaper in India.
24. During __the__ epidemic more people die.
25. __The__ old man was eager to know about __the__ wild elephants found in Myanmar.
26. During __the__ rainy season, I will go to London.
27. I shall buy __an__ umbrella for you.

EXERCISE NO. 11-B

Fill in the blanks with suitable 'Articles'.

1. Miss James is _an_ American lady but she wants to live with _an_ Indian family.

2. My cousin is _a_ university student.

3. Ganga is _the_ longest river in India.

4. _The_ earth moves round _the_ sun.

6. Mayuri has bought _an_ orange which is _a_ unique fruit.

7. _The_ Quran is _a_ holy book for _the_ Muslims.

8. Ashok _the_ great was _the_ wise king.

9. _A_ friend in need is _a_ friend indeed.

10. _A_ hunter was accused of hunting _the_ tiger.

11. Camel is _a_ ship of desert.

12. Honesty is _the_ best policy.

13. I have never seen _an_ untidy student in this school.

14. Gold is _the_ most precious metal.

15. Sketch _the_ figure of Abraham _the_ great philosopher.

16. _the_ Taj Mahal was built by Shahjahan.

17. _The_ Bible is _a_ holy book for _the_ Christians.

18. _The_ world is _a_ heaven for those who work hard.

19. _The_ M.P. was congratulated by _the_ President for getting _____ success in the general election.

20. Yesterday, Mr. Francis met _an_ African whose wife was _an_ Austrian but his mother was _an_ Indian.

EXERCISE NO. 11-C

Insert 'Article' wherever it is necessary :

1. Simple words act like oath.

2. Small leak can sink great ship.

3. Dew drops glitter in morning.

4. Live ass is better than dead lion.

5. Qutub Minar was built during Sultanate period.

6. I read Times of India every morning.

7. Nature is best physician and hunger is best sauce.

8. Nobody can pump ocean dry.

9. Lion is king of beasts.

10. Ink is useful article for students.

11. By hook or by crook, he will be Principal of this school.

12. I saw tiger prowling towards west.

13. Fruits that grow in Kashmir are very costly.

14. A man without patience is lamp without oil.

15. Bad workman never gets good tool.

16. Shakespeare was famous dramatist.

EXERCISE NO. 11-D

Cut the unnecessary and incorrect articles from the sentences :

1. An advice acts like the ointment.

2. To err is the human; to forgive is the divine.

3. The honesty is the best policy.

4. The Kalidas was the great dramatist of Sanskrit.

5. Football is the interesting sport.

6. The stars twinkle at night in the sky.

7. It is a most beautiful place I have ever seen.

8. The brass is an useful metal.

9. The Mother Teresa was the great social worker.

10. The Delhi is an historical city.

Figures of Speech

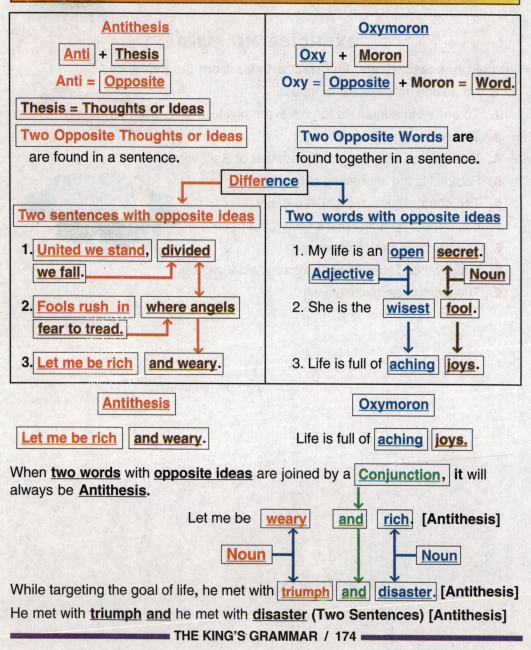

Antithesis	Oxymoron
Anti + Thesis	Oxy + Moron
Anti = Opposite	Oxy = Opposite + Moron = Word.
Thesis = Thoughts or Ideas	
Two Opposite Thoughts or Ideas are found in a sentence.	Two Opposite Words are found together in a sentence.

Difference

Two sentences with opposite ideas	Two words with opposite ideas
1. United we stand, divided we fall.	1. My life is an open secret. Adjective Noun
2. Fools rush in where angels fear to tread.	2. She is the wisest fool.
3. Let me be rich and weary.	3. Life is full of aching joys.

Antithesis

Let me be rich and weary.

Oxymoron

Life is full of aching joys.

When **two words** with **opposite ideas** are joined by a Conjunction, it will always be **Antithesis**.

Let me be weary and rich. [Antithesis]

Noun — Noun

While targeting the goal of life, he met with triumph and disaster. [Antithesis]

He met with **triumph and** he met with **disaster** (Two Sentences) [Antithesis]

Simile [As / Like]	Metaphor
It is a direct comparison between two different objects , things etc. using as / like.	It is an Implied Simile.
1. He is as brave as a lion.	1. He is a lion.
2. This room is as hot as a furnace.	2. This room is a furnace.

Alliteration = [All + letters]	Repetition
In this figure of speech 'A Letter' is repeated. (sound) 1st letter of a word is repeated.	In this figure of speech 'a Word', 'a Phrase' etc. is repeated.
1. The bright bird flew.	1. Two and Two make four.
2. Four fools fell in a fountain.	2. No stir in the air, no stir in the sea.

Pun = [Plural + One]	Tautology = [Two + Auto]
Plural + One = Pun	Two = 2 + Auto = Same
In this figure of speech	In this figure of speech
One Word has Two Meanings.	Two Words have One Meaning.
1. The happiness of life depends on 'Liver'.	1. Sign of the filth & the dirt.
Liver = [1] Part of a stomach. [2] One who lives.	Filth & Dirt are Synonyms.

Litotes	Irony

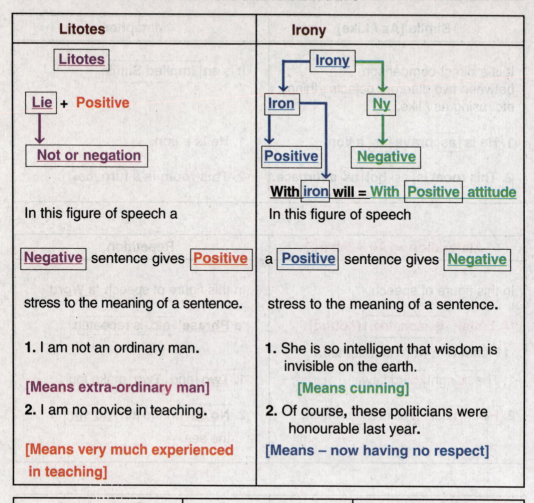

Litotes	Irony
Lie + Positive ↓ Not or negation	Iron ↓ Positive Ny ↓ Negative
	With iron will = With Positive attitude
In this figure of speech a	In this figure of speech
Negative sentence gives Positive stress to the meaning of a sentence.	a Positive sentence gives Negative stress to the meaning of a sentence.
1. I am not an ordinary man.	**1.** She is so intelligent that wisdom is invisible on the earth.
[Means extra-ordinary man]	**[Means cunning]**
2. I am no novice in teaching.	**2.** Of course, these politicians were honourable last year.
[Means very much experienced in teaching]	**[Means – now having no respect]**

Interrogation	Exclamation	Apostrophe
?	**!**	**O + Somebody !**
When questions are asked without expecting any answer, it is called 'Interrogation'	This figure of speech is used to draw attention through surprise.	This figure of speech is used to address some-body who is absent or dead.
Ex -1. How will you explain the life? **2.** How I can express it in words.	**Ex -1.** What a horrible place ! **2.** What a tragic character !	**Ex -1.** O God ! Please help me. **2.** O my friend ! I miss you.

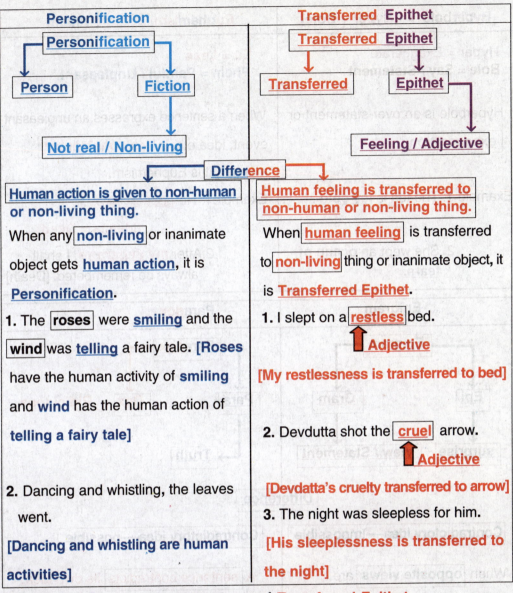

Personification	Transferred Epithet
Personification → **Person** / **Fiction** → **Not real / Non-living**	**Transferred Epithet** → **Transferred** / **Epithet** → **Feeling / Adjective**

Difference

Human action is given to non-human or non-living thing.	Human feeling is transferred to non-human or non-living thing.
When any **non-living** or inanimate object gets **human action**, it is **Personification**.	When **human feeling** is transferred to **non-living** thing or inanimate object, it is **Transferred Epithet**.
1. The roses were **smiling** and the wind was **telling** a fairy tale. [Roses have the human activity of **smiling** and **wind** has the human action of **telling a fairy tale**]	1. I slept on a restless bed. ↑ **Adjective** [My restlessness is transferred to bed]
	2. Devdutta shot the cruel arrow. ↑ **Adjective** [Devdatta's cruelty transferred to arrow]
2. Dancing and whistling, the leaves went. [Dancing and whistling are human activities]	3. The night was sleepless for him. [His sleeplessness is transferred to the night]

Difference between Personification and Transferred Epithet

Leaves are dancing and whistling. [Personification]
↑————**Verb (human action)**

He saw that the leaves were **sad** [Transferred Epithet]
↑——**Adjective (human feeling)**

The cloud has a **tongue** of fire and flame. [Personification]
↑——**a part of human body**

A part of human body given to non-human is also a '**Personification**'.

Hyperbole = [Hyper + Bole]	Euphemism = [Eu + Phem]
Hyper = Exaggerate **Bole** = Say / Statement Hyperbole is an over-statement or exaggeration. Example 1. The tea is <u>icy cold</u> . 2. She wept an <u>ocean of tears.</u>	**Eu = Less** **Phem = Painful / Unpleasant.** When a sentence expresses an unpleasant event, idea etc. in less unpleasant manner, it is Euphemism. Example1. He **passed away**. **[Means = Dead]** 2.After **my departure**, I shall always be remembered. [Death]

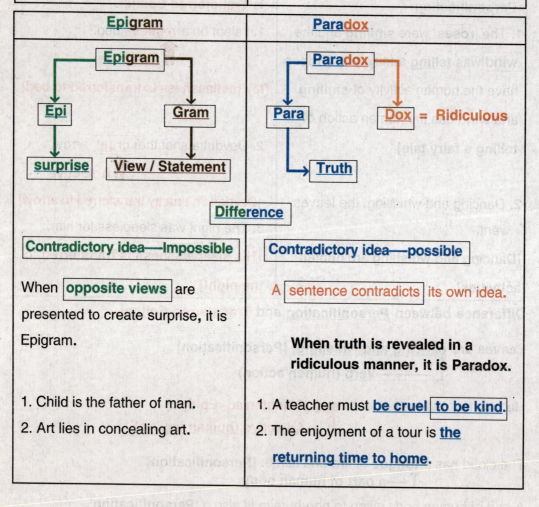

Epigram	Paradox
Epigram Epi — surprise Gram — View / Statement	Paradox Para — Truth Dox = Ridiculous

Difference

Contradictory idea——Impossible	Contradictory idea——possible
When opposite views are presented to create surprise, it is Epigram. 1. Child is the father of man. 2. Art lies in concealing art.	A sentence contradicts its own idea. **When truth is revealed in a ridiculous manner, it is Paradox.** 1. A teacher must be cruel to be kind. 2. The enjoyment of a tour is the returning time to home.

Synecdoche = [Synec + doche]	Metonymy = [Meto + Nymy]
Synec = Part Doche = Whole It is a │ substitution of word │ used as a part for the whole. Ex = I. Our hearts are peace. Heart = part of body. It indicates all the saints. II. His orchard's his bread. Bread = Part of food. It indicates the man's need.	Meto = Substitution. Nymy = Name. It is a │ substitution of name │. I. She must address the chair. Chair = chairman II. He is addicted to the bottle. Bottle = wine. III. The pen is mightier than the sword. The pen = Author. The sword = Soldier.

Inversion = [In + Verse]	Onomatopoeia
In = Not Verse = statement When a sentence is not written in correct order, it is Inversion. I. Never friend makes he. Correct order – He never makes friend.	On – Meto – Substitution. Poe – sound = on Substitution of sound When words suggest the sense of sound, it is Onomatopoeia. I. Zoom, Zoom, aeroplane flies. II. Tidy hinched and Tidy clinched.

The Figures of Speech.

Alliteration

A letter [sound] is repeated.
Sound of the 1st letter of a word is repeated.

1. With a [s]imple, [s]ign of [s]ound, [s]omething is mysterious.
2. [Sh]e was [sh]ivering with [sh]ock.
3. Over the [w]aiting [w]aves, there is a [w]arning.
4. The [b]lack sky was [b]laring to [b]urn [b]lue.
5. [S]imple [s]unlight [s]ilence is hovering there.

Repetition

A word or a phrase is repeated .

1. [So little] they rose , [so little] they fell.
2. [Up] , [up] , [up] the life climbs [up] .
3. Heigh [Tidy] ! ho, [Tidy] ! heigh, [Tidy] !
4. [Fill] , [fill] , [fill] , [fill] the pot soon.
5. To the Muslims I am [Hindu] . To the [Hindus] I am Brahmin.

Simile

1. [Like] a nightmare fled the night.
2. That beat into my ears [like] gong.
3. She was [as] merry [as] a rose.
4. He behaves [like] a silly mouse.
5. The fact is [as] clear [as] crystal.

Metaphor

1. Rock cut temples are the epics in stones.
2. Their waves were the light of life.
3. Tansen was called the chief jewel in his diadem.
4. Mirror is the eye of little God.
5. He is the lion.

Antithesis

a. Sentences/clauses with opposite ideas.

b. Two words with opposite ideas joined by a 'Conjunction'.

1. The ship can move , is still.

2. Sing also of the strikes, early and late.
   ↑ Conjunction

3. Let him be rich and weary.
   ↑ Conjunction

4. Many are called but few are chosen.
   ↑ Conjunction

5. Man proposes God disposes.
   ↑ but [Hidden Conjunction]

Oxymoron

Two words with opposite ideas used together in a sentence.

1. You have a terrific beauty.
2. This fellow is normally abnormal after the hot discussion.
3. The climax of the play was tragically comic.
4. His philosophy is morally immoral.
5. These ideas are simply complicated for us.

Irony

1. In abroad, <u>I am Indian but in India I do not know who I am</u>.
   ↑———————————————————— Ridiculous fact

2. To the <u>English I am wog, I do not know who am I</u>.
   ↑———————————————————— Ridiculous fact

3. But <u>I am glad, I really am</u>.
   ↑— Ridiculous fact

4. Doubtlessly, <u>morality shall die to see you</u>.
   ↑——————————— Ridiculous fact

Litotes

Negative sentence = Positive stress

1. My brother is ⬛ **not** ⬛ a ⬛ **savage** ⬛ in this society.
   Negative ↑   ↑**civilised**

2. The business men are ⬛ **no** ⬛ more ⬛ **fools** ⬛.
   Negative ↑   ↑**intelligent**

3. She is ⬛ **no** ⬛ more ⬛ **restless** ⬛ for her fortune.
   Negative ↑   ↑**tension-free**

4. His ideas are ⬛ **not** ⬛ ⬛ **immoral** ⬛ at all.
   Negative ↑   ↑**moral**

Interrogation

Rhetorical questions / Unanswered questions

1. Allow to sell me a couple?

2. Do you think I can listen all day to such stuff ?

3. What son shall I sing of you , my mother ?

4. Who can say who I am ?

5. What kind of place you have brought me my son ?

Exclamation

1. What a pity to injure him so !
2. What an idea to get the goal !
3. Father ! You come again !
4. Ah ! You will miss us.
5. What a wonderful phase of life !

Apostrophe

O Father ! guide us towards our destination.

Shakespeare ! You are really great.

Milton ! The World is visible through your words.

O life ! I shall find you somewhere.

O Dream ! Life is beautiful.

Hyperbole

Hyperbole : Exaggeration

1. You have eaten the goose with beaks and bones .
   ↑ ————————— Exaggeration

2. Out of the eyes of the hundred flowers .
   ↑— Exaggeration

3. The blood ran down to his toes .
   ↑——— Exaggeration

4. He made the blood to fly .
   ↑— Exaggeration

5. My hair do stand on end .
   ↑ — Exaggeration

6. She has wept an ocean of tears .
   ↑ —— Exaggeration

Personification

Human action is given to non-human.

1. I have chased the [shouting] wind along.

⬆

[**Human action**]

2. The darkness [flees].

⬆

[**Human action**]

3. A sentiment [arrives] from a distant friend.

⬆

[**Human action**]

4. And [the stars] began [to peep].

⬆

[**Human action**]

5. The [lightning] has a [tongue] of flame.

⬆

[**Part of Human body**]

6. The hoards of clouds [advance].

⬆

[**Human action**]

7. The leaves went [dancing] and whirling.

⬆

[**Human action**]

8. The [bird] [carries a message].

⬆ ⬆

[**Non-human**] [**Human action**]

Transferred Epithet

Human feeling which is transferred to non - human.

1. Devdutta loosened the cruel arrow.

Adjective ↑

2. Siddhartha loved the swan with his kind palm.

Adjective ↑

3. He used his criminal guns for this crime.

Adjective ↑

4. She threw away the unhappy flowers.

Adjective ↑

Euphemism

1. He soon fast asleep in their earthy bed.

Dead ↑

2. When we are gone away, you shall remember us.

Dead ↑

3. These are his last whispering words.

At the time of death ↑

4. I had heard his last grim call.

Death ↑

Metonymy

[Substitution of name]

1. Nobody can hurt the crown .

    ↑ **King**

2. The red coats have conquered the capital city.

    ↑ **British soldiers**

3. The bluejackets have lost the way in the sea wave.

    ↑ **Sailors**

4. The House will oppose this budget.

    ↑ **Members of Lok Sabha**

Synecdoche

1. Devdutta's arrow has hit the white wing.

    ↑ swan

2. There are so many hands to work in his factory.

    ↑ workers

3. O Lord, provide everybody the bread.

    ↑ livelihood

Inversion

A sentence is not written in correct prose order.

1. And to the Inchcape Rock they go.

   Correct order : And they go to the Inchcape Rock.

2. In the evening, it has died away.

   Correct order : It has died away in the evening.

3. Sunward I climb.

   Correct order : I climb sunward.

4. So many things you have not dreamed of.

   Correct Order : You have not dreamed of so many things.

5. Had once been his integrity put to test.

   Correct Order : His integrity had been once put to test.

Onomatopoeia : Sound

1. The babble rose and **burst** around.

Sound

2. The aeroplane is **zooming** in the sky.

Sound

3. The open window shuts with a **bang**.

Sound

4. It is the time for **jingle** - **tinkle**.

Sound

5. **Blaring** from the branches of trees.

Sound

6. The loose house sheet **clatter** and **clang**.

Sound   **Sound**

Climax
Ascending Order

entertains

plays

Sings

1. Sings , plays and entertains me night and day.

nor peace

no joy

no rest

2. I have no rest , no joy , nor peace .

the noise gathers

the houses fill

The street is clear

3. The street is clear , the houses fill , the noise gathers .

fell asleep

prayed

leaned

knelt

4. He knelt and leaned on the chair, he prayed and fell asleep .

Anticlimax
Descending Order

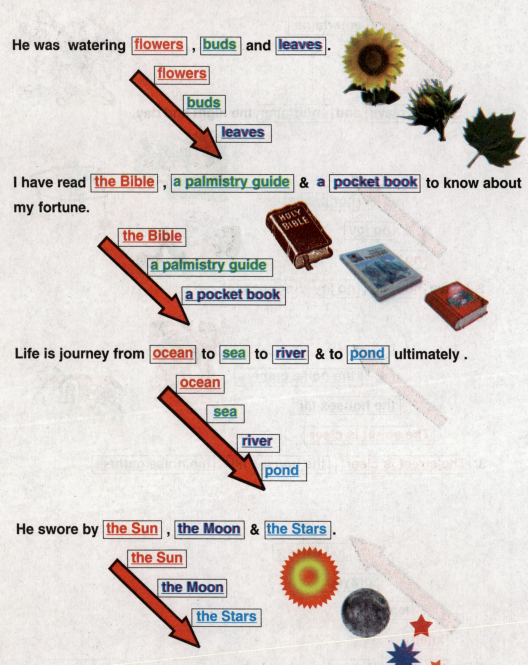

He was watering flowers , buds and leaves .

flowers

buds

leaves

I have read the Bible , a palmistry guide & a pocket book to know about my fortune.

the Bible

a palmistry guide

a pocket book

Life is journey from ocean to sea to river & to pond ultimately .

ocean

sea

river

pond

He swore by the Sun , the Moon & the Stars .

the Sun

the Moon

the Stars

Tautology

Two words : One meaning

1. With the **seers** and **prophets** , they followed him.

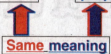

Same meaning

2. Said the mother **imperturbable** and **calm**.

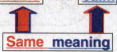

Same meaning

3. The fairy went **remote** and **far away**.

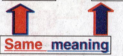

Same meaning

Pun

Pun :One Word with Two Meanings

1. **Rest** in the body lay.

Leisure/ rest	part of body
1st Meaning	2nd Meaning

2. The happiness of life depends on **liver**.

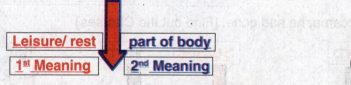

Life style	Part of body
1st Meaning	2nd Meaning

3. This terrorist **lies** in the jail.

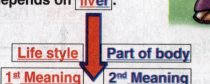

Telling lies	stays
1st Meaning	2nd Meaning

Clause

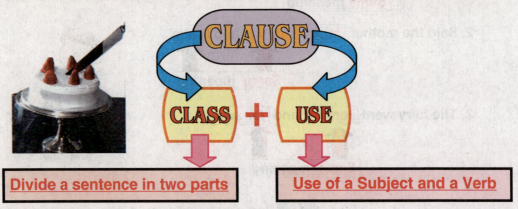

CLAUSE

CLASS + **USE**

| Divide a sentence in two parts | Use of a Subject and a Verb |

Divide a sentence in two parts. If a Subject in each part of the sentence and a Verb is used, each part is a Clause.

Definition

A Clause is a part of a sentence with a Subject and a Verb [finite] in each part.

Example : As she came, he had gone. [Find out the **Clauses**]

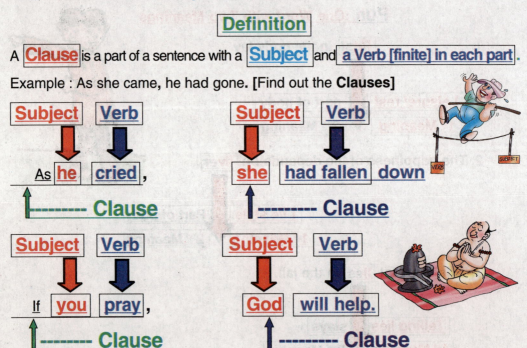

Subject	Verb		Subject	Verb
As he	cried,		she	had fallen down
└──────── Clause			└──────── Clause	

Subject	Verb		Subject	Verb
If you	pray,		God	will help.
└──────── Clause			└──────── Clause	

Principal and Subordinate Clause

What is a **Principal Clause?**

It is a part of a sentence which has | **a Subject** | and | **a Verb** | and has its own full
meaning without any **joining word**. [Conjunction] before it.

Ex. | **You will succeed** | if you work hard.

Principal Clause or Main Clause

| **You will get your money** | whenever you want.

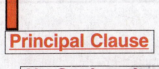

Principal Clause or Main Clause

Sometimes **Principal Clause** does not give complete meaning. In that case, if there is
no joining word [**Conjunction**] before the **Clause**, it will be the | **Principal Clause.** |

E.g. | **My hope is** | that I should get an award.

| **My hope is** | = Incomplete Meaning | **No Joining word before it** | = Principal Clause

Principal Clause

No Conjunction

| **Your idea is** | that they have to complete it secretly.

Principal Clause

No Conjunction

| **Her aim is** | that she should achieve the target anyhow.

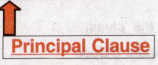

Principal Clause

Subordinate Clause

It is a part of a sentence with **a Subject, a Verb** (finite) and **a 'Subordinator' (in the beginning of clause).** It does not have its own complete meaning.

Subordinator is a conjunction or a joining word. It cannot help the clause to provide a complete meaning. Only principal clauses do so.

Subordinator

If it does not rain, **I shall meet you.**

Subordinate Clause

How to find **Subordinate Clause?**

The Clause with **Subordinator (in the beginning of a clause)** is always **a Subordinate Clause.**

Subordinator

Though he is poor, he is honest.

— Subordinate Clause

Subordinator

Come near, **so that** I can return your purse.

Subordinate Clause

Subordinator

Nobody has idea **how** the earth was created.

Subordinate Clause

Subordinator

I know the reason **why** you are late in the class.

Subordinate Clause

EXERCISE NO. 13-B

Find out the *'Principal Clause'* and *'Subordinate Clause'* from the following sentences :

1. Violence is just where kindness fails.
2. We talk little when vanity does not make us.
3. What is morally wrong, cannot be politically right.
4. When I grow, I want to be me only.
5. When a man meets his mate, the society begins.
6. What is well done, is done soon enough.
7. You show me the capitalist who is not a hard worker.
8. You cannot go far if you don't begin very near.
9. You cannot trace an enemy unless you are too friendly to them.
10. Those, who do not work hard, never get success in life.
11. Even if you get good marks, you may not get the golden crown of culmination.
12. Well done is better than well said.
13. We know the price of freedom if we pay for it.
14. The condition upon which, God has given liberty to man is eternal vigilance.
15. If you are sincere, you will surely succeed.

Kinds of Subordinate Clauses

1. Noun Clause

2. Adjective Clause

3. Adverb Clause

What is a **Noun Clause**?

A Clause that does the work of **a Noun** is called **a Noun Clause**.

I know that she had been waiting for you.

↑————————————— **Noun Clause**

What is **an Adjective Clause?**

A Clause that does the work of **an Adjective** is called **an Adjective Clause.**

Those, who work hard, will get success.

↑——————**Adjective Clause**

What is **an Adverb Clause**?

It is **a Clause** that does the work of **an Adverb** in a sentence.

I shall give you money, if you need .

↑——— **Adverb Clause**

How to differentiate :
Noun Clause, Adjective Clause and Adverb Clause.

Rule No. 1 : | Noun Clause : An Easy Approach |

| If **before the Subordinate Clause** | (or) | after the Subordinate Clause |

Is / Am / Are / Was / Were / Be is used, it will be a Noun Clause only.

Ex: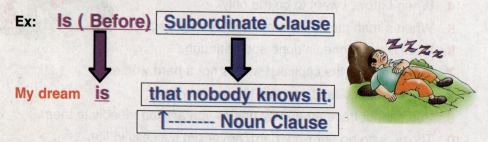

Is (Before) Subordinate Clause

My dream **is** that nobody knows it.
↑-------- Noun Clause

Ex: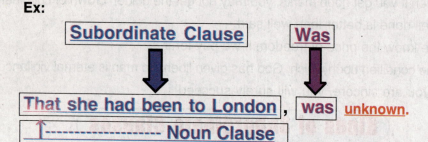

Subordinate Clause Was

That she had been to London , was unknown.
↑-------------------- Noun Clause

EX: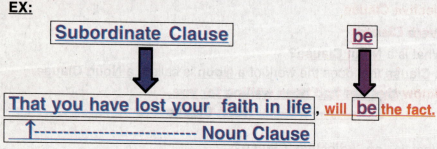

Subordinate Clause be

That you have lost your faith in life , will be the fact.
↑--------------------------- Noun Clause

EX: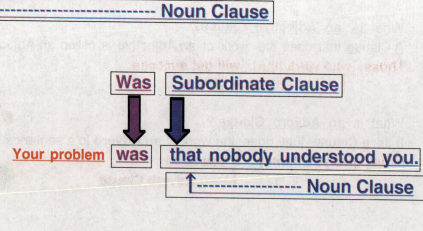

Was Subordinate Clause

Your problem was that nobody understood you.
↑------------------ Noun Clause

Rule No. 2 : If the **Principal Clause** is incomplete, the **Subordinate Clause** will be a **Noun Clause** only.

Ex.

↓ **Incomplete Principal Clause**

My life is | **what nobody knows it.**

↑--------- **Noun Clause**

↓ **Incomplete Principal Clause**

That he has killed a tiger | **is a secret**

↑ ------------- **Noun Clause**

Noun clause

[What question to the Principal Clause]

Ask what question to the **Principal Clause**. If you get answer in **Subordinate Clause**, it will be **a Noun Clause**.

↓ **Principal Clause**

She   knows   that I am a fool.

What does she know ? **Ans:** **That I am a fool.**

↑------ **Noun Clause**

Ex.

↓ — **Principal Clause**

Peter wants to explain   why he is late.

What does Peter want to explain? **Ans: why he is late.**

↑ ------**Noun Clause**

Ex.

↓ **Principal Clause**

Paul   was   told   that he will be the next monitor.

What was Paul told ? **Ans: that he will be the next monitor.**

↑ ------------ **Noun Clause**

Adjective Clause

When a <u>Clause</u> acts like an <u>Adjective</u>, it is an <u>Adjective Clause</u>.

Before the <u>Subordinate Clause</u>, mostly there is a <u>Noun</u> or <u>Pronoun</u>.

Or

<u>What question</u> cannot be framed with the help of **Principal Clause** and **Subordinate Clause** also does not respond to **what question** ?

Ex.

↓ --- Principal Clause

He lost the plan paper | which I had prepared.

What did he lose the plan paper ? [It is an improper question]

Noun

↓

He lost the | plan paper | which I had prepared.

↑----Adjective Clause

Ex.

↓-------------------------- Principal Clause

I want to learn Hindi from the teacher | who is experienced.

What do I want to learn Hindi from the teacher ? [Improper question]

Noun

↓

I want to learn Hindi from | the teacher | who is experienced.

↑ Adjective Clause

Another method to find the Adjective Clause

Ask what question to the **Subject** and **Verb** of **Principal Clause** and the rest part of **Principal Clause** will give you the answer.

Example:

↓ -------------------------------- Principal Clause

She | started | teaching Hindi to the foreigners | who were Germans.

↑-Subject ↑-Verb

What did she start? Ans : teaching Hindi to the foreigners.

Who were Germans = Adjective Clause.

Ex.

He, who works hard, **is sure to succeed.**

| Complement |

Principal clause = **He** **is** | sure | to succeed.

Subject- | |**-Verb** **[What ?]**

What is he sure to ? Ans: To succeed. **Who works hard. [Adjective Clause]**

| **Adverb Clause** |

Ask **when?/ where? / why? / How?** question to the **Principal Clause** and you will get answer in **Subordinate Clause.**

Learn by heart these **Subordinating Conjunctions** to find the

Adverb Clause: When, while, before, after, until, till, since, where, wherever, because, as, since, that, if, unless, so that, least, though, so, as, as if etc.

EXERCISE NO. 13-C

Find out the *'Principal Clause'* and *'Subordinate Clause'* from the following sentences and tell whether it is *'Noun Clause', 'Adjective Clause'* or *'Adverb Clause'* :

1. She has lost her ornaments because she is very careless.
2. You have attempted all the questions which shows your intelligence.
3. It is usual that he has been failed in the exam.
4. Snigdha, who is a very beautiful lady, deserves the title of Miss India.
5. She has known all the secrets which is dangerous for you.
6. That she was a foolish lady, is an open secret.
7. India won the match against Pakistan which was unexpected.
8. William Shakespeare, who was a great dramatist, has written Macbeth with much intelligence.
9. As they had been looking very suspicious, I informed the police.
10. She told me that the answer of one question is incorrect.
11. My aim is that I must expose the corrupt people.
12. I visited the Taj Mahal where everybody desires to visit once in a life.
13. The plant is growing up because the fertilizer has been used according to the instruction.
14. It has been cleared that you are empty-handed.
15. Roby hits me as she hates me.
16. Sam cried with joy when he heard the result of H.S.C. exam.
17. My father was very happy when he got promotion.
18. When India became independent, Indian people were very happy.

KINDS OF NOUN CLAUSES

It can be divided into **three** parts.

[A] Noun Clause: Of A Verb	[B] Noun Clause : Object of
1. Noun Clause: Subject of Verb	Noun Clause: Object of Participle
2. Noun Clause: Object of Verb	Noun Clause: Object of Infinitive
3. Noun Clause: Complement of Verb	Noun Clause: Object of Preposition

[C] Noun Clause: In Apposition to Noun

Noun Clause: Subject of Verb

Noun Clause + Verb = Noun Clause : Subject of a Verb

Ex.   Subordinator

That | she is a cheat, | is known to all.

↑ Subordinate Clause ↑   Main Clause [What ?]

What is known to all **?** Ans: That she is a cheat. **[Noun Clause]**

Subject

→ It   is known to all.

That she is a cheat   is known to all.

Noun Clause   + Verb = Noun Clause : Subject of Verb

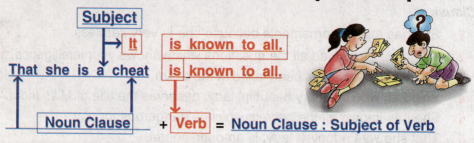

Subject

→ That   is   the greatest gift to me.

That you are my son   is   the greatest gift to me.

Noun Clause + Verb = Noun Clause : Subject of Verb

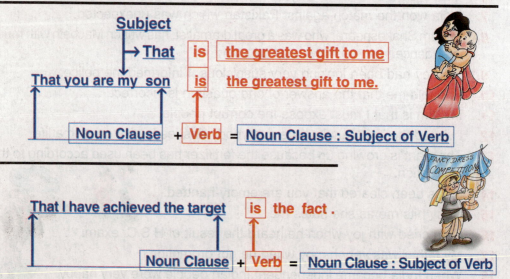

That I have achieved the target   is   the fact .

Noun Clause + Verb = Noun Clause : Subject of Verb

Noun Clause : Object of Verb

When **'Noun Clause'** is used after the Verb (Transitive), it is **Noun Clause: Object of a Verb.**

Transitive Verb: It transits the action or affects the object.

Verb [Transitive] + Noun Clause = Noun Clause : Object of Verb

Ex.

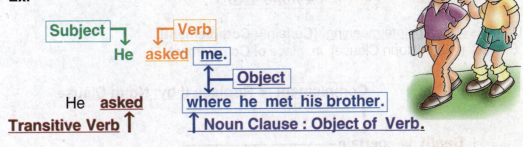

Subject He
Verb asked **me.**
Object

He **asked** where he met his brother.
Transitive Verb ↑ ↑ **Noun Clause : Object of Verb.**

Ex.

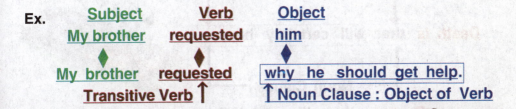

Subject	Verb	Object
My brother	requested	him

My brother requested why he should get help.
Transitive Verb ↑ ↑ **Noun Clause : Object of Verb**

Ex. You hoped that she would help you.
Transitive Verb ↑ ↑ **Noun Clause: Object of Verb**

Ex. Your sister **explained** how poor she is in English.
Transitive Verb ↑ ↑ **Noun Clause : Object of a Verb**

Ex. You have **cleared** that you are an innocent man.
Transitive Verb ↑ ↑ **Noun Clause : Object of Verb**

Noun Clause : Complement of Verb

Sub + Verb = a Sentence = He writes [A Complete Sentence]

Sometimes **Subject** and **Verb** fail to provide complete meaning then **Complement** completes meaning in the sentence.

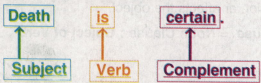

Death	is	certain.
Subject	**Verb**	**Complement**

Death is = Incomplete meaning [Certain = **Complement**]
Subject + Verb [Noun Clause] in place of Complement.

Complement = Replace it by **Noun Clause**

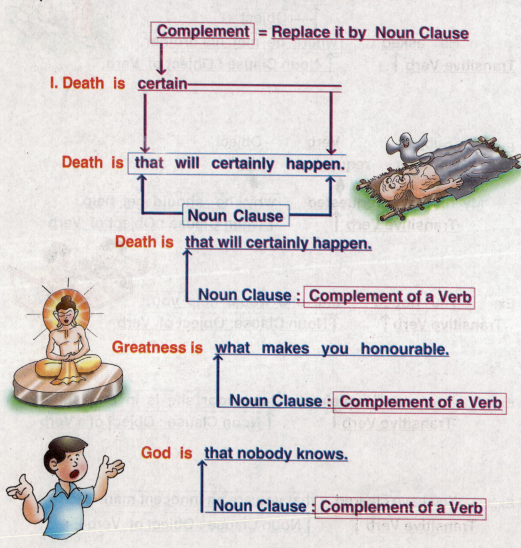

I. Death is certain

Death is that will certainly happen.

Noun Clause

Death is that will certainly happen.

Noun Clause : Complement of a Verb

Greatness is what makes you honourable.

Noun Clause : Complement of a Verb

God is that nobody knows.

Noun Clause : Complement of a Verb

Before Subordinate Clause if Preposition / To + Verb / Verb- ing **is used, it will be Noun Clause. [When 'What' question is asked to the Principal Clause, Subordinate Clause should be the answer]**

Noun Clause as an Object of :

a. a Preposition

b. an Infinitive

c. a Participle

NOUN CLAUSE : OBJECT OF A PREPOSITION

Preposition + Noun Clause

1. You should be determined **to** what you decide.

— Noun Clause

Preposition

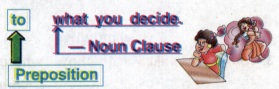

Ans: What you decide = Noun Clause : Object of a Preposition

---

2. You must be fully involved **in** what you do.

— Noun Clause

Preposition

What you do = Noun Clause : Object of a Preposition

---

3. They will be happy **for** why I am restless.

— Noun Clause

Preposition

Why I am restless = Noun Clause : Object of a Preposition

---

4. My friends helped me **with** whatever they had.

Preposition Noun Clause : Object of a Preposition

whatever they had = Noun Clause : Object of a Preposition

NOUN CLAUSE : OBJECT OF INFINITIVE

To + Verb (1st form) = Infinitive

1. **The thief wanted** → *Infinitive* | to tell | **why he had stolen money**.
   ↑ Noun Clause : Object Of Infinitive

2. **She wished** → *Infinitive* | to know | **how she can get success.**
   ↑ Noun Clause : Object Of Infinitive

3. **Your brother likes** → *Infinitive* | to show | **where the accident had occurred**.
   ↑ Noun Clause : Object Of An Infinitive

4. **Sita desires** → *Infinitive* | to explain | **why she was late**.
   ↑ Noun Clause : Object Of Infinitive

Noun Clause : Object of the Participle

When a Verb is used as an Adjective, it is a Participle.

E.g. → **Adjective** Rolling | → **Noun** stone gathers no moss.
   ↑ Participle

Participle + Noun Clause = Noun Clause : Object of a Participle

Example:

1. **She praised him for** | presenting | **that he had an excellent plan.**
   ↑ Participle ↑ Noun Clause

2. **You compelled her for** | saying | **that she was weak in French.**
   ↑ Participle ↑ Noun Clause

3. I appreciate her for clearing   that he is an efficient person.

                         Participle   **Noun Clause**

4. Titus has helped the students in proving   that they are better.

                         Participle   **Noun Clause**

Noun Clause: In Apposition to a Noun

When Noun Clause clarifies or explains about Noun, Pronoun etc.,
it is **Noun Clause : In Apposition to a Noun**.

Noun

E.g: **The truth,**   that she is a doctor,   is not known to anybody.

Noun

The news,   that India has lost the match,   is not true.

                         Noun Clause

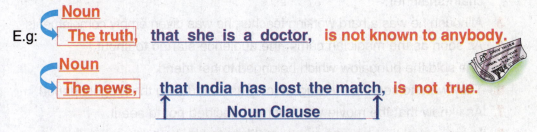

Kinds of Adverb Clauses

Adverb Clause of time : Till, Until, Since, After, Before, When, While.

Adverb Clause of Place : Where, Wherever, Whereas.

Adverb Clause of Reason : As, Since, Because, That.

Adverb Clause of Condition : Unless, If.

Adverb Clause of Purpose : So that, Lest.

Adverb Clause of Concession : Even though, Although, Though.

Adverb Clause of Comparison : As, than.

Adverb Clause of Manner : As if.

Adverb Clause of Result : So.

Examples:

1. Miss Smith is happy because she has passed the exam.

                 Adverb Clause of Reason

2. You should do exercise so that you will be fit.

                 Adverb Clause of Purpose

3. She did not work hard so she failed.

                 Adverb Clause of Result

4. **Although** he is poor, he is honest.

↑ **Adverb Clause of Concession**

5. **Nick was talking** **as if** she were a fool.

↑ **Adverb Clause of Manner.**

EXERCISE NO. 13-D

Find out the *'Subordinate Clauses'* and tell their kinds:

1. Those, who don't fear, achieve the target.
2. While she was waiting for a bus at the bus stop, she saw an empty handed chain-snatcher.
3. Although he was a hard working teacher, he was given empty complements.
4. As soon as the magician came, the audience started to shout.
5. She sold the bungalow which belonged to her friend.
6. They went to see the building which was built during the Moghul period.
7. As I know that the movie was boring, I decided not to see it.
8. He accepted that he was caught red-handed by the police.
9. As the war started, the soldiers were ready to attack.
10. Tell me, how he will speak about the evil of his friends.
11. Show me the bungalow that was gifted by your friend.
12. Boys, who are handsome, try to become models.
13. It was an explosive situation as nobody was ready to bell the cat.
14. We met the politician who had two faces.
15. I appreciate you for clearing that she is a helpful lady.

EXERCISE NO. 13-F

***Identify the Clauses,* name them and tell their kinds also:**

1. If you have faith, you can achieve your goal.
2. I thank you for helping me as I was in such a critical stage of my life.
3. Students, who don't talk much, are seen lost in the depth of thoughts.
4. Please call the doctor while I am going to phone for the ambulance.
5. She is sad because there is hodge-podge in her plan.
6. Peter goes wherever Sam goes.
7. She must understand why she has been failed.

8. It is a fact which can be a good news for you.

9. I hate you for saying that you are hollow-hearted.

10. The news, that she has become Miss India, has surprised me.

11. She should listen to what he instructs.

12. Keep your eyes on him as he is a hard-hearted fellow.

13. As you have no patience, you can count the chicken before they are hatched.

14. She does it because she is hawk-eyed.

15. Unless you go to the college, you will not get the result.

16. As there is hue and cry, you cannot get into final inclusion.

17. She has not been admitted as she is not very serious.

18. If it rains, I shall not be able to come.

19. You will succeed whenever you attempt towards your goal.

20. Though she has itching palm, she cannot earn money.

21. Nothing happens to those who have courage.

22. Tell him the truth before you go to the police.

23. If you do so, I shall punish you.

24. He, who deceives his friends, deceives himself.

25. Prayers never inconvenience to anybody.

26. Uneasy lies the head that wears the crown.

27. He, who finds wisdom, is always happy.

28. He, who is slow to anger, never loses his wits.

29. He, who does not support you, is against you.

30. He, who eats till he is sick, should fast till he is well.

31. Those, who live in glass houses, should not throw stones at others.

32. Those, who seek only for faults, cannot see anything.

33. The fruits, that grow in our garden, are not for sale.

34. Those, who seek wisdom, are kind-hearted.

35. God helps those who help themselves.

36. Those, who do not work, must starve.

37. Those, who are too sharp, cut their own finger.

38. It is the ill wind that blows good to nobody.

39. Those, who have a pure heart, inherit the kingdom of love.

40. Napoleon, whom French honour, died at Helena.

41. As the crow opened the beaks to sing, the fox snapped the cheese up.

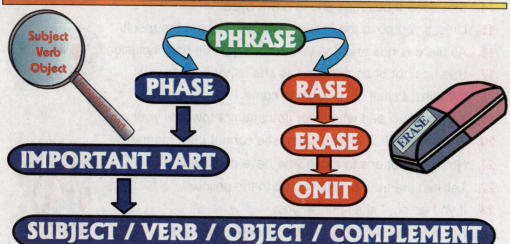

PHRASE

PHRASE

PHASE — **RASE**

IMPORTANT PART — **ERASE** — **OMIT**

Subject Verb Object

SUBJECT / VERB / OBJECT / COMPLEMENT

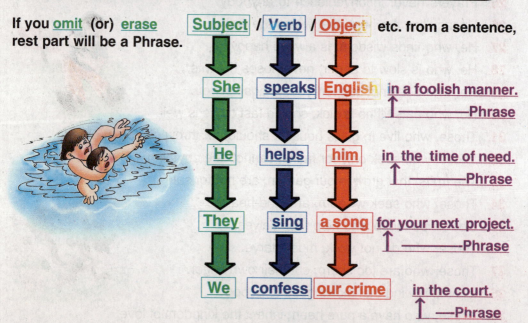

If you <u>omit</u> (or) <u>erase</u> <u>Subject</u> / <u>Verb</u> / <u>Object</u> etc. from a sentence, rest part will be a Phrase.

<u>She</u>	speaks	English	in a foolish manner. —Phrase
<u>He</u>	helps	him	in the time of need. —Phrase
<u>They</u>	sing	a song	for your next project. —Phrase
<u>We</u>	confess	our crime	in the court. —Phrase

A Phrase is a part of a sentence without **a Subject, Verb, Object or Complement**.
<u>Phrase</u> does not contain a <u>Subject</u> and a <u>Verb</u>.

A <u>Clause</u> contains a <u>Subject</u> and a <u>Verb</u> (Sometimes the subject is hidden)

NOUN, NOUN PHRASE & NOUN CLAUSE

Noun – All that you can see, feel or think is a <u>Noun</u>.

Ex = Ram, a boy, a tree, a bus, a train, sorrow etc.

Noun Phrase – Noun Phrase is a part of sentence without <u>Subject</u> and <u>Verb</u> and it always acts as a **Noun.**

Noun Clause – Noun Clause is a part of sentence with <u>Subject</u> and <u>Verb</u> and it always acts as a **Noun.**

Example:

What does she desire ?

She desires some | **food.**
↑ Noun

She desires | **to have some food.**
↑   Noun Phrase

She desires | **that she would like to have some food.**
↑ ———————————— Noun Clause

Example:

What does he like ?

He likes | **cricket.**
↑ Noun

He likes | **to play cricket.**
↑ Noun Phrase

He wishes | **that he could play cricket.**
↑ ——————— Noun Clause

What do we know ?

We love | **honesty.**
↑ — Noun

We love | **to be honest.**
↑— Noun Phrase

We love | **what is known to be honesty.**
↑ ——————— Noun Clause

EXERCISE NO. 14-A

Pick out the *'Noun Phrases'* from the following sentences:

1. Thinking about the great thoughts precedes good actions.
2. Cheats prefer cheating honest people only.
3. My dream to get the Noble Prize surprises everybody.
4. She has decided to punish her friends.
5. The cunning leaders love to cheat people.
6. Walking in open air provides me comfort.
7. The poor beggar decided not to beg anymore.
8. I prefer such an idea.
9. Has she ever been to an open place to have fresh air?
10. She accepts doing such criminal acts.
11. Her sister wished to speak to my parent.
12. To preach such great thoughts, is a graceful attempt.
13. To preach a fool, is not easy
14. She denies creating any problem.
15. To crack jolly jocks, is good for us.
16. We enjoy singing sad songs.
17. Early to rise is a good habit.
18. Promise to smile again.
19. She refuses to accept the fact.
20. Miss Newbolt denies stealing the ornaments..
21. To sing such melodious song is graceful.
22. She desires to create a history.
23. Crows prefer stealing sweet bread.
24. Do you prefer eating breakfast early ?

ADJECTIVE, ADJECTIVE PHRASE & ADJECTIVE CLAUSE

Adjective – It tells about the quality of **Noun** or **Pronoun**. This is a **black** cow.

Adjective Phrase – It is a **Phrase** that acts like an **Adjective.**

Adjective Clause – It is a **Clause** that acts like an **Adjective.**

EX:

She is an **intelligent** girl.
↑ Adjective

She is the **girl** **with intelligence.**
Noun↑. ↑ Adjective Phrase

She is the **girl** **who has intelligence.**
Noun↑. ↑ — Adjective Clause

EX:

He has a **golden** pen.
↑ Adjective

He has a **pen** **made of gold.**
Noun↑. ↑ Adjective Phrase

He has a **pen** **which is made of gold.**
Noun↑. ↑ Adjective Clause

EX:

Bill Gates is a **wealthy** man.
↑ Adjective

Bill Gates is a **man** **with a great wealth.**
Noun↑. ↑ Adjective Phrase

Bill Gates is a **man** **who has a great wealth.**
Noun↑. ↑ Adjective Clause

EX:

There is a **blue** jackal.
↑ Adjective

There is a **jackal** **with blue skin.**
Noun↑. ↑ Adjective Phrase

There is a **jackal** **who has blue skin.**
Noun↑. ↑ Adjective Clause

ADVERB, ADVERB PHRASE & ADVERB CLAUSE

Adverb : **An Adverb** is a word that adds some meaning to a **Verb, an Adjective** or another **Adverb**.

Adverb Phrase : **A Phrase**, which acts like an **Adverb**, is an **Adverb Phrase**.

Adverb Clause : **A Clause**, which acts like an **Adverb**, is an **Adverb Clause**.

Ex.

They talked wisely. [Adverb]

They talked in a wise manner [Adverb Phrase]

They talked as if they were wise men. [Adverb Clause]

Ex.

Sachin played nicely at Sharjah. [Adverb]

Sachin played in a very nice style at Sharjah. [Adverb Phrase]

Sachin played as nicely as he could at Sharjah. [Adverb Clause]

Ex.

You have spoken intellectually . [Adverb]

You have spoken in an intellectual manner . [Adverb Phrase]

You have spoken as if you were an intellectual person . [Adverb Clause]

Ex.

The students were answering politely . [Adverb]

The students were answering in a polite manner . [Adverb Phrase]

The students were answering as if they were very polite. [Adverb Clause]

Ex.

They fought bravely. [Adverb]

They fought in a brave manner . [Adverb Phrase]

They fought as if they were brave men . [Adverb Clause]

EXERCISE NO. 14-B

Find out the *'Adjectives'* / *'Adjective Clauses'* / *'Adjective Phrases'* from the following sentences:

1. God punishes them who cheat honest people.
2. The cause, why these people are respected, is clear to everybody.
3. The fact, which is unknown, is a secret.
4. Those people, who live for others, are always adored.
5. People, who live in glass houses, should not throw stones at others.
6. Nobody knows about his idea of cheating.
7. I have seen a girl with a black purse.
8. She has bought a bungalow without any fence.
9. A leader, with his supporters, was arrested by the police.
10. A TV, stolen from your shop, has been found in my backyard.

EXERCISE NO. 14-C

Find out the 'Nouns' / 'Noun Clauses' / 'Noun Phrases' from the following sentences:

1. I know that a fool is only original in the world.
2. She wishes to know my reality.
3. I desire that I should become a Guinness Record Holder.
4. He hates to waste his time.
5. We seldom surprise how you succeed so easily.
6. Peter denies stealing my purse.
7. Everyone knows how you earn money.
8. Hercules loves preaching all the time.
9. Simon enjoys singing songs in the morning.
10. The man, who has misguided us, seems to be a paper tiger.

EXERCISE NO. 14-D

Find out the *'Adverbs'* / *'Adverb Clauses'* / *'Adverb Phrases'* from the following sentences:

1. Krish fought with great courage.
2. If you are a wolf whistler, you will be punished.
3. Robert behaved in a very silly manner.
4. As you take bull by horns, you have to face the horrible result.

5. He was looking for a milch cow so that he should not work hard.
6. She has presented it in a very beautiful style.
7. Your monkey tricks are presented without much wisdom.
8. He was unwisely making monkey of him.
9. He was eating like a horse so that he might become healthy.
10. You have to hit the bull's-eye so that you may get the goal.
11. You have separated sheep from the goats in a very unwise manner.
12. If you want to prove your honesty, you should have clean hands.

SIMPLE, COMPLEX & COMPOUND SENTENCES

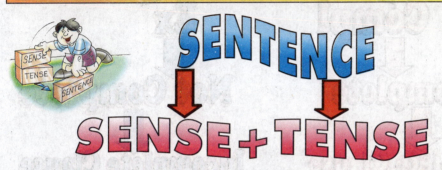

SENTENCE
SENSE + TENSE

A group of words that has a complete sense and a tense is a **Sentence**.

Common Definition : A group of words that has a complete meaning is called **a Sentence**.

Example : **1.** She is going to meet you.   **2.** You have been waiting for me.

SIMPLE SENTENCE
SIMPLE
SIM + PLE
SUBJECT PREDICATE

A Sentence that has **a Subject** and **a Predicate** is called **a Simple Sentence.**

 Subject   **Main Verb**

She   has   taken my book. [Simple Sentence]

                    Predicate

 Subject   **Main Verb**

You   play   football   with   my   friends. [Simple Sentence]

                    Predicate

Complex Sentence

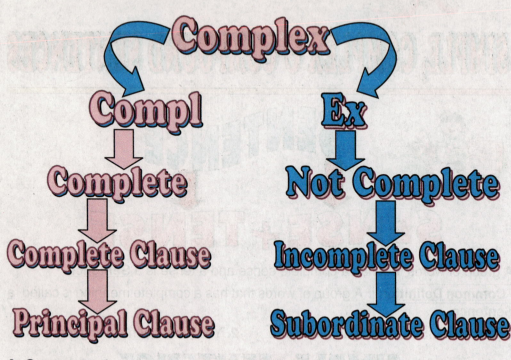

Complex

Compl → **Complete** → **Complete Clause** → **Principal Clause**

Ex → **Not Complete** → **Incomplete Clause** → **Subordinate Clause**

A Sentence that has **a Principal Clause** and one or more than one **Subordinate Clauses** is **a Complex Sentence.**

↓————— Incomplete Meaning   ↓————— Complete Meaning

When | her money | was picked , | she | was | sleeping.

| Subject | Verb | | Subject | Verb |

| Subordinate Clause | | Principal Clause |

Complex Sentence

↓— Incomplete Meaning   ↓————— Complete Meaning

If | you | study , | you | will | succeed.

| Subject | Verb | | Subject | Verb |

| Subordinate Clause | | Principal Clause |

Complex Sentence

Compound Sentence

Compound

Complete

Round

Complete

Complete

Coordinate Clauses

Coordinate Clauses

Round off = complete

When 2 or more **Clauses** with complete meanings are used together, it is called a **Compound Sentence**.

A Compound Sentence consists of two or more **Coordinate Clauses** joined by a **Coordinator** or a **Coordinating Conjunction**.

Coordinate Clauses : When both the **Clauses** give complete meaning, they are called **Coordinate Clauses** -

Coordinator = And/But/Or/Nor/Nevertheless/As well as/Not only—but also **etc.**

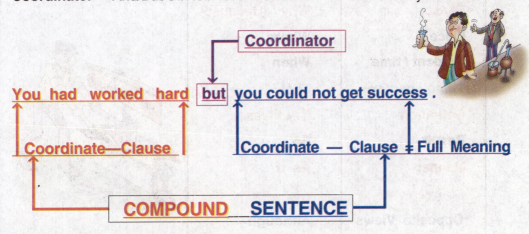

Coordinator

You had worked hard **but** **you could not get success** .

Coordinate—Clause

Coordinate — Clause = Full Meaning

COMPOUND SENTENCE

TRANSFORMATION
Simple To Complex Sentence

Subject   Verb   **Principal Clause = Main Clause**

| **He** | **sold** | his mother's necklace. **[Simple Sentence]**

How to solve?

Subject   Verb   Object

| He | | sold | his mother's | necklace. |

[Separate it from Subject, Verb & Object]

He sold the necklace   his mother   Use a

Main Clause

| Subordinator | Verb | | Preposition |
| Which | belonged | | to |

Ans: **He sold the necklace** which **belonged** to his mother.

Past

He sold the necklace   which   belonged to his mother.

Main Clause   Subordinate Clause

Complex Sentence

How to select the Subordinator ?

Thing	Which
Person	Who
Reason	Why [Because]
Place	Where
Incident / time	When
Thing / person	That
Condition	If / unless
Result	So
Manner	As if
Comparison	As / than
Opposite Views	Although

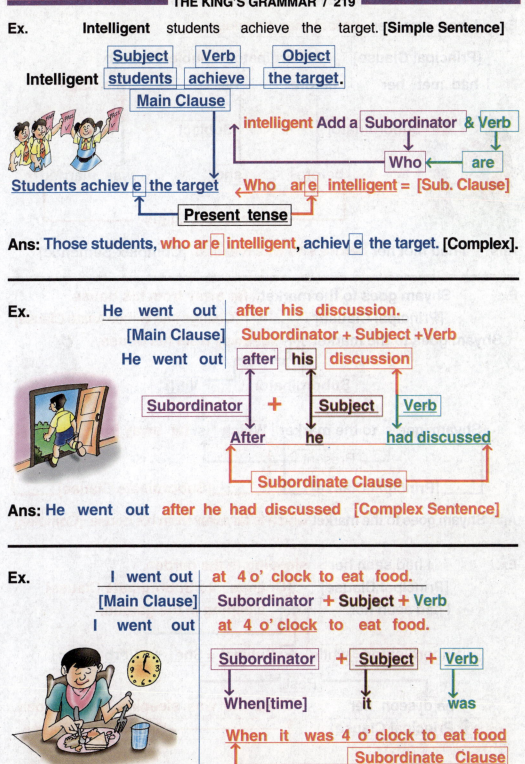

Ex. **Intelligent** students achieve the target. **[Simple Sentence]**

Subject	Verb	Object

Intelligent | students | achieve | the target.

Main Clause

intelligent Add a Subordinator & Verb

Who ← are

Students achiev e the target , Who are intelligent = [Sub. Clause]

Present tense

Ans: **Those students, who are intelligent, achieve the target. [Complex].**

Ex. He went out | after his discussion.

[Main Clause] Subordinator + Subject +Verb

He went out | after | his | discussion

Subordinator + Subject Verb

After he had discussed

Subordinate Clause

Ans: **He went out after he had discussed [Complex Sentence]**

Ex. I went out | at 4 o' clock to eat food.

[Main Clause] Subordinator + Subject + Verb

I went out | at 4 o' clock to eat food.

Subordinator + Subject + Verb

When[time] it was

When it was 4 o' clock to eat food

Subordinate Clause

Ans: **I went out when it was 4 o'clock to eat food. [Complex Sentence]**

Ex.   I had met her before her marriage.

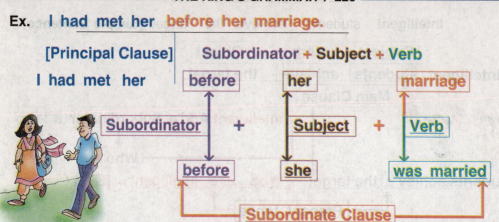

[Principal Clause]   Subordinator + Subject + Verb

I had met her   before   her   marriage

Subordinator   +   Subject   +   Verb

before   she   was married

Subordinate Clause

Ans: I had met her **before she was married.** [Complex Sentence]

Ex.   Shyam goes to the market, far away from his house.
          [Principal Clause]   [Change into Subordinate Clause]

Shyam goes to the market   far away from his house.

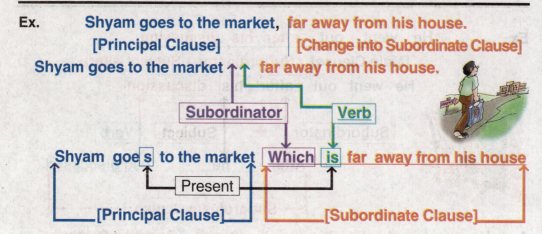

Subordinator   Verb

Shyam goes to the market   Which   is   far away from his house

Present

[Principal Clause]   [Subordinate Clause]

Ans: Shyam goes to the market **which is far away from his house.** [Complex]

Ex.   I had seen her   sleeping in the garden.
          [Principal Clause]   [Change into Subordinate Clause]

I had seen her   sleeping in the garden.

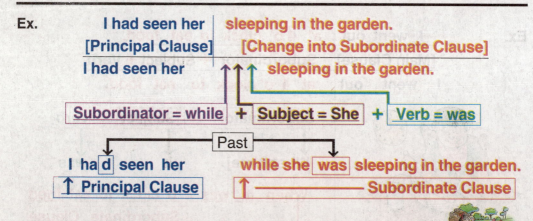

Subordinator = while   +   Subject = She   +   Verb = was

Past

I had seen her   while she was sleeping in the garden.

↑ Principal Clause   ↑ ——————— Subordinate Clause

Ans: I had seen her while she was sleeping in the garden.

[Complex Sentence]

While is used in Continuous tenses.

Ex. **She is too lazy to help me.**

Present | Past   [too —— to = so —— that]

too – to = can | could + not

She is so lazy that she cannot help me. [Complex Sentence]

EXERCISE NO. 15-A

Transform the *'Simple Sentences'* into *'Complex Sentences'* :

1. She knows the truth.
2. They cleared the fact to me.
3. He demolished his father's house.
4. Foolish students waste their time in watching cricket.
5. Please understand the meaning of your life.
6. She searches her lost purse.
7. They are too foolish to solve the problem.
8. After the minister's termination, all the cabinet ministers are shocked.
9. Because of his hard working nature, he can achieve the target.
10. Edward will not expose the secret without my suggestion.
11. The inspector saw her cheating him in the office.
12. On her departure, I could see tears in her eyes.
13. I am too tired to walk with you now.

COMPLEX SENTENCES TO SIMPLE SENTENCES

Divide a sentence into two parts Principal Clause & Subordinate Clause

Do not do anything with the Principal Clause.

Cut the Subordinator and use a Preposition e.g. because = because of

Change the Subject and Verb into Adjective + Noun. Or use to or Ing

Change the Subject [e.g. He = his She = her They = their]

Replace Subordinator = Preposition

Ex. : **Andy was sad because he lost a pen.**

Main Clause | Subordinate Clause = Adjective + Noun

Andy was sad | because he lost a pen

Possessive = his + Noun

Ans: Andy was sad because of his lost pen. [Simple Sentence]

Ex.

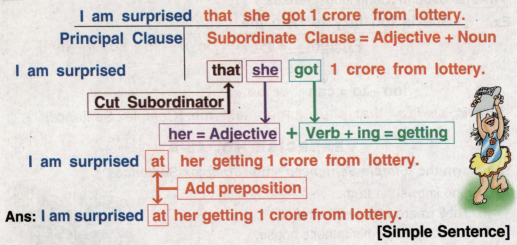

I am surprised that she got 1 crore from lottery.
Principal Clause | **Subordinate Clause = Adjective + Noun**

I am surprised | that | she | got | 1 crore from lottery.

Cut Subordinator

her = Adjective **+** Verb + ing = getting

I am surprised at her getting 1 crore from lottery.

Add preposition

Ans: I am surprised at her getting 1 crore from lottery.
[Simple Sentence]

Ex.

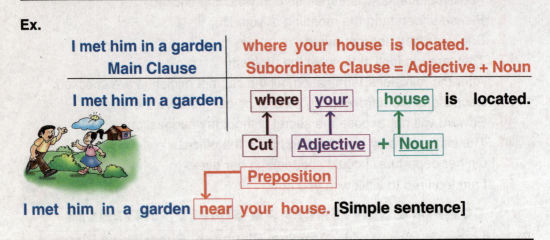

I met him in a garden | where your house is located.
Main Clause | **Subordinate Clause = Adjective + Noun**

I met him in a garden | where | your | house | is located.

Cut | **Adjective** **+** **Noun**

Preposition

I met him in a garden near your house. **[Simple sentence]**

Ex.

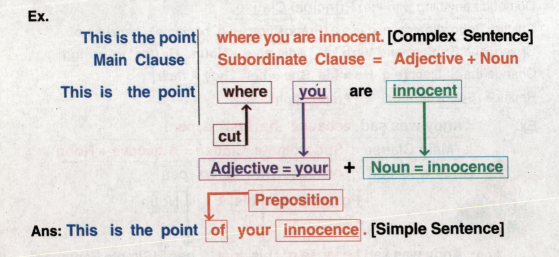

This is the point | where you are innocent. **[Complex Sentence]**
Main Clause | **Subordinate Clause = Adjective + Noun**

This is the point | where | you | are | innocent

cut

Adjective = your **+** Noun = innocence

Preposition

Ans: This is the point of your innocence. **[Simple Sentence]**

Ex.

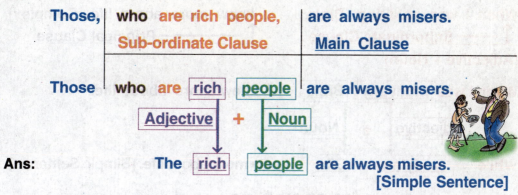

Those, | who are rich people, | are always misers.
Sub-ordinate Clause | Main Clause

Those | who are rich people | are always misers.
Adjective + Noun

Ans: The rich people are always misers.
[Simple Sentence]

Ex.

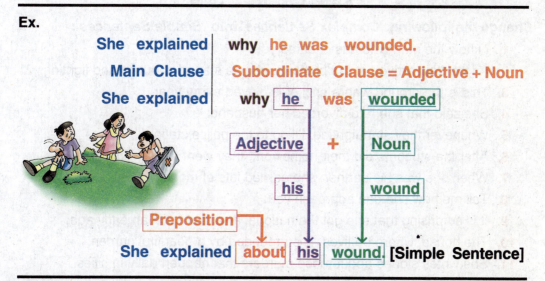

She explained | why he was wounded.
Main Clause | Subordinate Clause = Adjective + Noun

She explained | why he was wounded
Adjective + Noun
his + wound
Preposition

She explained about his wound. [Simple Sentence]

Ex.

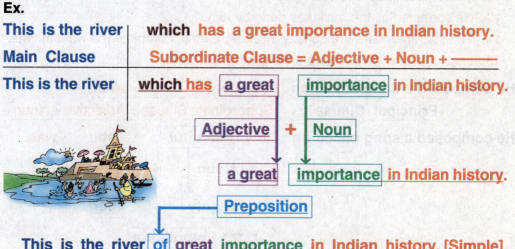

This is the river | which has a great importance in Indian history.
Main Clause | Subordinate Clause = Adjective + Noun + ———

This is the river | which has a great importance in Indian history.
Adjective + Noun
a great importance in Indian history.
Preposition

This is the river of great importance in Indian history. [Simple]

Example:

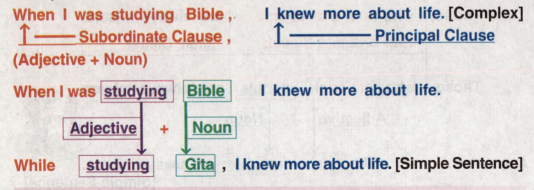

When I was studying Bible , I knew more about life. [Complex]
↑ —— Subordinate Clause , ↑ ————— Principal Clause
(Adjective + Noun)

When I was [studying] [Bible] I knew more about life.

[Adjective] + [Noun]

While [studying] [Gita] , I knew more about life. [Simple Sentence]

EXERCISE NO. 15-B

Change the following *'Complex Sentences'* into *'Simple Sentences'*:

1. I know the man who has cheated you.
2. As the train arrived at the platform, people started shouting and fighting.
3. This is the ground where cricket is played every year.
4. She said that she had divorced her husband.
5. Whenever they start fighting, I'll go to the police station.
6. After the students did their homework, they went to play cricket.
7. When she was his partner, she earned lots of money.
8. Tell me how she can approach you.
9. It is surprising that she got the national award at such an early age.
10. The house, where he lives, is surrounded by a beautiful garden.
11. She writes stories about those murders that happen daily in cities.
12. I have no money that I can give you.
13. He corrected all the mistakes done by him.
14. The staff members are so lazy that they cannot complete the work in time.
15. I saw that she was singing a song with her friends.

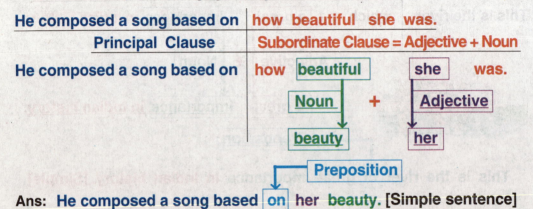

He composed a song based on	how beautiful she was.
Principal Clause	**Subordinate Clause = Adjective + Noun**

He composed a song based on how [beautiful] [she] was.

[Noun] + [Adjective]

[beauty] [her]

[Preposition]

Ans: He composed a song based [on] her beauty. [Simple sentence]

Cut indefinite word - Cut helping verb - Cut subordinator = Simple sentence

Ex.

In case of it there etc.= Indefinite words take other part as main.

Indefinite word   Main Part

It is well known that he is an artist.

| Indefinite word | Verb | Subordinator |

Cut It is well known that he is an artist.

Ans. He is a well known artist. [Simple Sentence]

Ex.

As the exam was over, the students were free.

Subordinate Clause   Principal Clause

Adjective + Noun

As the exam was over. the students were free.

Noun + Adjective

Preposition

the exam   end

The students were free at the end of exam. [Simple Sentence]

Ex.

Subordinate Clause   Principal Clause

How long her brother will survive is doubtful.

The duration of her brother's survival is doubtful.

Adjective + Noun

The duration of her brother's survival is doubtful. [Simple Sentence]

Ex.

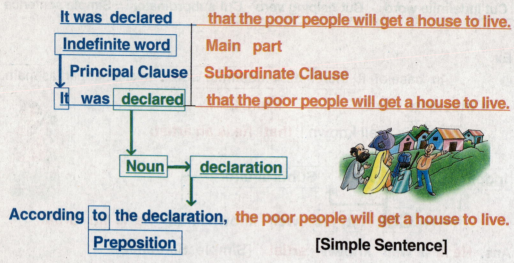

It was declared | that the poor people will get a house to live.

Indefinite word | Main part

Principal Clause | Subordinate Clause

It was declared | that the poor people will get a house to live.

Noun → declaration

According to the declaration, the poor people will get a house to live.

Preposition | [Simple Sentence]

Ex.

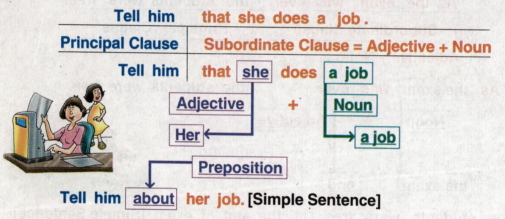

Tell him | that she does a job.

Principal Clause | Subordinate Clause = Adjective + Noun

Tell him | that she does a job

Adjective + Noun

Her ← → a job

Preposition

Tell him about her job. [Simple Sentence]

Ex.

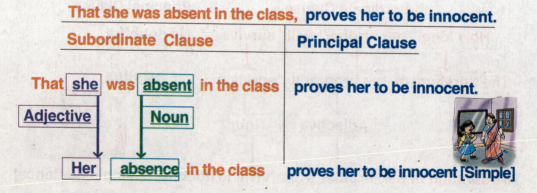

That she was absent in the class, proves her to be innocent.

Subordinate Clause | Principal Clause

That she was absent in the class | proves her to be innocent.

Adjective | Noun

Her absence in the class | proves her to be innocent [Simple]

Adjective Clause

Complex to Simple Sentences

Ex.

She has no money **that she can give him.**

Cut ~~Subordinator~~ cut ~~Subject~~ cut ~~helping verb~~ = **Simple Sentences**

She has no money that she   can give him.

She has no money **to give him.** [Simple Sentence]

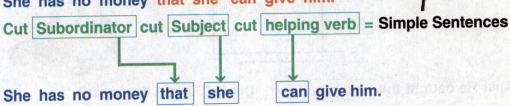

Ex.

Main Clause	Subordinate Clause = Adjective + Noun
Don't forgive	who is **your** **enemy**
	Adjective + **Noun**
	Don't forgive **your** **enemy**. [Simple Sentence]

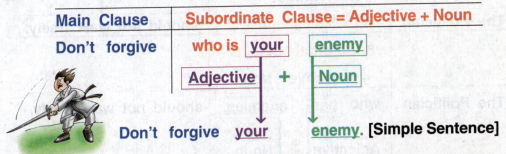

Ex.

The watch, **that I bought from America,** is very costly.

Main Clause

The watch | that I bought from America | **is very costly**

Subordinate Clause = | [Main Clause]

Adjective + Noun

That **I** bought from **America** | **the watch** is very costly

Adjective + **Noun**

My **American** | **the watch** is very costly.

Ans: My American watch is very costly. [Simple Sentence]

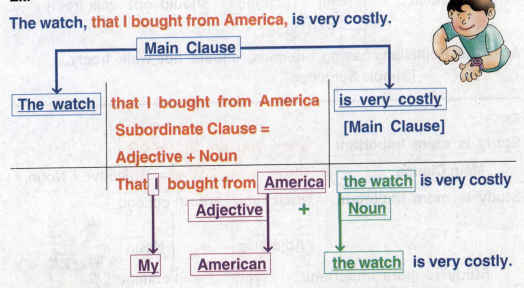

Ex.

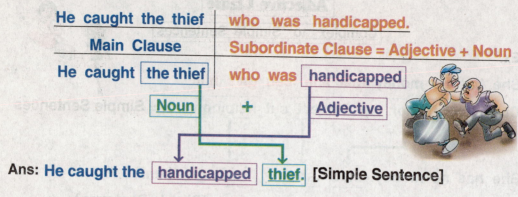

He caught the thief	who was handicapped.
Main Clause	Subordinate Clause = Adjective + Noun
He caught the thief	who was handicapped
Noun	+	Adjective

Ans: He caught the **handicapped** **thief.** [Simple Sentence]

Ex.

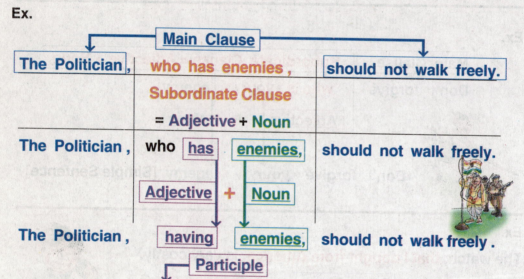

	Main Clause	
The Politician ,	who has enemies ,	should not walk freely.
	Subordinate Clause	
	= Adjective + Noun	
The Politician ,	who has enemies,	should not walk freely.
	Adjective + Noun	
The Politician ,	having enemies,	should not walk freely .
	Participle	

Ans: The Politician , having enemies, should not walk freely.
       [Simple Sentence]

Ex.

Study is more important	when you are in college.
Main Clause .	Subordinate Clause = Adjective + Noun
Study is more important	when you are in college
	Adjective + Noun
Study is more important	your in college

Ans: Study is more important in your college. [Simple Sentence]

Ex.

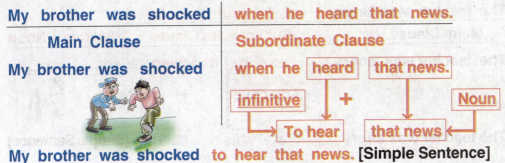

My brother was shocked	when he heard that news.
Main Clause	**Subordinate Clause**

My brother was shocked | when he | heard | that news.

infinitive **+** Noun

To hear | that news

My brother was shocked to hear that news. **[Simple Sentence]**

Ex.

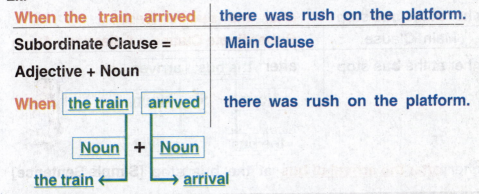

When the train arrived	there was rush on the platform.
Subordinate Clause =	**Main Clause**
Adjective + Noun	

When | the train | arrived | there was rush on the platform.

Noun **+** Noun

the train ← → arrival

Ans: At the arrival of train , there was rush on the platform.
[Simple Sentence]

Ex.

In case of if Clause = If Clause is the main part

So cut **If** .

Main Clause = To + Verb + Noun

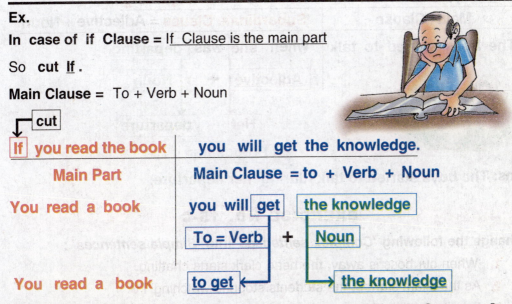

cut

If you read the book	you will get the knowledge.
Main Part	**Main Clause = to + Verb + Noun**

You read a book | you will get the knowledge

To = Verb **+** Noun

You read a book | to get ← → the knowledge

Ans: You read a book to get the knowledge. **[Simple Sentence]**

Ex.

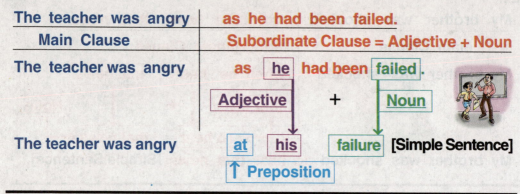

The teacher was angry	as he had been failed.
Main Clause	Subordinate Clause = Adjective + Noun
The teacher was angry	as he had been failed.
	Adjective + Noun
The teacher was angry	at his failure [Simple Sentence]
	↑ Preposition

Ex.

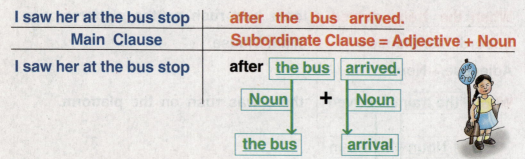

I saw her at the bus stop	after the bus arrived.
Main Clause	Subordinate Clause = Adjective + Noun
I saw her at the bus stop	after the bus arrived.
	Noun + Noun
	the bus arrival

I saw her after the arrival of bus at the bus stop [Simple Sentence]

Ex.

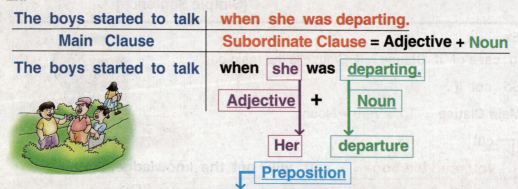

The boys started to talk	when she was departing.
Main Clause	Subordinate Clause = Adjective + Noun
The boys started to talk	when she was departing.
	Adjective + Noun
	Her departure
	Preposition

Ans: The boys started to talk during her departure.

EXERCISE NO. 15-C

Change the following 'Complex sentences' into 'Simple sentences' :

1. When our boss is away, the head clerk starts chatting.
2. As the exam started, the students stopped watching TV.
3. I shall complete the work properly if I charge money.

4. Once the opportunity is lost, it is lost forever.

5. She has no money that she can give you.

6. This is the place where Napoleon was born.

7. I have seen the man who was cheating you.

8. My brother, who is a famous doctor, has been awarded by the President.

9. Childhood is the time when a child needs to be cared and loved.

10. She has bought the garden which belonged to my father.

11. The Manager was unhappy because the staff members were not active.

12. While there is courage, there is a struggle.

13. He can go wherever he wishes to go.

14. I am so hungry that I cannot stay here for a single minute.

15. She had suspected that her fast friend was very poor.

16. Tell me clearly that you have made the mistake.

17. She does not know when her friend will return.

18. The President ordered that the killer must be hanged.

19. He was very careless so he lost his gold medal.

20. She told me why she had come to Mumbai.

21. Although her health is very poor, she is doing her duty properly.

22. The book is too old to republish it.

23. I forgot her while I was making a list of guests.

24. They thought that they would achieve the target easily.

25. Rocky does not know when he was born.

26. She cleared me that I was confused.

27. As he is a good cricketer, he is expected to win the match for his team.

28. Doctors hope that she will recover soon.

29. The robbers attacked because they wanted to snatch my ornaments.

Compound to Complex Sentence

Rule 1: Cut Coordinator = And/But/Or/Nor/Nevertheless/
As well as/Not only ———— but also **etc.**

Rule 2: Use Subordinator = When/Although/As/Because/Even if **etc.**

How to select the Subordinator.

Place = Where / Wherever

Time = When / till / until / since [According to the sentence]

Condition = If / Unless

Result = So

Reason = Because

Purpose = So that

Concession = Although / Even though [Opposite sentences]

Comparison = Than

Incident = When

Rule 3. **Add–Use the Subject** according to the sentence.

If the sentence begins with **Verb [1st.form], use 'You'** as a **Subject.**

Coordinator

Ex. **Write a letter and get the reply.(Write =Verb 1st form =You)**

Cut

You write a letter you get a reply. [Condition = if]

Ans: If you write a letter, you will get a reply. [Complex Sentence]

Ex. **He did not work hard but achieved the target. [Compound]**

Cut Subordinator	Add Subordinator_____
but	Although (different opposite ideas)

(**opposite views = although**)

Although   **Coordinator**

He did not work hard but achieved   the target.

Ans: Although he did not work hard, he achieved the target. [Complex]

Ex.

I met him in the garden | and | remembered my childhood. [Compound]

[Cut] Coordinator	[Add] Sub ordinator
And	when [Indicating time]

when ⟶   Coordinator

I met him in the garden | and | remembered my childhood. [Compound]

Ans: When I met him in the garden, I remembered my childhood.

[Complex Sentence]

Ex.

She lives near the school | and | teaches English there. [Compound]

[Cut] Coordinator	[Add] Subordinator
and	where [indicating place]

Coordinator

She lives near the school | and | teaches English | there.

Sub ordinator = Where

Ans: She lives near the school | where | she teaches English.

[Complex Sentence]

Compound Sentence

Ex.

He has joined coaching classes | and | he stopped teaching at home.

[Cut] Coordinator	[Add] Subordinator
and	because [indicating reason]

Because   Coordinator

He has joined coaching classes | and | he stopped teaching at home.

Because he has joined coaching classes, he stopped teaching at home.

[Complex Sentence]

Ex.

She has lost some money	**but** not the wealth. [Compound]
[Cut] Coordinator	[Add] Subordinator
but	still [indicating present state]

(Subordinator) still   Coordinator

She has lost some money **but** not the wealth. [Compound Sentence]

She has lost some money <u>still</u> she has wealth. [Complex Sentence]

Ex.

I did a crime to earn money	**and** I am suffering now. [Compound]
[Cut] Coordinator	[Add] Subordinator
and	So [indicating result]

Coordinator

I did a crime to earn money **and** I am suffering now. [Compound]

so (Subordinator)

I did a crime to earn money **so** I am suffering now. [Complex]

Ex.

Cut

She went to buy vegetables **but** she bought some fruits. [Compound]

Coordinator .

Ans: **Although** she went to buy vegetables, she bought some fruits.

Subordinator {Different things}

[Complex Sentence]

EXERCISE NO. 15-D

Change the *'Compound sentences'* given below into *'Complex sentences'*.

1. Open the bag and you will get the grapes of Nasik.
2. Her mistakes were pointed out but not corrected by her.
3. They have to complete the work in time or they will be punished.
4. Do as she suggests you or you will fail to get a good result.
5. She got a letter of her missing son and wept bitterly.
6. Guide not, punish not.
7. My brother has bought a bungalow and it is located near the graveyard.
8. Rick has got the 1st prize but we don't want to declare it.
9. They hope to achieve the goal and, therefore, they have planned this programme.
10. You must be quick or you will not be able to complete the work in time.
11. She has been very late and for this I am sorry.
12. The sentence was correct but we could not justify it.
13. He had lost his money but he got it in her purse.
14. Sanjay met his friend at the bus stop and immediately he took a taxi.
15. Sam must return back early or her parents will be worried.
16. An old saint lives in a cave and nobody knows it.
17. He has insulted me but I will not do the same to anybody.
18. Get out or I shall beat you.
19. She will achieve the target or die.
20. My boss is overloaded with work, consequently he could not find these mistakes.
21. I desired to become an actor therefore I came to Mumbai.
22. Consult the doctor or her disease will be fatal.
23. Meet that fellow and you will come to know more about her.
24. She is shocked and, therefore, she fell unconscious.
25. Crime causes disorder and it is quite unfortunate for our country.
26. The fox praised the crow for his golden voice and took the bread away.
27. He got the gold medal in the Asian Games and never turned back all through his life.
28. Sam is very rich but he is a miser.
29. She is trying to bring dream come true in real life yet it is not possible.
30. Yukta may not be very beautiful but her nature is very good.

Complex to Compound Sentence

You will get **two types** of <u>**Complex Sentences**</u>.

Complex Sentence: | Beginning with Subordinate Clause |

Complex Sentence: | Beginning with Principal Clause |

Complex Sentence: Beginning with Subordinate Clause

Ex.
Cut ↓

| As soon as | I saw robbers, I informed the police.

Subordinator ↑   **[Complex]**

I saw robbers | and | informed the police. **[Compound]**

Coordinator ↑

Ex.
Cut ↓

| Unless | she takes medicine, she will not recover. **[Complex]**

Subordinator ↑

She | must | take medicine | or | she will not recover. **[Compound]**

compulsion ↑   Coordinator ↑

Ex.

Cut ↓

| Because | he has committed a crime, he will be imprisoned.

Subordinator ↑   **[Complex]**

and, so (result) ↓

Ans: He has committed a crime | and, so | he will be imprisoned.

Coordinator ↑   **[Compound]**

Ex.
Cut ↓

| As | she was disobedient, I complained against her.

Subordinator ↑   **[Complex]**

and , therefore (Consequence) ↓

Ans: She was disobedient | and, therefore | , I complained against her.

Coordinator ↑   **[Compound]**

Ex.

Cut ↓

Since you are confused, you must not do it. [Complex]

Subordinator ↑

↓ **and thus(cause)**

Ans: You are confused **and, thus** you must not do it. [Compound]

Complex Sentence : **Beginning with Principal Clause**

Ex.

Main Clause = Principal Clause

It was amazing that she won the gold medal. (Complex)
↑Principal Clause ↑ -------------------- Subordinate Clause

Exchange the place of **Principal Clause** and **Subordinate Clause**

Subordinator

⬇

That she won the gold medal, was amazing. [Complex]
↑ -------------Subordinate Clause ↑Principal Clause

Coordinator (and)

⬇

Ans: She won the gold medal **and** it was amazing. [Compound]

Ex.

Subordinator

⬇

She accepted **that** she had made a silly mistake. [Complex]
↑Cut

Coordinator

⬇

She had made a silly mistake **and** she accepted so. [Compound]

Ex.

I work hard | so that | I can achieve the target of my life. [Complex]
↑ Principal Clause | ↑ ---------------- Subordinate Clause

Exchange

Subordinator

Cut

So that I can achieve the target of my life, I work hard.
↑-------------------------- Subordinate Clause ↑ Principal Clause

willingness   Coordinator (Result)

I want to achieve the target of my life and, so I work hard.
[Compound Sentence]

Ex.   Subordinator (cut)

I can prove it in the court | that | he is a cheat. [Complex]
↑ —— Principal Clause | ↑ ------ Subordinate Clause

Exchange

Co- ordinator

He is a cheat | and | I can prove it in the court. [Compound]

Ex.   Subordinator(cut)

My mother comes to college | so that | she may know about my progress.
↑ —— Principal Clause | ↑ ----------- Subordinate Clause (Complex)

     Coordinator (result)

May = | desires |
My mother desires to know about my progress | and so | she comes to
college.   **[Compound]**

Ex.

| Subordinator | (cut)

She was insulted | where | she hated everybody. (Complex)
↑ — Principal Clause | ↑---------- Subordinate Clause

Exchange

| Coordinator | (result)
↓

She hated everybody | and, so | she was insulted there. (Compound)

EXERCISE NO. 15-E

Change the following 'Complex sentences' into 'Compound sentences' :

1. As soon as Rockey finished his work, he tried to approach his boss.
2. If she talks to me very rudely, I shall reply in the same manner.
3. Unless you try again and again, you will never achieve the goal.
4. Although the hunter shot the tiger, he could not find the body.
5. I am justifying that the sun is larger than the earth.
6. He was waiting for 1st April so that he might make her "April fool".
7. If she does not take care of her purse, she will lose her money.
8. She is more a painter than an actress.

9. As you sow, you shall reap so.
10. I am confident that he is criminal.
11. He bought 6 bananas after he had purchased some vegetables.
12. It is shocking that she has not returned home till now.
13. If he does his duty, he will get salary in time.
14. She is responsible for what she has done.
15. As soon as she orders, it will be carried out.
16. She went to bank so that she might clear her accounts.
17. Her face shows that she is frustrated.
18. I know what I have to do.
19. Any thing that gletters is not gold.
20. You must feel sorry as you have misbehaved with your parents.
21. The news, that the Prime Minister was killed, shocked me.
22. People, who live in glass houses, should not throw stones at others.
23. He is a cheat so he must be imprisoned.
24. She can complete it as it is very easy.

25. As Barry is intelligent, she can find these errors very easily.
26. Although Geffry attempted well, she could not pass the M.H.C.E.T. exam.
27. Ian, who is a famous administrator, can only unite them.
28. Miss Bell is so beautiful that she can become Miss India.
29. It all happened as I had predicted.
30. They are happy as they are hard working.
31. The information, that my friend is a cheat, shocked me.
32. Because she was insulted, she left the party.
33. You will not be able to meet him unless you catch the bus now.
34. He cannot help her because he is very poor.
35. Everybody knows that the earth moves round the sun.

Transformation: Simple to Compound Sentence

Rules:

1. Divide the sentence into **two parts** and get the <u>Clause</u>.
2. Add <u>a Subject</u> and <u>a Verb</u> to the rest part of the sentence and frame a sentence.
3. Use a **Coordinator** to join the sentences.
4. **Cut Preposition**

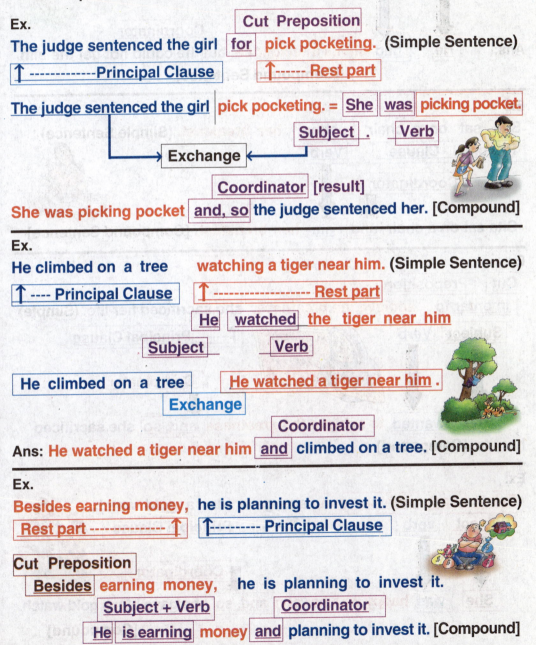

Ex.

Cut Preposition

The judge sentenced the girl **for** pick pocketing. **(Simple Sentence)**

↑ ------------Principal Clause   ↑------ Rest part

The judge sentenced the girl | pick pocketing. = She **was** picking pocket.

Subject . Verb

→ Exchange ←

Coordinator [result]

She was picking pocket **and, so** the judge sentenced her. **[Compound]**

Ex.

He climbed on a tree   watching a tiger near him. **(Simple Sentence)**

↑ ---- Principal Clause   ↑------------------- Rest part

He **watched** the tiger near him

Subject   Verb

He climbed on a tree   He watched a tiger near him .

Exchange

Coordinator

Ans: He watched a tiger near him **and** climbed on a tree. **[Compound]**

Ex.

Besides earning money, he is planning to invest it. **(Simple Sentence)**

Rest part -------------- ↑   ↑--------- Principal Clause

Cut Preposition

Besides earning money,   he is planning to invest it.

Subject + Verb   Coordinator

He **is earning** money **and** planning to invest it. **[Compound]**

Ex.

With all his intelligence, he could not get the aim. **(Simple Sentence)**

Rest part ----------------↑   ↑ --------- **Principal Clause**

| Cut | Preposition |

With all his intelligence, he could not get the aim.

Subject   Verb   ↑--------------- **Principal Clause**

Coordinator

Ans: He   had all his intelligence but he could not get the aim.

[Compound Sentence]

Ex.

Sita sat on a chair eating her breakfast. **(Simple Sentence)**

Principal Clause   **Verb**

Coordinator

Sita sat on a chair and ate her breakfast. **[Compound Sentence]**

Ex.

| Cut | Preposition |

In order to achieve the greatness, she sacrificed her life. **(Simple)**

Subject   Verb   ↑------ **Principal Clause**

Coordinator

She   wanted to achieve the greatness and, so she sacrificed her life. **[Compound]**

Ex.

Being happy with her son, she gave him a gold watch.

Subject   Verb   ↑--------- **Principal Clause**

Coordinator

She   was happy with her son and, so she gave him a gold watch.

[Compound]

EXERCISE NO. 15-F

Change the 'Simple sentences' given below into 'Compound sentences' :

1. Having killed the tiger, she went back to her friend's house.
2. You should work to earn.
3. Notwithstanding her beauty, she could not get the crown of Miss India.
4. He was fined for his bad habits.
5. Listening to the radio, he was remembering his parents.

6. Because of his property, people respect him in this village.
7. She should consult the doctor to get the medicine.
8. Besides creating problems, she has never accepted her faults.
9. You should meet him to know the fact.
10. I shall complain to the Principal for doing it.
11. Seeing the quarrel between two friends, she got a good lesson.
12. Notwithstanding his good approach, he could not get the party ticket.
13. In spite of being a good doctor, he could not save the patient.
14. They should work hard to survive.
15. Failing to complete the work in time, he was fined and scolded.
16. The drama, being over, the audience went back to home.
17. Having no money in my pocket, I went to my office.
18. Being a rich fellow, he never helps poor people.
19. She will not pay fees only under critical condition.
20. He is too tired to walk any more.
21. Madona is happy after getting the best actress award.
22. The birthplace of Napoleon is unknown.
23. Our teachers have no suggestion to give you.
24. They must take medicine to survive.
25. In the event of being lazy, he will be fined.
26. Notwithstanding his good nature, nobody likes him in the office.
27. He was insulted in the party for his bad habits.
28. Besides driving his car, he was making a plan to establish a new business.
29. In spite of his bad habits, nobody dislikes him.
30. Because of his bravery, he is well known all over the world.

Synthesis

Synthesis

Synthesis

Syn   Thesis

Add (or) Join   Thoughts (or) ideas

When two or more thoughts, ideas, sentences etc are joined, it is called **Synthesis**.

1. Synthesis: Simple sentence.

2. Synthesis: Complex sentence.

3. Synthesis: Compound sentence.

Synthesis : Simple sentence

Using : Participle [Verb + ing]

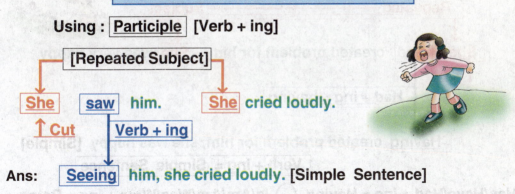

[Repeated Subject]

She saw him.   She cried loudly.

↑ Cut   Verb + ing

Ans: Seeing him, she cried loudly. [Simple Sentence]

Ex.

The thief was tortured. He ran away from the jail.

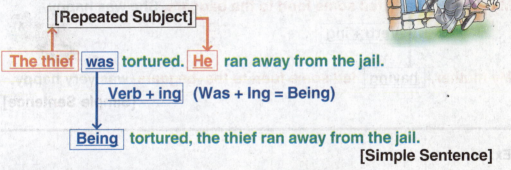

[Repeated Subject]

The thief was tortured. He ran away from the jail.

Verb + ing   (Was + Ing = Being)

Being tortured, the thief ran away from the jail.

[Simple Sentence]

Note: Is / Am / Are / Was / Were + ing = Being

Has / Have / Had + ing = Having

Ex.

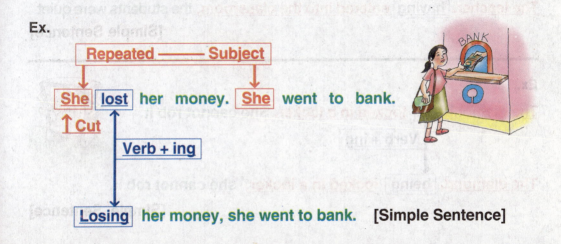

Repeated ——— Subject

She lost her money. She went to bank.

↑ Cut   Verb + ing

Losing her money, she went to bank.   [Simple Sentence]

Ex.

Repeated ——————————————— Subject

She | had | created problem for him. | She | was very happy.

↑ Cut

Had + ing = having

Having | created problem for him, she was happy. **[Simple]**

Verb + ing = Simple Sentence

Has/Have/Had + ing = Having ◯ Is/Am/Are/Was/Were + ing = Being

---

Ex.

My mother | had | fed some food to the beggars. She was happy.

Verb + ing

My mother, | having | fed some food to the beggars, was very happy.

[Simple Sentence]

Ex.

The teacher | had | entered into the classroom. The students were quiet.

Verb + ing

The teacher, | having | entered into the classroom, the students were quiet.

[Simple Sentence]

Ex.

The diamond | is | locked in a locker. She cannot rob it.

Verb + ing

The diamond, | being | locked in a locker, she cannot rob it.

[Simple Sentence]

Ex.

The students [are] told to stay in the class. They cannot go home.

[Verb + ing]

The students, [being] told to stay in the class, cannot go home.

[Simple Sentence]

Ex.

His parents [were] out. The house was locked.

[Verb + ing]

His parents, [being] out, the house was locked.   [Simple Sentence]

Ex.

She [has] lost her pen in the classroom. She found it near the college gate.

[Verb + ing]

[Having] lost her pen in the classroom, she found it near the college gate.

[Simple Sentence]

If you get 'Ing' in the second sentence, join from there.

Ex. I saw her. She was watching a football match.

Ans: I saw her watching a football match.

EXERCISE NO. 16-A

Join the sentences given below into *'Simple sentences'*.

1. The Prime Minister was injured. He was carried to the Royal Hospital.
2. It has rained cats and dogs. The crops were ruined.
3. He has given his decision. He returned back to his office.
4. She is ill. She cannot go out for picnic.
5. He has a good idea. It will be implemented soon.
6. I helped you. I have lost my image.
7. She is very intelligent. She does not expect any kindness from anybody.
8. The President was injured. He was admitted in the Royal hospital.
9. Greg wants to help me. He called me at home.
10. My father has cleared the fact. He went to the church.
11. Sanjay earns more money. He writes stories.
12. She scolded me. I was watching TV at my home.
13. You have cheated an honest man. He was attempting to prove his honesty.
14. He has lost the match. He decided not to play anymore.
15. My brother decides to help her. He wanted to know about her problems.

EXERCISE NO. 16-B

Join the sentences given below using *'Participles'* into *'Simple sentences'*.

1. She was returning back from her college. She met him near the temple.
2. He has taken your book. He sold that book in the market.
3. I lost my money- bag in the train. I went to the police station.
4. They have corrected all the errors. They will succeed in implementing their plan.
5. She cooked food. She served lunch. She cleaned the utensils.
6. He was warned by the police. He surrendered immediately.
7. She is an intelligent girl. She is very hard working. She will pass the I.A.S. exam.
8. I was talking to your Principal. I saw all the students shouting in the class.
9. Napoleon came. He attacked. He conquered.
10. The businessman bought a building. He sold it with 20% profit.
11. The student was 10 minutes late. Principal did not allow him to attend the class.

12. She watched the match. It was very exciting. People were enjoying it.

13. He could not pass the exam. He is weak in Moral Science.

14. She has cleared the truth. She is being punished.

15. She went to London. She wished to become a writer.

16. The militants had caught him. He was killed after 2 days.

17. She was preparing breakfast. She saw a bee in the boiling milk.

18. Tony had written answers very badly. She was given less marks in all the subjects.

19. A pilot alighted from the aeroplane. He informed the wing commander about his successful attack over the enemies.

20. The thief has accepted his guilt. He will be sent to jail.

21. She is right. She is not sure about it.

22. The train was delayed. I could not reach office in time.

23. The boy was badly beaten by his teacher. He was unconscious.

24. She gave me a cup of tea. She went to prepare breakfast in the kitchen.

25. Hitler was informed about his defeat. He shot himself.

Synthesis: Simple Sentence
To + Verb

Ex.

Your brother is very foolish. He cannot pass the exam.

Very = too   Using infinitive = [to+Verb]

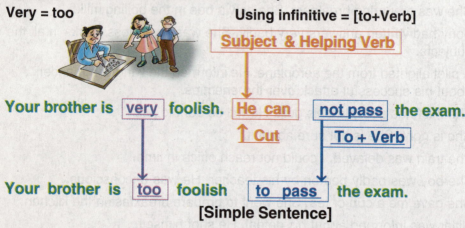

Your brother is [very] foolish. [He can] [not pass] the exam.

↑ Cut   To + Verb

Your brother is [too] foolish [to pass] the exam.

[Simple Sentence]

Ex.

I have lots of wealth. I can enjoy my life.

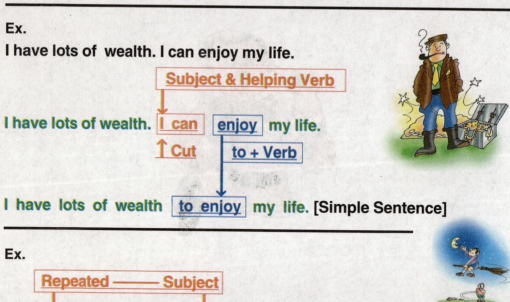

Subject & Helping Verb

I have lots of wealth. [I can] [enjoy] my life.

↑ Cut   to + Verb

I have lots of wealth [to enjoy] my life. [Simple Sentence]

Ex.

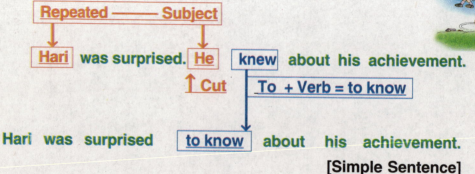

Repeated ——— Subject

[Hari] was surprised. [He] [knew] about his achievement.

↑ Cut   To + Verb = to know

Hari was surprised [to know] about his achievement.

[Simple Sentence]

Example:

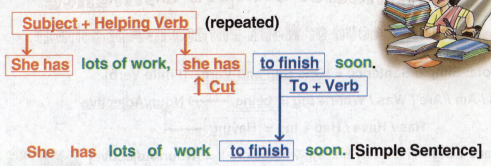

Subject + Helping Verb (repeated)

She has lots of work, **she has** **to finish** soon.

↑ Cut   To + Verb

She has lots of work **to finish** soon. **[Simple Sentence]**

EXERCISE NO. 16-C

Join the sentences given below into *'Simple sentences'* by using *'Infinitive'*.

1. She keeps a cool mind. She can handle the situation very well.
2. I had a book. I could get the highest marks.
3. She has a credit card. She wants to pay the whole amount.
4. He wants to open the secret. He wishes to get the chair of chairman.
5. She is too poor. She cannot buy a piece of bread.
6. My father heard of my achievement. He is very pleased.
7. Sam wants to become a doctor. He studies in Wilson College.
8. You must surrender. You will be getting police protection.
9. The criminal took out the pistol. He was willing to kill the merchant.
10. She will not return your money. She is very cunning.
11. She has two guards. They take care of her flat.
12. They do not have a single pen. They cannot write a letter to their parents.
13. You have an excellent plan. You can tell it to your boss.
14. The teachers held a meeting. They wanted to get more salary.
15. He opened his eyes. He wanted to know the fact.
16. She closes her eyes. She wanted to recall her childhood friends.
17. She provided an easy touch. She was willing to clarify the open secret.
18. She was promising him a moon. She did so in order to cheat him.
19. He was listening to her with half ear. He did so in order to avoid her idea.
20. She was killing the goose laying golden eggs. She wanted to ruin herself.

Synthesis: Simple Sentence
Using: Noun or Noun Phrase in Apposition

Note: Simple Sentence = One Sub and Verb. [Finite Verb]

Is / Am / Are / Was / Were + Ing = being ⟶ Noun/Adjective

Has / Have / Had + Ing = Having ⟶ (to Noun/Adjective)

Verb + ing without any helping verb before it = [Noun/Adjective]

In one sentence we can use only Noun and Adjective

[Or the word that modifies Adjective]

Ex.

Kalidas was the greatest play writer. He wrote many plays in Sanskrit.

⟶ Repeated Subject

Kalidas was the greatest play writer. He wrote many plays in Sanskrit.

Verb + ing = being ↑ Cut

Ans. Kalidas, being the greatest play writer, wrote many plays in Sanskrit.

[Simple Sentence]

Ex.

Pt. Jawaharlal Nehru was born on 14 Nov. He was the first Prime minister of India.

Solution: Pt. Jawaharlal Nehru was born on 14 Nov. [Main Sentence]

Repeated Subject and Verb

He was the first Prime Minister of india.

↑ Cut

Ans. Pt. Jawarharlal Nehru, the first Prime Minister of India, was born on 14ᵗʰ November. [Simple Sentence]

Ex.

Gold is the most precious metal. It shines very brightly.

Solution:

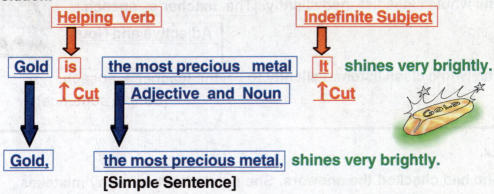

Helping Verb   Indefinite Subject

Gold | is | the most precious metal | It | shines very brightly.

↑ Cut   Adjective and Noun   ↑ Cut

Gold,   the most precious metal, shines very brightly.

[Simple Sentence]

Ex.

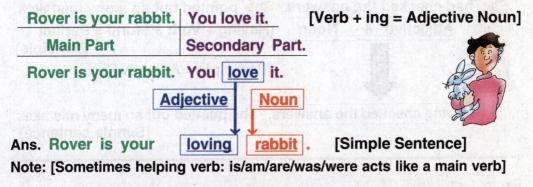

Rover is your rabbit. | You love it.   [Verb + ing = Adjective Noun]

Main Part | Secondary Part.

Rover is your rabbit. You love it.

Adjective | Noun

Ans. Rover is your | loving | rabbit .   [Simple Sentence]

Note: [Sometimes helping verb: is/am/are/was/were acts like a main verb]

Ex.

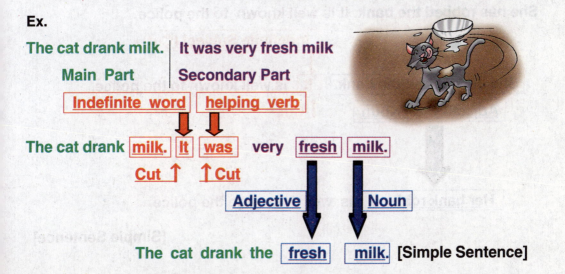

The cat drank milk. | It was very fresh milk

Main Part | Secondary Part

Indefinite word | helping verb

The cat drank milk. It was very fresh milk.

Cut ↑   ↑ Cut

Adjective   Noun

The cat drank the fresh milk. [Simple Sentence]

Some other examples:

The whole class listened silently. The teacher delivered the speech.

The whole class listened silently. | The teacher's speech. |

                    Adjective and Noun

The whole class listened silently to   **the teacher's speech.**

                          [Simple sentence]

Ex.

She had checked the answers. She pointed out so many mistakes.

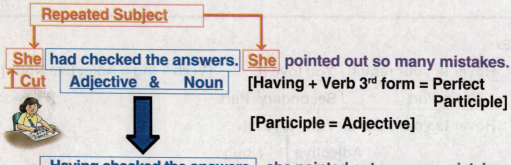

Repeated Subject

She | had checked the answers. | **She** | pointed out so many mistakes.

↑**Cut**   **Adjective & Noun**   **[Having + Verb 3rd form = Perfect Participle]**

[Participle = Adjective]

Having checked the answers, she pointed out so many mistakes.

                          [Simple sentence]

Ex.

She has robbed the bank. It is well known to the police.

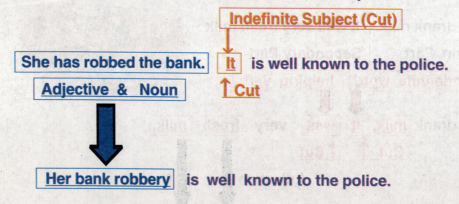

Indefinite Subject (Cut)

She has robbed the bank. | **It** | is well known to the police.

Adjective & Noun   ↑**Cut**

Her bank robbery is well known to the police.

                          [Simple Sentence]

Ex.

He achieved the gold medal.	She knew it.	She was surprised.
His achievement of the gold medal	knowing	

Adjective + Noun

Preposition

Ans: **On** knowing his achievement of the gold medal, she was surprised.

[Simple Sentence]

EXERCISE NO. 16-D

Join the sentences by using 'Nouns' or 'Phrases in Appositions'.

1. Mr. Sam stays in New York. He is a well-known lecturer in Wilson College.
2. Mr. Rao is a well-known poet. He has written 500 poems in Tamil language.
3. Plato was a great philosopher. He used to preach about the truth of life.
4. Mahatma Gandhi is our father of nation. He was born on 2nd October.
5. He has killed a tiger. That tiger is said to be a man-eater.
6. Ravindranath Tagore was a great poet. He got the Nobel Prize for "Geetanjali".
7. I saw a movie. It was produced by Richard.
8. Yukta has been crowned as Miss World. She lives at Mulund near my bungalow.
9. Jack is my puppy. Everybody loves him.
10. Your bungalow is located at Juhu. Its name is "My Home."
11. The policeman has caught a notorious criminal. He used to pick pocket five years before.
12. Sachin is my best friend. His batting is well known all over the world.
13. Sir William wrote 'Macbeth'. It is one of the well-known plays in English.
14. I like gold very much. It is the most precious metal.
15. It is feared. She will kill me for my mistake.
16. It is unfortunate. I have lost my gold watch.
17. We must remember. Old is gold.
18. Her thought has enlightened my mind. Honesty is the best policy.
19. Your preaching has guided us to our goal. Work is worship.
20. It is hoped. I shall win the gold medal for my contribution in the field of the language.

Synthesis: Simple Sentence
Using: Adverb & Adverbial

Adverbial: It is a part of a sentence that does the work of **an Adverb**.

Example:

She has studied Shakespeare . **She has studied it in deep.**

Ans. She has studied Shakespeare │ deeply │ . [Adverb]

Note: The use of Preposition can make 2 sentences into **a Simple Sentence.**

Ex. The windows are shut. It is clear.

│ Adverb │
↓

The window are │ clearly │ shut.

Ex. My brother killed the snake. He took only a few minutes.

│ Adverbial │
↓

My brother killed a snake only │ in a few minutes. │ [Simple Sentence]

Ex. Your son did not do his homework. It was yesterday.

│ Adverbial │
↓

Ans : Your son did not do his homework │ yesterday. │ [Simple]

EXERCISE NO. 16-E

Join the sentences given below into *'Simple sentences'* by using *'Adverbs or Adverbials.'*

1. She has lost her ornaments. She is very careless.
2. You have attempted all the questions. It shows your intelligence.
3. He has been failed in the exam. It is usual.
4. Kanika is a very beautiful lady. That is certain.
5. She has known the secret. She took no time to do so.
6. He helped her last month. That was his foolishness.
7. India won the match against Pakistan. It was unexpected.

8. I have read 'Hamlet', Sir William has written it with much intelligence.

9. They had been waiting for us. They look very suspicious.

10. She told me the answer of only one question. She did it in the previous exam.

11. He is very cruel. He killed her with a knife.

12. I visited the Taj Mahal. I often visit there.

13. The plant is growing up because of fertilizer. The growth is very fast.

14. She has cleared the confusion. She did it with much intelligence.

15. Rambo hit me. She had no reason for doing so.

SYNTHESIS : COMPLEX SENTENCE

It means that '**One Sentence**' will be the '**Principal Clause**'. The other sentence will be changed into '**Subordinate Clause**'.

Complex sentence = Principal Clause + Subordinate Clause

There are three types of Subordinate Clauses :

1. Noun Clause
2. Adjective Clause
3. Adverb Clause

Subordinators :

Place = Where

Condition = If

Reason = Why

Time = When

Number = How many

Indefinite state = Whether

Otherwise = Except that.

That is very common in Noun Clauses.

Noun Clause

Ex. **She will meet me. It is not definite.**

Subordinator

Ans. It is not definite that she will meet me. [Complex Sentence]

Check Noun Clause ? What question to the Principal Clause

What is not definite?   Ans: That she will meet me = Noun Clause.

Ex.

He will show the ┃style.┃ Sachin hits the ball.

┃Subordinator┃

He will show ┃how┃ Sachin hits the ball. [Complex Sentence]

┃Check the answer:┃

What will he show ?

Ans: How Sachin hits the ball = Noun Clause

Ex.

Jackie Chan is a great actor. **It is well known .**

┃Subordinator┃ [General Statement]

It is well known┃that┃ Jackie Chan is a great actor. [Complex Sentence]

What is well known? Ans: That Jackie Chan is a great actor = Noun Clause

---

Ex.

Susan is hadicapped. **She is a good teacher.**

┃Subordinator┃ [General Statement]

Except ┃that┃ Susan is hadicapped, she is a good teacher. [Complex]

Ans: Except ┃that┃ Susan is hadicapped, she is a good teacher. [Complex]

Ex.

You are a killer. **She does not know.**

┃Subordinator┃ [Indefinite state]

She does not know ┃whether┃ you are a killer. [Complex Sentence]

What does she not know ? Ans: Whether you are a killer.= Noun Clause.

EXERCISE NO. 16-F

Join the following sentences into *'Complex sentences'* :

1. Somebody was approaching. I was roaming around to see it.
2. Come back. You are a butterfly.
3. Sachin Tendulkar has proved. Cricket is not a game of fate.
4. See yourself. I have sacrificed my life for you.
5. Tell me. I can solve this problem.
6. It is the fact. She is the Nobel Prize winner.
7. I saw. He had done a crime at seven bungalow.
8. She appreciates me for detecting. He is a thief.
9. Your teacher wants to know. You have been failed in your exam.
10. The news has reached us. India has won the Sahara Cup.
11. The truth is known to the whole society. He is not a cheat.
12. I know. You have created a history in the world of English language.
13. She admits. She has seen the **pickpocket** who was handicapped.
    (**Pickpocketer** is a wrong word)
14. It is my belief. I shall be remembered for my achievement.
15. He denied. He had been to his friend's house.

ADJECTIVE CLAUSE

Selection of Subordinator:

Person = Who
Thing = Which
Reason = Why
Place = Where
Object = Whom [Person]

He is a killer. He has been imprisoned for ten years.

He, who has been imprisoned for ten years, is a killer.　　**[Complex]**

　　Subordinator

Person = Who

Ex.

My brother has studied Chinese. It is spoken by the largest number of population.

Subordiator

Ans: My brother has studied Chinese which is spoken by the largest number of population.   [Complex Sentence]

Ex.

He is Mr. Batra, a friend of mine. I received him from the airport.

Subordinator

He is Mr. Batra, a friend of mine, whom I received from the airport.
[Complex]

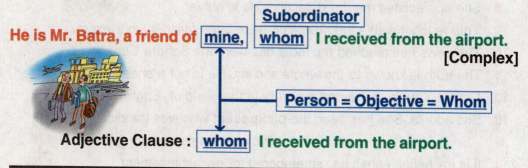

Person = Objective = Whom

Adjective Clause : whom I received from the airport.

Ex.

I do not know the reason. She cheated me.

Noun	Subordinator	[reason]

I do not know the reason why she cheated me.

Adjective Clause : Why she cheated me.

EXERCISE NO. 16-G

Join the following sentences into *'Complex sentences'* :

1. I started guiding them. They had lost the way of life.
2. She gave up the idea of creating problems. She had come for.
3. Nothing happens to the kids. They are properly fed and cared.
4. People always complain against them. They are lazy people.
5. You started cheating them. They are poor people.
6. You should not throw stones at others. Your house is also made of glass.
7. Mrs. Thatcher is an iron lady. She is very rich and wealthy.
8. Your bungalow needs much repair and maintenance. It is 10 years old.
9. He is a criminal. He wants to live like a good citizen.
10. The passengers were taken to the police station. They had no tickets.
11. I found my watch under my bed. I had lost it yesterday.
12. My brother has seen the lady in the court. She was accused of having black money.
13. She lives in a village. She was born there.
14. It was the lost moment. It was lost for ever.
15. She has no suggestion. She cannot give any suggestion.

Adverb Clause

Subordinators:

Place: Where / Wherever
Reason: Because / As / Since
Condition: If / Unless
Purpose: So that / Lest
Concession: Though / Although
Result: So
Manner: As / As if
Comparison: Than
Time/Event/Incident etc.: When/Since/Before/After/Till/Until.

Example:

The teacher arrived. She had left the college

Subordinator [incident]

The teacher arrived before she had left the college. [Adverb Clause]

[Complex Sentence]

Ex.

He cooked food for her friend. He cooked till midnight.

Subordinator [Time]

He cooked food for her friend | till | it was midnight. [Adverb Clause]

[Complex Sentence]

Ex.

He is a lazy fellow. He cannot get a job.

Subordinator [reason]

As | he is a lazy fellow, he cannot get a job. [Adverb Clause]

[Complex Sentence]

Ex.

Henry works very hard. He desires to get gold medal.

Subordinator [Purpose]

Henry works very hard | so that | he may get gold medal. [Adverb Clause]

[Complex Sentence]

Ex.

She reached near the church. Her father had left the church.

Subordinator [incident]

When | she reached near the church, her father had left. [Adverb Clause]

[Complex Sentence]

EXERCISES NO. 16-H

Join the following sentences into '*Complex sentences*' :

1. He will help me. I shall not get my aim.
2. You ran so slowly. You could not catch me.
3. The priest appeared in the church. The Moon was shown in the sky.
4. My brother smiled. He saw me coming with the gold medal.
5. The students paid no attention to the teacher. They were busy in gossiping with their friends.
6. You like to help me. You cannot help me.

7. I cannot teach in that class. All the students are very careless and disobedient.

8. You open her purse now. You will find a gold watch made in Japan.

9. You work hard. You can achieve the goal very easily.

10. The hunter shot a lion in a dense forest. The lion was only wounded.

11. He wishes to become Einstein. He works hard day and night.

12. She talks to my friends. She talks like a dictator.

13. The Titanic sank into the Atlantic Ocean. All the crew members were killed in that accident.

14. The fox started to praise the crow. The hungry fox needed a piece of bread, stolen from a confectioner's shop.

15. The chief guest did not arrive. The function started on time.

16. I have my life. I have my hope to get my goal.

17. My grandfather is very tired. He cannot sit with you for any suggestion.

18. She makes a promise. She keeps it at any cost.

EXERCISE NO. 16-I

Join the following sentences into 'Complex sentences' :

1. Lataji is a great singer. She is the queen of melody. She is the soul of Indian classical music.

2. Folk songs have been derived from various sources. The root of these songs is unknown. They have been composed by the great music composers.

3. The troops of France were often commanded by Napoleon. He was a brave warrior. The tales of his heroism and glory are well known.

4. There is no villain in this play. John is the central character.

5. The music is based on the situation of film. He works very hard.

6. Kanika would travel to Mumbai. She would not buy a ticket. It is a foolish idea.

7. He was badly shaken. He tried to think of some other way. He wanted to cheat her.

8. They got down from the bus. They followed Mr. Sharma. They wanted to rob his money-bag.

9. Let us make faces. The faces should look to be sad. We can win his sympathy very easily.

10. They saved their fare. They did so to watch the movie. It was a horrible idea.

11. The students were punished. They went to complain to their parents. They could not get proper judgment from the Principal.

12. They were walking past a bungalow. They sold flowers to the owner. The bungalow was under construction.

13. They saw ten businessmen. They were discussing a plan. They were eating their lunch.

14. I have got the work of preaching the lesson of truth. It can be a difficult work. It can be a fatal work.

15. He admitted it. He had done a crime. He started weeping bitterly.

16. She paid money to the cab driver. She got out of the cab. She thanked the cab driver.

17. She promised me yesterday. She would never gossip in the class.

18. She had taught grammar to the students. She was 18 years old then.

19. You can sell your bungalow. You can sell your property. You can sell your moral. You are a cheat.

20. They are the unfortunate people. They kill their time. The time will kill them without any mercy.

21. We should not change the religion. God is one. He lives in the soul of honest people only.

22. You are honest. You are hard working. Nobody can snatch your success from you.

23. Her heart leaps up. She sees peacocks dancing. They dance under the shower of rain.

24. History accepts this fact. Triumph does not mean to win every battle.

25. Do you know ? Diamond cuts diamond.

26. You should do. Your teacher suggests you to do.

27. I reached the platform. The train had left.

28. The speed of the car was very high. It was out of control. It crashed against the bridge. It fell into the river.

29. Your nature is unique. Nobody can understand it. It is well known to everybody.

30. My students do not like me. I punish them. They do not do their homework.

31. She gave a suggestion to us. It was a good suggestion. It was full of so many guidelines for our future.

32. I reached late to my office. I was 2 hours late.

    My boss scolded me for that reason.

33. My brother is going to U. K. My sister is already there. She wants to become a scientist.

34. They have joined army. They want to become warriors. They wanted to kill their enemies.

35. She sold a house. The house was mine. She wanted to earn more money.

36. You have a good health. You go to gym. You do daily exercises there.

37. He approached the task in a different way. He failed.

38. The body cannot perform its function. It is abundantly supplied with all the essential nutritional factors.

39. Food is one of the most essential factors. It builds our body and mind.

40. I would make the announcement. I reached the office.

41. You are likely to be punished. You do not express your regret.

42. There are two opposite views about woman. They have been repeatedly exploited by the men.

SYNTHESIS: COMPOUND SENTENCE

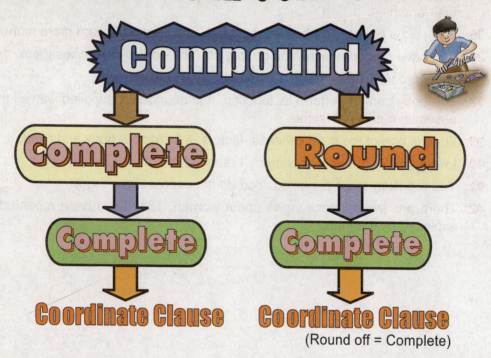

Compound

Complete → **Complete** → **Coordinate Clause**

Round → **Complete** → **Coordinate Clause**

(Round off = Complete)

A Compound sentence consists of two or more '**Coordinate Clauses**' having complete meaning.

Coordinate Clause – **A Clause,** which co-ordinates the other **Clause** and has a complete meaning, is a **Coordinate Clause.**

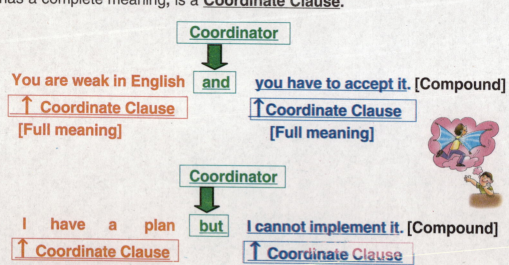

Coordinator

You are weak in English **and** you have to accept it. [Compound]
↑ Coordinate Clause   ↑ Coordinate Clause
[Full meaning]   [Full meaning]

Coordinator

I have a plan **but** I cannot implement it. [Compound]
↑ Coordinate Clause   ↑ Coordinate Clause
[Full meaning]   [Full meaning]

Compound Sentence: More than Two Sentences

How will you solve ?

Ex.

I was walking past a bungalow. The bungalow was under decoration.

I saw ten decorators. They were busy in their discussion.

Step 1: Join first two sentences without using any **Subordinator or Co-ordinator** and be careful there must be only **one Subject** and one finite or main verb .

Ex.

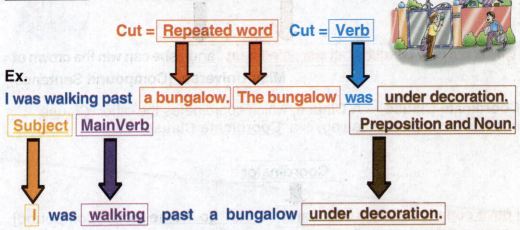

Step 2 : Join the rest **two sentences** in the same manner.

Rule: You can cut verbs : is / am / are / was / were etc. as often they are used as a helping verb or main verb.

Ex.

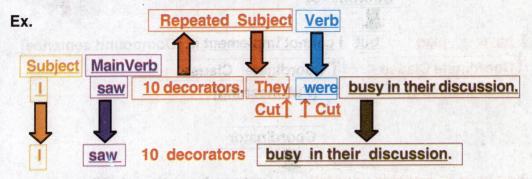

Step 3: Now join both the sentences by the help of a Coordinator.

I was walking past a bungalow under decoration and saw ten decorators busy in their discussion. [Compound Sentence]

Compound Sentence : More than Two Sentences

Ex.

She is beautiful. She is intelligent. She can win the crown of Miss Universe.

Step 1: Join the first two sentences as a Simple sentence.

[Only one '<u>Subject</u>' and one '<u>Main Verb</u>']

| She is beautiful + She is intelligent | | Coordinator |

She is not only beautiful but also intelligent and she can win the crown of Miss Universe. [Compound Sentence]

Coordinate Clause – **A Clause,** which coordinates the other '<u>Clause</u>' and has a complete meaning, is a '<u>Coordinate Clause</u>'.

Coordinator

I have completed my work and I can go home now. [Compound]
↑ Coordinate Clause ↑ Coordinate Clause
[Full meaning] [Full meaning]

Coordinator

I have a plan but I cannot implement it. [Compound sentence]
↑ Coordinate Clause ↑ Coordinate Clause
[Full meaning] [Full meaning]

Coordinator

You have to dedicate yourself or you can leave the job. [Compound]
↑ Coordinate Clause ↑ Coordinate Clause
[Full meaning] [Full meaning]

EXERCISE NO. 16-J

Combine each set of sentences into a *'Compound sentence'* :

1. We can travel by bus. We can travel by train.
2. He is a fool. He is a useless fellow.
3. Tony is a richman. He has a farmhouse in London.
4. Miss Marina was my classmate. She became a bank officer. She forgot her parents.
5. The boy was my friend. The boy was terminated from the college.
6. He came to Delhi. He meets the Prime minister.
7. I may go to the class. I may play football.
8. Silvia stood first in the class. She was given a prize.
9. Clive loves nature. Clive loves painting.
10. She will have to face the problem. Her parents will have to face the problem.

EXERCISE NO. 16-K

Combine the *'Simple sentences'* given below into *'Compound sentences'* :

1. They were looking worried before the programme. They presented the show properly.
2. They were caught by the people. They were taken to the police station.
3. The aeroplane had crashed. Nobody was alive.
4. The film 'Terror' is very popular among the youths. It is banned by the government.
5. He can go to the exhibition. Your father can go to the exhibition.
6. The minister could travel by a plane. The minister could travel by a train.
7. Chhabi is very active. Chhabi is intelligent also.
8. Hurry up. You will not be able to catch the bus.
9. Football is a very popular game. The entire country enjoys it.
10. Donald is weak in Maths. Donald is weak in Social Studies too.
11. Most of the people talk about Lara Dutta. You are unknown to it.
12. Sam lost his bag. Sam complained to the police. Sam did not get it.

EXERCISE NO. 16-L

Combine into the *'Compound* sentences' :

1. Henry was a poor man. He agreed to help her.
2. You must act accordingly. You may leave the office.

3. He killed the tiger. He could not get the dead body.

4. You should work to earn. You may leave the job.

5. She got one million. She donated all her money to the poor people.

6. This is the house. He built it within one year.

7. Harry saw the photographs. He remembered his lost friend.

8. He is rude. The people do not like him.

9. Rocky is willing to get the solution of his psychological problem. He should consult Dr. Sinha.

10. Ruby creates disturbance. She never accepts her mistakes.

11. She wanted to see the '**Hanging Garden**'. She should go with him now.

12. Get out. I shall complain to the Principal.

13. The S.P. saw the quarrel between the police inspector and the constable. He suspended the police inspector.

14. He had a good approach. He could not get the party ticket.

15. He is a good lecturer. The students respect him.

16. They should work hard. They will not survive in Mumbai.

17. Divya could not complete her work in time. She was fined and scolded.

18. The film was over. The audience went back to home.

19. I had no money in my pocket to buy a ticket. I got the ticket from my friend.

20. He is a miser. He will not help the needy people.

21. He is facing a crucial condition. He will not be able to pay his school fee.

22. He is very tired. He will not complete his work in time.

23. Rosy got the best actress award. She is happy.

24. You have robbed me. It is not known to anybody.

25. I have no suggestion. I cannot suggest you anything regarding this project.

26. He should take medicine. He can survive.

27. He is indifferent regarding his work. He will be warned.

28. She has a sober nature. Nobody likes her in the society.

29. He was insulted in the party. He gave anti-party remarks.

30. He was making a plan to establish a garment factory. He has taken loan.

EXERCISE NO. 16-M

Join the sentences given below into '*Compound* sentences' using *Coordinators*:

1. Barry was returning back from club. Mr Charkin met him near the market.

2. She has taken my sari. She gave that sari to a beggar.

3. Mr. Bush lost his purse in the bus. Mr. Bush went to the police station.

4. They are confident. They will succeed in working out their plan.

5. She cooked food. She served the dinner. She cleaned the utensils.

6. The criminal was warned by the police. The criminal surrendered immediately.

7. Alana is an intelligent girl. She is laborious. She will pass the medical exam.

8. My father was talking to the Principal. My father was asking him about my career.

9. Napoleon came. He attacked. He conquered.

10. Mr. Blair bought a building. Miss Maria sold it with 20% profit.

11. I was 20 minutes late. The class teacher did not allow me to attend the class.

12. Miss Rege watched the game. It was very interesting. People were enjoying it.

13. Edward could not pass the exam. He is weak in general knowledge.

14. She has cleared the truth. She had nothing more to say.

15. She went to London. She wished to become a writer.

16. The robbers had caught him. He was murdered immediately.

17. She was preparing breakfast. She saw a cockroach in the plate.

18. Miss Joy had written answers very badly. She hasn't got good marks in all the subjects.

19. The pilot alighted from the aeroplane. He informed the wing commander about his successful attack over enemies.

20. The thief has accepted his guilt. He will be sent to police custody.

21. He is right. He is not sure about it.

22. The bus was late. I could not reach the party in time.

23. The thief was badly beaten by the boys in blue. He became unconscious.

24. She gave me snacks. She went to prepare lunch in the kitchen.

25. Anil was informed about his termination.
He applied for a new job.

EXERCISE NO. 16-N

Join the sentences given below and rewrite as *'Compound sentences'* :

1. Harry packed his luggage. He went to the airport.
He waited for the aeroplane.

2. Maria got up in the morning. She went to church. She prayed for your better health.

3. This chemical curbs pests. It can improve the soil. It proves to be a blessing to the farmers.

4. Priya listens very cautiously to my problems. The problems are very complicated. She is trying to find the solution as soon as possible.

5. You walked straight for about ten minutes. You then turn to the right. You walk for about two minutes. You then turn left.

6. You should remind him. He is new to the place.

7. My friends were demanding for the justice. They did so in front of the judge. They got the right judgment within no time.

8. They could eat in the morning. They could eat bread and butter. I had arranged well after taking their suggestions.

9. You reply to these questions.You wait for the guidance.

10. I was near the bus stop. I saw a lady watching me very suspiciously.I approached her to introduce myself. She was a police officer. She was looking for a pickpocket.

11. Raj tried to stand up. He was finding it difficult.

12. I had gone out for fishing. I was never thinking of a trout.

13. He was given the best medical treatment. His condition steadily grew worse.

14. All his work is being finished in time. He has a long interval for rest in the evening.

15. He went about the streets of Athens. He was preaching logic.

16. Search operations were continuing. They wanted to locate more bodies.

17. The boy would have been badly injured. The height was about 18 feet. He had been taught how to jump by me. He landed safely on his feet.

18. We explored a few passages. We explored the dark tunnels in the royal palace. We explored thousands of little dungeons. We always forget all those sights.

19. Almitra had never seen the Mexican city before. This city was very wonderful. It seemed very amazing and enjoying.

20. She had brought her car to Mumbai. She enjoyed the driving very much. One day she lost her car. It was carried away by the Towing Van of B. M. C.

21. I had worked hard. I referred to so many books. I could not get passing marks. It was unfortunate.

22. Balance sheet was not urgent. My boss scolded me. There was no reason. He wanted to terminate me.

23. I saw a chainsnatcher. He was trying to sell a golden chain. It was my wife's chain. I went to the police station to inform the police.

24. V. Richards' batting is a landmark in the world of cricket. He is a great cricketer.

25. She is a beautiful girl. She is intelligent. She is going to guide an illiterate fool.

26. The road to Kolkata was blocked. It was blocked because of heavy rainfall. I had to meet my friends very urgently.

27. The teacher saw the students throwing stones. He scolded everybody. The damages were charged from their parent.

28. Sana opened her lunch box. She ate two pieces of bread. She did it very promptly.

29. Bhavna bought some books from this shop. She took it to her home. She placed it on the table. She studied it well.

30. Because of the surprise check, he tried to jump from a fast moving bus. He was caught by the T.C. It was quite unfortunate for him.

EXERCISE NO. 16-O

Use *'Coordinator'* or *'Subordinator'* according to the instructions given in the brackets and join the sentences.

1. Peter is going to join B.A.R.C. He is the most brilliant student in college. **[Use Subordinator]**

2. He can clear each and every confusion. Robert does not give me much importance. **[Use Coordinator]**

3. We scolded each other. Afterwards, we realized our mistakes. We cleared the misunderstanding. **[Use a Subordinator and a Coordinator]**

4. She entered into the college compound. She heard a loud noise of the students demanding for more periods. **[Use Coordinator]**

5. Her room is not enough for more than 4 people to sleep. All the family members sleep there only. It is the only room. They have taken it on rental basis. **[Use Subordinator & Coordinator]**

6. Mr. Loyed went to Kolkata to meet my elder brother. There she had a peculiar type of experience. **[Use Subordinator]**

7. Silvia enjoys playing cricket whole day. He hates watching cricket on T V. **[Use Coordinator]**

8. He worked hard to achieve his aim. He did it with confidence. **[Use Subordinator]**

9. She bought the photo of Goddess Durga. She worshipped her. She prayed her to get her blessing. **[Use Coordinator]**

10. She is a Principal. She wants to meet the Education Minister regarding her college problems. **[Use Coordinator]**

11. I have no money. I cannot pay you anything. **[Use Subordinator]**

12. There are five kitten in my house. I love them very much.
     [Use Subordinator]

13. Rosy is a foolish girl. I know her very well. **[Use Coordinator]**

14. Kanika was very serious. She was taken to hospital. **[Use Coordinator]**

15. The waiter smashed the glass. The waiter left. **[Use Coordinator]**

16. Phone me on Friday. I will inform you about the result.
     [Use Coordinator]

17. They have ten books. They have to sell them within two days.
     [Use Subordinator]

18. Simon accepted Buddhism. Simon preached it all over the world.
     [Use Coordinator]

19. Miss Batra can achieve her target. She works hard. She concentrates on the study. **[Use Subordinator/Coordinator]**

20. She did not continue her coaching classes. She got good marks in all subjects. **[Use Subordinator]**

21. They might have prepared plans and programmes. They must not have applied them practically. **[Use Coordinator]**

22. Are Indians being treated well in America? Are Indians being treated as foreigners? **[Use Coordinator]**

SEQUENCE OF TENSES

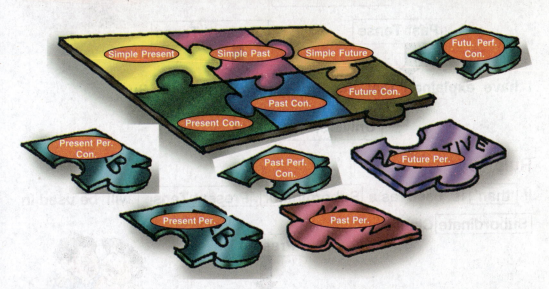

Rule - 1 :

When Principal Clause is in **Past Tense, 'Subordinate Clause'** should be in **Past Tense.**

[Exception =universal truth, general truth etc.]

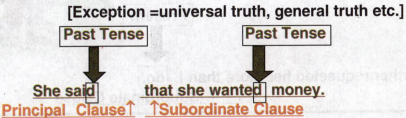

| Past Tense | Past Tense |

She said   **that she wanted money.**
Principal Clause↑   **↑Subordinate Clause**

Rule - 2 :

If there is **universal truth /general truth** etc. , **'Subordinate Clause'** will be in **'Present tense'.**

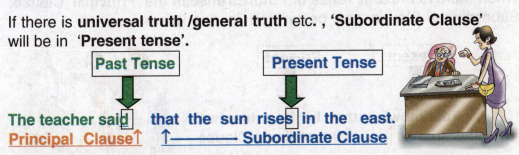

Past Tense   **Present Tense**

The teacher said   **that the sun rises in the east.**
Principal Clause↑   **↑———— Subordinate Clause**

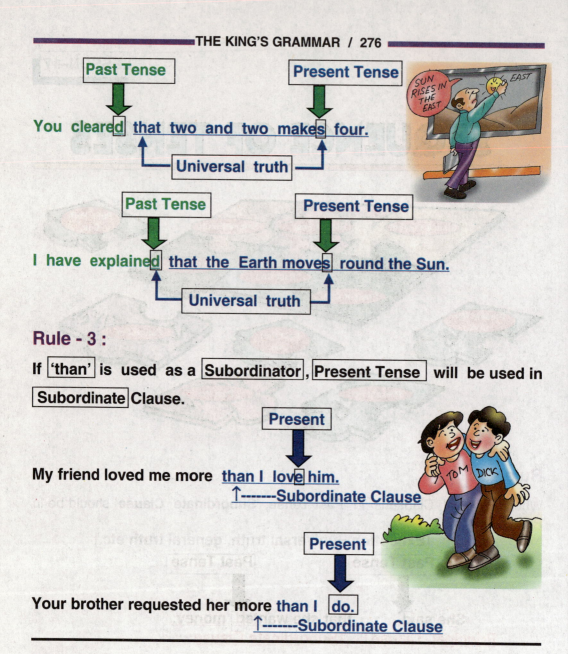

Past Tense → **Present Tense**

You clear**ed** that two and two mak**es** four.

Universal truth

Past Tense → **Present Tense**

I have explaine**d** that the Earth move**s** round the Sun.

Universal truth

Rule - 3 :

If 'than' is used as a Subordinator, Present Tense will be used in Subordinate Clause.

Present

My friend loved me more than I lov**e** him.
↑-------Subordinate Clause

Present

Your brother requested her more than I do.
↑-------Subordinate Clause

Rule - 4 :

When there is Present Tense or Future Tense in the Principal Clause, Subordinate Clause can be written in any tense.

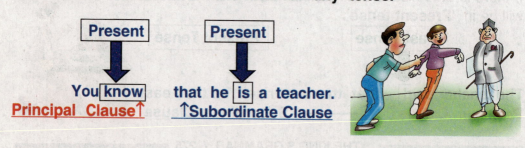

Present **Present**

You know that he is a teacher.
Principal Clause↑ ↑Subordinate Clause

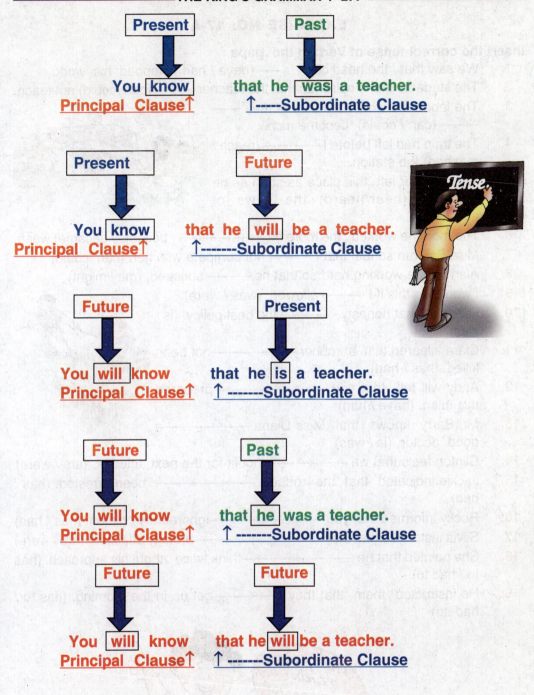

EXERCISE NO: 17-A

Insert the correct tense of Verb in the gaps :

1. We saw that the head clerk —— (have / had) stopped his work.
2. The students make noise so that the teacher ———(can /could) not teach.
3. The labourers work hard so that they —————(can / could) become rich.

4. The train had left before I ———— (reach / reached) the station.
5. The minister left this place as soon as he ———— (hear/heard) the news of accident.
6. The more he worked , the more he ———— (become / became) weak.
7. Miss Bell ran so fast that I ——— not compete with her. (can /could)
8. Alan will be working hard so that he ——— succeed. (may/might)
9. I would do this if I ——— allowed. (was / were)
10. Dick said that honesty ——— the best policy. (is / was)
11. Clara cleared that a robber —————not been killed. (has / had)
12. Andy will tell that you —————prepared this plan. (have / had)
13. Mr. Barry knows that Miss Diana ————a good doctor. (is / was)
14. Clinton feels that we ————not fit for the next attempt. (are / were)
15. Jackie indicated that the robber ———— been arrested. (has / had)
16. Rocky informed that you —————ignored my opinion. (has / had)
17. Silvia instructed that they —————brutally attacked. (are / were)
18. She pointed that he —————think twice about his approach. (has to / had to)
19. He instructed them that they —————get up in the morning. (has to / had to)

Transformation of Sentences

No sooner---

Too---

Hardly-- when

Unless

As soon As

If -- not

Hardly —— When. No sooner —————— than. As soon as.

How to Transform?   **As soon as**

Ex. | Cut | | When |

1.   **As soon as** the driver **stopped** the bus, all people started to fight.

| Hardly had | | Verb 3rd form = Stopped (Past Participle) |

Ans: **Hardly had** the driver stopped the bus **when** all people started to fight.

| Cut | | When |

2.   **As soon as** my brother **left** me, I found his lost money.

| Hardly had | | Verb 3rd form | = | left | (Past Participle)

Ans : **Hardly had** my brother left me **when** I found his lost money.

Cut		When

3. **No sooner did** I **reach** the college **than** it started to rain.

Hardly had	Verb 3rd form = reached (Past Participle)

Ans : **Hardly had** I **reached** the college **when** it started to rain.

Cut		When

4.
As soon as he **returned** back to home, he found that everything was robbed.

Hardly had	Verb 3rd form = reached (Past Participle)

Ans: **Hardly had** he **returned** back to home **when** he found that everything was robbed.

Cut		When

5.
No sooner did he **start** the speech **than** people started throwing stones at him.

Hardly had	Verb 3rd form = Started

Ans: **Hardly had** he **started** the speech **when** people started throwing stones at him.

Hardly ...... when

Join the sentences using **Hardly —— When**
Ex.
1. He had thrown the net. A fish was caught.

	When

He **had** thrown the net a fish was caught.

Hardly had	when

Hardly had he thrown the net **when** a fish was caught.

2. I had entered the zoo. I saw a tiger.

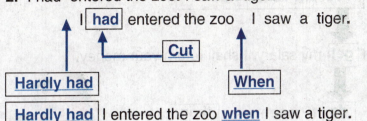 

Hardly had I entered the zoo **when** I saw a tiger.

---

3. She had got up from the bed. The cock started crowing.
Hardly had she got up from the bed **when** the cock started crowing.

She got the news of death . She became very sad .
Hardly had she got the news of death **when** she became very sad.

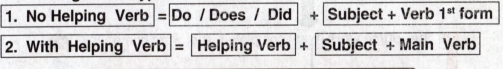

No sooner ——— than

How to Transform ?
You will get two types of sentences.

| 1. No Helping Verb | = | Do / Does / Did | + | Subject + Verb 1st form |

| 2. With Helping Verb | = | Helping Verb | + | Subject + Main Verb |

No Helping Verb = Do / Does / Did

Example:

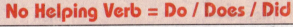

Past Tense = did

1. As the police came, the crowd dispersed.

No sooner .. did (Past) than

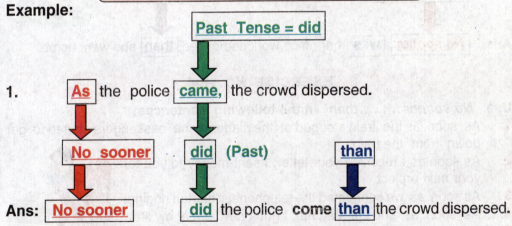

Ans: No sooner did the police come than the crowd dispersed.

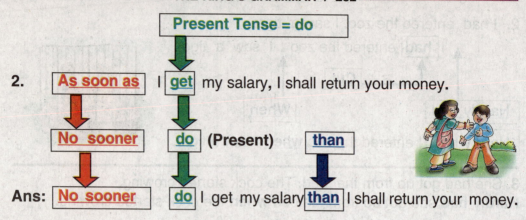

Present Tense = do

2. | **As soon as** | I | **get** | my salary, I shall return your money.

| **No sooner** | | **do** | (Present) | | **than** |

Ans: | **No sooner** | | **do** | I get my salary | **than** | I shall return your money.

Helping Verb

Helping Verb = is / am / are / was / were / has / have / had / shall / will etc.

Example:

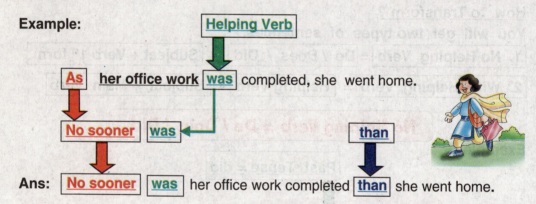

Helping Verb

| **As** | **her office work** | **was** | completed, she went home.

| **No sooner** | **was** | | | | **than** |

Ans: | **No sooner** | **was** | her office work completed | **than** | she went home.

EXERCISE NO.18-A

Use *'No sooner ....than'* in the following sentences:

1. As soon as the train stopped at the platform, the passengers started to get down from the train.
2. As soon as I received your letter, I sent money to you for your next project.
3. As soon as we connected the telephone, it started ringing.
4. As soon as she cheated me, I got a new aim of my life.
5. I got the gold medal. All the people started to clap.
6. As soon as you entered into the room, all the people were shocked and surprised.
7. I reached at the main gate of your bungalow. I saw your dad coming towards me with a gun in his hand.
8. She will come to know about my honest nature. She will cheat me.
9. As soon as I caught the thief, he introduced himself to be the relative of a policeman.

10. As soon as the book was published, the writer became famous.
11. Your friends came to meet you. They found you very busy with your family.
12. The commander ordered his army to attack. A never-ending battle started.
13. As soon as he bought a cheap and cheerful toy, the child smiled brightly.
14. As soon as he started feeling as cool as cucumber, he switched off the A.C.
15. As soon as the child cried for the Moon, his mother dropped a coin into the glass full of water.
16. As soon as he saw a crystal clear picture of Jesus, he started praying.
17. As soon as he crossed his fingers, he started getting succeess.
18. As soon as he started dreaming about the crowning glory, he found himself in deep trouble.

REMOVE TOO

B. You will get **Present Tense or Past Tense**

Present tense = **so…. that …. Subject + cannot**

Past tense = **so … that …… Subject + could not**

Example :

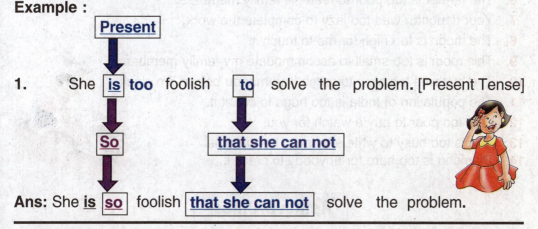

Present

1. She **is** **too** foolish **to** solve the problem. [Present Tense]

So → **that she can not**

Ans: She **is** **so** foolish **that she can not** solve the problem.

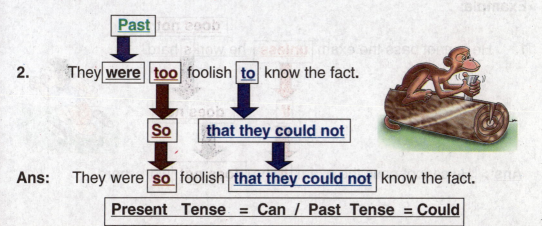

Past

2. They **were** **too** foolish **to** know the fact.

So **that they could not**

Ans: They were **so** foolish **that they could not** know the fact.

Present Tense = Can / Past Tense = Could

3. She **is** too tired to cook food. **[Present Tense]**

Ans: She is **so** tired **that she cannot** cookfood .

4. She is **too** beautiful.

↕

She is **very** beautiful.

EXERCISE NO. 18-B

Remove 'too' from the following sentences:

1. She is too illiterate to guide me.
2. Jack is too young to be the captain for his cricket team.
3. The knife is too blunt to cut vegetables.
4. You are too ignorant to your studies.
5. He was too late to attend the meeting.
6. The farmer is too poor to feed his family members.
7. Your daughter was too lazy to complete the work.
8. The moon is too high for me to touch it.
9. This room is too small to accommodate my family members.
10. The bus was too slow to reach Kathmandu before 7 o'clock.
11. The population of India is too huge to count it.
12. I am too poor to buy a watch for you.
13. She is too busy to write a letter to her parents.
14. Diamond is too hard for anybody to crack it.

Remove Unless

Example:

does not

1. He cannot pass the exam **unless** he work**s** hard.

↓   ↓

If   **does not**

↓   ↓

Ans : He cannot pass the exam **if** he **does not** work hard.

2. She cannot win the match <u>unless</u> she <u>is</u> supported by her team.

If   **not**

Ans : She cannot win the match if she is not supported by her team.

Use Unless

3. He will not meet them if he is **not** being respected.
Cut↑

Ans: He will not meet them unless he is being respected.

4.   She may not get the book if you **do not** guide her.
Cut↑

Ans : She may not get the book unless you guide her.

5.   How could he complete his work if she **did not** help him ?
Cut↑

Ans: How could he complete his work unless she helped him ?

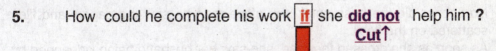
EXERCISE NO.18-C

Remove 'Unless' from the following sentences:
1. I cannot do anything unless I talk to my parents.
2. She could not cook well unless she joined cooking classes.
3. They will not stop accusing her unless you support them.
4. He can lose his temper unless you return him his money.
5. Miss Joseph could not feed the poor students unless her father had given her money.
6. Rick may not come to meet you unless you say sorry to him.
7. The tiffin might not be prepared in time unless she gets up early.
8. The battle would not have been won unless our soldiers fought bravely.
9. Barry may not sing a song unless you play guitar.
10. Sam will not pass the exam unless he works hard.

EXERCISE NO.18-D

Use 'Unless' in the following sentences :
1. How will you help him if you do not have any money?
2. Where does she live if she is a stranger in this city?
3. She will not come to party if he does not invite her.
4. He may pass the exam if he works hard.
5. They might create problems if you are too liberal.
6. France can win the match if Brain plays well.
7. The staff would be late if you were absent .
8. You can earn more money if you spend more time.
9. She will not get entry if she does not reach in time.
10. The workers will go for a strike if they do not get bonus.

EXERCISE NO.18-E

Use 'Hardly —— when' in the following sentences:
1. As she reached near the door, she heard a horrible cry.
2. No sooner did we enter the Principal's office than we found him being punished.
3. No sooner did the President arrive than all the workers started clapping.
4. As soon as I locked the gate, I heard the telephone bell ringing.
5. No sooner did the rain stop than the birds were seen flying in the sky.
6. As soon as the tiger roared, all the wild animals hid somewhere in the forest.
7. No sooner did the boss enter the office than he saw the papers and files scattered on the floor.
8. As soon as she crossed the road, she saw her husband being kidnapped by the goons.
9. No sooner did the juggler play flute than the monkey started to dance.
10. As soon as Miss Joy entered into the hall, all were surprised to see her.
11. No sooner was the moon shown in the sky than she opened her window to count the stars.
12. No sooner did the rain start than peacocks started to dance.
13. As soon as she left the job, she got a lottery of Rs. 1 crore.
14. As soon as he tried to grease his palm, he was caught red-handed.
15. As soon as she met a culture vulture, she became happy.
16. No sooner did he point the mistake than he started behaving like a dead duck.
17. As soon as he tried to dice with death, he started getting success.
18. No sooner did he start playing devil than people started opposing him.
19. As soon as he scolded them, they started acting like die flies.

MODAL AUXILIARIES

| Mood | + | All |

Modal Auxiliaries present all kinds of moods in sentences.

	Function	Modal Auxiliary
1.	Permission	may
2.	Ability	can, could
3.	Capacity	can, could
4.	Possibility	may, can
5.	Past possibility	might / could have
6.	Unfulfilled desire	might / could have
7.	Compulsion / Necessity	must

8.	Lesser possibility	might
9.	Suggestion / Advice	should / ought to
10.	Duty / Obligation	should / ought to /must
11.	Moral duty / Obligation	ought to
12.	Polite request	would
13.	Challenge	dare [be brave enough to]
14.	Desire / Unfulfilled duty/ Probability	ought to
15.	Inference	should
16.	Assumption	will
17.	Degree of dissatisfaction	might
18.	Promise/ Command	I / we + will . Rest all subjects + shall.
19.	Determination / Threat	I / we + will . Rest all subjects + shall.
20.	Willingness	will
21.	Insistence	will / shall
22.	Discontinued habit / Past habit	used to
23.	Volition	will
24.	Impossibility	cannot
25.	Improbability	may not
26.	Logical certainty	must
27.	Characteristic habit	will

Rule : Shall, Will, Should, Would, Can, Could, May, Might, Must, Ought, Need, Dare, Used to etc. These auxiliaries are used with the first form of verb only.

USES OF CAN

Can shows Present Condition.
Subject + Can + Verb 1st form
Example:
1. She can help you regarding exams.
2. You can come here before 2 o' clock.
   Any **subject** can be used with 'can'.
A. Verb 1st form is always needed with 'can'.
B. Can expresses : Power / Ability / Capacity.

Example:
1. The Manager **can** increase your salary. **[Power]**
2. I **can** solve the problems easily. **[Ability]**
3. He **can** lift 100 kgs weight. **[Capacity]**

USES OF COULD

"Could" shows Past Condition.
Subject + could + Verb 1st form
Example:
1. She could understand me.
2. You could pass the exam.

'Could' is Past of 'can'

A. **'Could' is used with any subject.**
B. **'Could' takes first form of verb only.**

Could Expresses : Polite request / Power / or Ability.

Example:
1. Could you return my book please**? [Request]**
2. Could you help me**? [Request]**
3. My brother could beat him. **[Power]**
4. You could drive a car . **[Ability]**

MAY

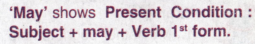

'May' shows **Present Condition :**
Subject + may + Verb 1st form.

Example:
1. He may give you money.
2. She may come here.
A. **'May' can be used with any Subject .**
B. **'May' always takes the 1st form of Verb.**

May Expresses: Permission / Possibility / Purpose / Wish.

Example:
1. May I come in sir **? [Permission]**
2. It may rain. **[Possibility]**
3. She takes coaching so that she may pass the exam. **[Purpose]**
4. May you achieve success **! [Wish]**

Might

Might is **Past** of **May** but it also indicates **'Present Condition.'**
Subject + might + Verb [1st form]
Example:
1. He might know you well.
2. They might help my friend.
A. **Might is used with 'Any Subject'.**
B. **Might always takes the 1st form of Verb.**

Might Expresses:

Remote Possibility / Permission & Possibility in the Past.
Example:
1. Your brother is studying. He might pass the exam.
   [Remote Possibility]
2. I have stolen her money. She might complain.
   [Remote Possibility]
3. The commander said that they might be attacked.
   [Possibility in Past]
4. He said that she might get success. **[Possibility in Past]**

OUGHT TO

Ought shows **Present Condition**
Subject + Ought to + Verb [1st from]
Example:
1. My father ought to help me.
2 . I ought to work hard.
A. **'Ought to'** is used with **Any Subject.**
B. **'Ought to'** is used with the **1st form of Verb.**

Ought to Expresses :

A. **Moral obligation**
B. **Strong Possibility**
C. **Unfulfilled duty / Desire**
Example:
1. She ought to have paid fees.
2. You ought to have taken money.

MUST

Must shows Present Condition.

Subject + Must + Verb [1st from]

Example:

1. She must take medicine.

2. You must meet his father.

A. 'MUST' is used with any Subject.

B. 'Must' is used with the 1st form of Verb

Must Expresses:

Necessity / Obligation / Prohibition / Certainty of belief.

Example:

1. You must go to the doctor as you are ill. [Necessity]

2. She must look after her parents. [Obligation]

3. You must not go out during your duty hours. [Prohibition]

4. She must be a leader. [Certainty of belief]

NEED

Sub + need + ...

Example:

1. You need my help.

2. They need some money.

'Need' is used with Any Subject.

NEGATIVE

Example:

1. You need not go there.

2. They need not try to meet you.

Need expresses: Necessity / Obligation / Compulsion

Example:

1. You need my guidance. [Necessity]

2. The parents need support. [Obligation]

3. They need tickets to travel by train.

[Compulsion]

WILL

Will shows future.

Subject + will + Verb (1st form)

Example:

1. You will remember me for my help.
2. They will come here to meet you.

A. Will is used with any subject except [I / We]

B. If will is used with I or we, in that case it shows determination, threat, challenge etc.

Will expresses : Promise/ Willingness / Determination / Threat.

Example:

1. I will kill you. **[Threat]**
2. We will beat them. **[Threat]**
3. I will break the records. **[Challenge]**
4. We will pass the exam. **[Determination]**

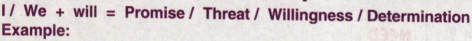

I / We + will = Promise / Threat / Willingness / Determination

Example:

1. He will try to help you. **[Simple Future]**
2. They will sing a song. **[Simple Future]**

WOULD

Sub + would + Verb [1st form]

Example:

1. Your friend would come to meet you.
2. She would like to continue her hard work.
3. They would play in the evening.
4. My brother would be very happy to see you.

A. Would is used with any Subject.

B. Verb 1st form is used after Would

Example :

1. He would **like** to eat food.

        Verb 1st form

C. We use would in Past tense.

Example:

1. I **desired** that I **would** become a doctor.

        Past Tense

2. They **promised** that she **would** get a chance.

⬆ **Past tense**

Would Expresses

Happening in the Past / Polite request / Frequent activities in Past.

Example:

1. My father would go to college to know about me each day.
[Frequent activities in Past]
2. Last month, every Monday, your son would be absent.
[Frequent activities in past]
3. Would you please give me some money ?
[Polite request]
4. Would you please sing a song? **[Polite request]**

SHALL

Shall indicates Future tense.
Subject + Shall + Verb (1ˢᵗ form)
'Shall' is used with **I / We.**

Example:
1. I shall help you. **[Simple Future]**
2. We shall win the match. **[Simple Future]**
If 'Shall' is used with **any subject except , I / We, it shows** : Promise / Threat / Willingness / Determination.

Example:

1. He shall not follow the rules. **[Threat]**
2. You shall be killed. **[Threat]**
3. You shall have to keep the words. **[Promise]**

SHOULD

Subject + Should + Verb [1ˢᵗ form]
Example:
1. She should be present here.
2. You should return back .
'Should' can be used with **any Subject**
'Should' is used with the 1ˢᵗ form of Verb.
Should expresses : Advice / Suggestion

Example:
1. You should reach school in time.
2. He should take guidance.
3. Your father should look after her.

Should expresses : Inference

Example:

1. She should have achieved the success.
2. I should have become a doctor by this time.

Should expresses :Duty / Obligation

Example: 1. You should be disciplined.
2. You should take care of your parents.

EXERCISE NO. 19 - A

Fill in the blanks with appropriate 'Modal Auxiliaries':

1. She ——————behave like a sick parrot in front of the boss to get his sympathy . **[Use modal auxiliary showing advice]**

2. He ——————tell you a story of ghosts to make your hair stand on the end. **[Use modal auxiliary showing possibility]**

3. You —————— not blame him as he is like a straight arrow. **[Use modal auxiliary showing obligation]**

4. Studying in such a filthy environment ——————be difficult. **[Use modal auxiliary showing logical certainty]**

5. Nobody ——————avoid the king of terror. **[Use modal auxiliary showing capacity]**

6. He ——————return the bank loan otherwise he will be in a queer street. **[Use modal auxiliary showing certainty]**

7. You ——————remain dumb as a lamb during the meeting. **[Use modal auxiliary showing certainty]**

8. She ——————retaliate as her condition is just like a hen with one chick. **[Use modal auxiliary showing possibility]**

9. Donald —————— feel as high as a kite after drinking wine. **[Use modal auxiliary showing lesser possibility]**

10. Peter ——————get a golden hello from his fast friend. **[Use modal auxiliary showing lesser probability]**

11. I ——————to born with a silver spoon in my mouth to become your friend . **[Use modal auxiliary showing desire]**

12. He ——————not upset the apple cart as he is a very gentle fellow. **[Use modal auxiliary showing improbability]**

13. Life ——————not be a road of roses but I don't careit. **[Use modal auxiliary showing improbability]**

14. Dick ——————go to church in the morning. **[Use modal auxiliary showing discontinued habit]**

15. You ——————accept the fact that beggars cannot be choosers. **[Use modal auxiliary showing logical certainty]**

16. He ——————tell a cock and a bull story during dinner time. **[Use modal auxiliary showing characteristic habit]**

17. A beggar ——————not ride on a horseback with a golden crown. **[Use modal auxiliary showing impossibility]**

18. I ——————clearly see the beginning of the end in this project. **[U se modal auxiliary showing capacity]**

19. My heart ——————bleed to see your poverty and poor physical condition. **[Use modal auxiliary showing assumption]**

EXERCISE NO.19-B

Do as directed in the brackets.

1. I have to work for my family members. **[Use modal auxiliary showing obligation]**

2. You can continue study in order to achieve your destination. **[Use modal auxiliary showing advice]**

3. They need to be protected. **[Use modal auxiliary showing desire]**

4. The remaining journey has to be undertaken on foot or pony. **[Use modal auxiliary showing necessity]**

5. You can go to bed early so that you are fresh in the morning. **[Use modal auxiliary showing duty]**

6. Be prepared always to pay the price. **[Use modal auxiliary showing necessity]**

7. You keep a cool mind and handle the situation. **[Use modal auxiliary showing suggestion]**

8. You work hard to acquire the goal of life.

    [Use modal auxiliary showing degree of dissatisfaction]

9. They use a credit card to buy a gold watch.

    [Use modal auxiliary showing advice]

10. He opens the secret by this time without being afraid of any thing.

    [Use modal auxiliary showing duty]

11. I shall kill you for your immoral character.

    [Use modal auxiliary showing threat]

12. She buys a gold watch for you.

    [Use modal auxiliary showing moral obligation]

13. Sanjay becomes a doctor and serves the poor people.

    [Use modal auxiliary showing duty]

14. You shall continue your father's business to please him.

    [Use modal auxiliary showing obligation]

15. You surrender yourself immediately.

    [Use modal auxiliary showing command]

16. She will not return your money.

    [Use modal auxiliary showing possibility]

17. The teachers get more salary because of their great contribution.

    [Use modal auxiliary showing obligation]

18. I shall implement your plan at any cost.

    [Use modal auxiliary showing determination]

19. You can obey your elders.

    [Use modal auxiliary showing advice]

20. You tell it to your boss about this event.

    [Use modal auxiliary showing duty]

USES OF HELPING VERBS & MAIN VERBS

HELPING VERBS

A. Is / Am / Are
B. Was / Were
C. Has / Have / Had
D. Shall / Will
E. Shall have / Will have

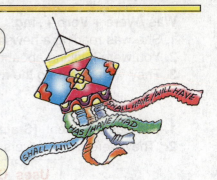

Is / Am / Are

Uses of Is / Am / Are [Present Tense]

A. **Is = He / She / It** & Singular Noun [Subject]
Are = We /You / They & Plural Noun [Subject]
Am = I
Is /Am / Are should be used with **Verb - Ing** for action.
Is / Am / Are + Verb - ing [Action]

ACTION

1. She is writing a letter. [Action]
2. I am trying to solve the problem. [Action]
3. They are waiting for you. [Action]

STATE

1. He is a student. [State]
2. I am a teacher. [State]
3. You are very happy. [State]

EXERCISE NO. 20- A

Write whether the following sentences are presenting 'State' or 'Action':

1. She had a good idea about this project.
2. He had been trying to know the truth.
3. He will continue his work with honesty.
4. Your brother is very eager to meet you.
5. Bhavana was willing to expose the secret.
6. My friend has a book to study for the exam.
7. Meghna is looking for a better opportunity to get the aim.
8. Miss Rice was an intelligent girl.
9. They are trying to prove that I am not a good teacher.
10. Miss Panchal is not a good doctor.

WAS / WERE [Past Tense]

Was / Were / + -Ing .
Was = He / She / It / I / Singular Subject.
Were = We / You / They / Plural Subject.

ACTION

Was /Were + Verb + -ing
1. She was reading a newspaper. [**Action**]
2. You were thinking about me. [**Action**]
3. They were crossing the river. [**Action**]

STATE

1. He was a student. [**State**]
2. They were good players. [**State**]

Uses Of = Has / Have / Had.

| Has | is used with He / She / It & Singular Subject [**Present Tense**]
Example: He has lost money.

| Have | is used with I / We / You / They & Plural Subject [**Present Tense**]
Example: I have lost my money.

| Had | is used with any Subject = Singular **or Plural**.
Example: IT HAD BEEN LOST.
I HAD LOST MY MONEY.

HAS	HAVE	HAD	
Present Perfect	Present Perfect	Past Perfect	+ **VERB 3ᴿᴰ FORM**
Singular	Plural / I / You	Any SUBJECT	(Past Participle)

1. She **has** **taken** my pen. [**Present Perfect**]
↑**Verb 3ʳᵈ form**

2. You **have** **lost** your moral. [**Present Perfect**]
↑**Verb 3ʳᵈ form**

3. They **had** **prepared** a plan. [**Past Perfect**]
↑**Verb 3ʳᵈ form**

POSSESSIVE VERB

When **Has / Have / Had** are used as '**Main Verb**', they show possession.
You cannot use any '**Verb**' [Main Verb] after **Has / Have / Had** in this case.

1. She ha**s** a book. **[Present]**
2. You hav**e** a pen. **[Present]**
3. They ha**d** an idea. **[Past]**

   Has = He / She / It/ & Singular Subject.
   Have = I / We / You / They & Plural Subject
   Had = All Subjects.

USES OF NOT

1.   She   **has**   a   dog.

     She   **does**   not   **have**   a   dog.

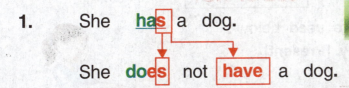

2.   You **have** a pen.

     You **do** not **have** a pen.

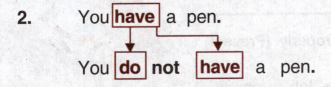

3.   They **had** an   idea.

     They **did** not **have** an idea.

EXERCISE NO. 20-B

Use 'not' in the following sentences:

1.   I have to meet my friend.
2.   Miss Bond has a beautiful doll.
3.   You had an old house to sell.
4.   We have some mistakes to show you.
5.   They had to understand my problem.
6.   She has a good project to earn money.
7.   They have cunning thoughts.
8.   Your brother has to go to Rome.
9.   I had nothing to do with this project.
10. He has a cunning idea.

DO / DOES / DID

[As a Main Verb]

[Present Tense] Does = He / She / It & Singular Subject.

[Present Tense] Do = I / We / You / They & Plural Subject.

[Past Tense] Did = Any subject

1. She does her duty. [Present]
2. They do the job properly. [Present]
3. I did everything in time. [Past]
4. All the boys did it according to the instruction . [Past]

USE OF NOT

Above sentences are used below :

1. **She does her duty. [Present]**

   She does not do her duty.

___

2. **They do the job properly. [Present]**

   They do not do the job properly.

___

3. **I did my work in time. [Past]**

   I did not do my work in time.

YES / NO QUESTION

1. **She does her duty.**

   Does she do her duty?

___

2. **They do the job for money.**

   Do they do the job for money?

3. All the boys did their homework.

Did all the boys do their homework?

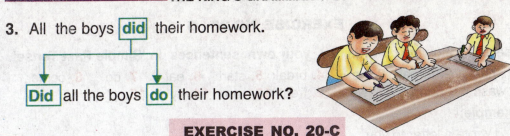

Fill do / does / did in the gaps according to the instructions given in the brackets :

1. He _____ everything for money. **[Past]**
2. She _____ nothing to get success. **[Present]**
3. They _____ work hard to get the confidence. **[Present]**
4. I _____ my home work in time. **[Past]**
5. Your brother _____ the household work without anybody's help.

   [Present]
6. My friends _____ nothing. **[Past]**
7. God _____ nothing for those people who _____

   nothing for themselves. **[Present]**
8. She _____ her work to get more fame. **[Past]**

Change the following sentences into 'Negative' and 'Interrogative' sentences:

1. He does everything for his family members.
2. She did nothing to achieve the target.
3. They do official work to survive better.
4. I do my work very sincerely.
5. The cheats did their cheating very clearly.
6. Your enemies did everything to defeat me.
7. You do nothing in time.
8. Miss Donwalker does her work properly.
9. You do your job for yourself.
10. I did it for you.

Write 8 sentences of your own by using 'do / does / did'.

Use the following words in your own sentences in 'Simple Past Tense'.

1. got   2. came   3. chose   4. blew   5. beat   6. rang   7. ran
8. shot   9. sang   10. cooked   11. wrote   12. won   13. sank   14. knew
15. dug.

EXERCISE NO.20- G

Use the following words in your own sentences in 'Simple Past Tense'.

1. write **2.** forget **3.** go **4.** break **5.** start **6.** eat **7.** do **8.** come
9. wash **10.** drink **11.** wear **12.** treat **13.** run **14.** fly **15.** play.

Example:

1. I wrote a letter to you.

EXERCISE NO.20- H

Change the following sentences into 'Simple Past Tense':

1. The children go to school in time.
2. I watch TV at my house.
3. She sits under the tree.
4. You write a letter to your brother.
5. The teacher suggests the students to work hard.
6. Henry brings a book from his class.
7. They brush their teeth in the morning.
8. My grandmother tells a story to me.
9. Rocky gets a present from his father.
10. The girls quarrel in the garden.

USE OF DID NOT

Sub + did not + Verb [1st form]

A. **"Did not"** can be used in **Simple Past Tense** only.

B. **"Did not"** can be used with any **Subject, Singular or Plural.**

Example:

1. She did not go to college.
2. I did not go to college.
3. You did not go to college.
4. We did not go to college.
5. They did not go to college.

We have to use the **1st from of Verb** with **did not.**

1st form	2nd form	3rd form
Go	Went	Gone

Reason :   She play**ed.**

She **did** not **play.**

EXERCISE NO. 20-I

Use 'did not' with the <u>Verbs</u> given below and maks sentences in Simple Past Tense:

1. kick **2.** win **3.** go **4.** sleep **5.** kill **6.** meet **7.** fight **8.** work **9.** get **10.** give **11.** sing **12.** write **13.** speak **14.** remember **15.** teach.

Example:

You jumped in the garden.

You did not jump in the garden.

EXERCISE NO. 20-J

Use 'did not' in the following sentences :

1. She told me the whole story.
2. I wrote a letter to you.
3. They sang a song on the stage.
4. My brother worked hard to pass the exam.
5. We read a book under the tree.
6. He drank water in the room.
7. You corrected your mistakes yesterday.
8. Hick cleared all his accounts.
9. Miss Rosy danced very nicely.
10. He came here to meet you.

VERB

USES & FORMS

Oral – Verbal – Verb = To tell

A Verb is a word that tells about the activity or state of **Subject / Agent** etc.

She is writing a letter. **[Action]**

She is a good teacher. **[State]**

KINDS OF VERBS

There are two kinds of Verbs.

(A) Helping Verb.

(B) Main Verb.

Helping Verb : It is a **Verb** that helps the **Main Verb** to complete the meaning in a sentence.

Main Verb : A word that shows the main activity of the **Subject , Agent** etc. is called **a Main Verb.**

1. She <u>is</u> <u>writing</u> a letter.

   Is = Helping Verb & **Writing** = Main Verb

2. You <u>have</u> <u>taken</u> my pen.

   Have = Helping Verb & **Taken** = Main Verb

3. She <u>has</u> <u>lost</u> her money .

   Has = Helping Verb & **Lost** = Main Verb

4. They <u>will</u> <u>go</u> to the college.

   Will = Helping Verb & **Go** = Main Verb.

EXERCISE NO. 20-K

Find out the '<u>Helping Verbs</u>' & '<u>Main Verbs</u>' from the sentences given below:

1. She has taken all my money.
2. He has a pen to write a letter.
3. You will have been singing a song.
4. They had a plan to destroy the whole business.
5. It was raining cats and dogs during last night.
6. She has helped me.
7. Having completed his work, he went out to enjoy a party.
8. He found it more irksome.
9. Talkers are no good doers.
10. The ability to laugh together is the essence of love.
11. Get out from my room.
12. Honesty is the best policy.
13. The greatest prayer is patience.
14. Diamond cuts diamond.
15. The wicked people are never clever.
16. There has been no cosmetic for beauty like happiness.
17. Truth fears no trial.
18. Truth is the only road paved by God towards heaven.
19. We gain freedom when we have paid the full price for our right to live.
20. Well done is better than well said.

MAIN VERB

<u>Main verb</u> is the main activity or state of **<u>Subject</u>**.

Example :

Hari **<u>reads</u>** a book.

She **<u>is</u>** a good student.

When there is **no** **<u>Main Verb</u>** then helping verb acts as **a** **<u>Main Verb</u>**.

Example:

She **does** her duty.
    ↑**Main verb**

You **have** a book.
    ↑**Main verb**

They **had** to come here.
    ↑**Main verb**

Use of Singular Present Form of Verb

Goes**s**
Sing**s**
Correct**s**
Play**s**
Remember**s**
Forget**s**
Wait**s**
Write**s**
Jump**s**

1. It is also called as the 5th form of verb .

2. It is called '**Singular Present**' form because it can only be used with '**Singular** <u>Noun</u>' and '**Singular** <u>Pronoun</u>'. (He / She / It only)

Example: He gives my book to you. [Singular Pronoun]

5 FORMS OF A VERB

There are 5 forms of a <u>**Verb**</u> :

1.	1st **form = go**	**play**	**write**	**(Original or base form)**
2.	2nd **form = went**	**played**	**wrote**	**(Past Form)**
3.	3rd **form = gone**	**played**	**written**	**(Perfect Form)**
4.	4th **form = going**	**playing**	**writing**	**(Continuous Form)**
5.	5th **form = goes**	**plays**	**writes**	**(Singular Present Form)**

Hick knows the truth. [Singular Noun]

The 5th form of Verb is only used in Simple Present Tense and Positive sentences only.

In Negative / Interrogative & Wh question = No Verb s/es will be used.

[Except Helping Verbs]

1. He writes a letter. [Positive]

He does not write a letter. [Negative]

Does he write a letter ? [Interrogative]

What does he write ? [WH Question]

EXERCISE NO. 20-L

Use the Verbs in your own sentences:

1. goes   2. writes   3. plays   4. teaches   5. jumps   6. waits   7. comes
8. loves   9. meets   10. hates   11. sleeps   12. locks   13. rises   14. shines
15. cooks.

Uses of the Continuous form of Verb

[Verb + ing]

Throwing

Singing

Playing

Driving

Looking

Reading

Talking

Fighting

Verb-ing form is used with is, am, are, was, were, be, been .

It is also called the 4th form of Verb.

1st form	2nd form	3rd form	4th form	5th form
Help	Helped	Helped	Helping	Helps

The 4TH form of Verb is also called -ing form of Verb. It is used in Continuous Tenses only.

USES

1. **Is / Am / Are + Verb -ing = [Present Continuous]**
   1. She is coming here to meet you.
   2. I am waiting for you.
   3. They are making noise.

2. **Was / Were + Verb + ing = [Past Continuous]**
   1. She was going to college.
   2. They were sleeping in my house.

3. **Will / Shall + be + Verb -ing = [Future Continuous]**
   All Subject / I / we.
   1. I shall be waiting for you.
   2. You will be doing your duty.

Uses of Been

1. **Has / Have + been + Verb -ing** [Present Perfect Continuous]
   He / She / It & Singular <u>Noun</u> = <u>Has</u>
   I /We / You / They & Plural noun = Have

   1. He has been reading a book.
   2. You have been singing a song.

2. **<u>Had</u> been + Verb -ing = [Past Perfect Continuous]**

   Any Subject can be used [Singular or Plural] with had.
   1. He had **<u>been</u>** watch**ing** TV at his house.
   2. You had **<u>been</u>** pray**ing** to God.
   3. They had **<u>been</u>** do**ing** home work.

Future Perfect Continuous

I shall have been playing football.
Mr. Hardy will have been studying properly.

Note:

As a "Main Verb" Verb - ing cannot be used without
'**<u>Helping Verb</u>.**'

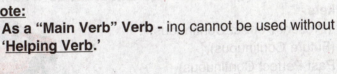

EXERCISE NO. 20-M

Use Verb -ing form according to the instructions given in the brackets:

1. She ——————— (sleep) in the classroom for two periods.
   [Present Perfect Continuous]
2. You ——————— (write) a poem for yourself. **[Future Continuous]**
3. It ——————— (rain) since 2 o' clock. **[Past Perfect Continuous]**
4. They ——————— (wait) for you at the railway platform. **[Past Continuous]**
5. He ——————— (read) a book to know the truth of life.
   [Present Continuous]
6. My brother, Ravi ——————— (dance) very nicely. **[Past Continuous]**
7. Geeta ——————— (do) lots of business dealings to earn more money.
   [Present Perfect Continuous]
8. The pilot ——————— (fly) his aeroplane to thrill them.
   [Future Perfect Continuous]
9. The Super market ——————— (open) in order to provide people the cheapest product. **[Present Perfect Continuous]**
10. My mother ——————— (get) medical treatment in the hospital.
    [Past Continuous]
11. The storm ——————— (raise) up very fast in this area.
    [Future Continuous]
12. Your father ——————— (ask) so many questions regarding my family members.
    [Future Continuous]

EXERCISE NO. 20-N

Change these sentences into 'Past Continuous', 'Future Continuous', 'Present Perfect Continuous', 'Past Perfect Continuous' and Future Perfect Continuous tense :

1. She is writing a letter to your father.
2. You are playing football to win the match.
3. They are doing their work.
4. It is raining cats and dogs.
5. Your friends are coming to meet you.

EXERCISE NO. 20-O

Use the verbs in your sentences in the same tense as it has been instructed in the brackets.

1. Marry (Present Perfect Continuous)
2. Have (Future Continuous)
3. Wait (Past Perfect Continuous)
4. Drive (Future Perfect Continuous)
5. Jump (Present Continuous)

6. Hunt (Past Continuous)
7. Pray (Future Continuous)
8. Teach (Future Perfect Continuous)
9. Solve (Past Perfect Continuous)
10. Watch (Present Perfect Continuous)
11. Correct (Present Perfect Continuous)
12. Prepare (Future Continuous)
13. Complete (Past Continuous)
14. Knock (Future Perfect Continuous)
15. Do (Past Continuous)
16. Throw (Present Continuous)
17. Teach (Present Continuous)
18. Drink (Present Perfect Continuous)
19. Learn (Future Continuous)
20. Help (Past Perfect Continuous)

USES OF THE PERFECT FORM OF VERB
Helping Verbs begin with "H" Letter

Have
Shall have
Had
Will have   Should have
Would have
Might have
Can have
May have
Could have   Must have

It is also called the 3rd form of Verb.
[H]

1ST form	2nd form	3rd form	4th form	5th form
Go	went	Gone	going	goes

A. **Verb 3rd form** is used with the helping verbs beginning with **[H]** letter
e.g. **h**as / **h**ave / **h**ad / will **h**ave / shall **h**ave
can **have** / could **h**ave / should **h**ave / would **h**ave
could **h**ave / may **h**ave / might **h**ave / **h**aving
(**h** letter has been underlined)

Example:

1. She **h**as created so many problems. **[Present Perfect]**
2. They **h**ave lost a purse. **[Present Perfect]**
3. Harry **h**ad closed the door. **[Past Perfect]**
4. He will **h**ave taken my book. **[Future Perfect]**
5. You would **h**ave presented it. **[Conditional Perfect]**

B. **The 3rd form of Verb is used in Passive Voice for all Tenses.**

1. She kills a tiger. **[Active]**

   Verb 3rd form
   A tiger is │ **killed** │ by her. **[Passive]**

2. He │ **played** │ cricket. **[Active]**

   Cricket was │ **played** │ by him . **[Passive]**
   Verb 3rd form

EXERCISE NO. 20-P

Fill in the blanks with the 'Verbs' according to the instructions given in the brackets:

1. I ....(do) my homework in time. **(Present Perfect)**
2. She ...(correct) all the mistakes. **(Past Perfect)**
3. My friends ...(complete) this file for the next project. **(Future Perfect)**
4. They ...(know) the truth. **[Conditional Perfect (must)]**
5. Your staff ...(complete) their office work by 2 o' clock. **(Future Perfect)**
6. Mr. Pat .... (show) all the mistakes to me. **(Past Perfect)**
7. Bob ....(prepare) food for me. **(Present Perfect)**
8. Your secrets ....(exposed) by your family members. **(Present Perfect)**
9. His brother ...(guide) me regarding my future plans. **(Future Perfect)**
10. You ....(try) to get the goal. **(Past Perfect)**

Uses of The Past Form of Verb

USES OF THE 2nd FORM OF VERB

1ST form	2nd form	3rd form	4th form	5th form
Speak	Spoke	Spoken	Speaking	Speaks

[Past form]

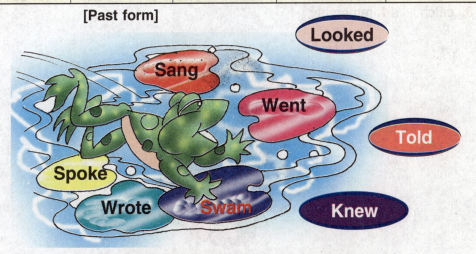

2ND FORM of Verb[Past form]

1. Verb 2nd form is used in Simple Past Tense without helping verb.
   She spoke English very well.
2. We cannot use Verb 2nd form in Negative / Interrogative sentences/ Wh questions.

She did not <u>write</u> a letter. [Negative]
     ↑1st form of Verb

Did she <u>write</u> a letter ? [Interrogative]
     ↑1st form of Verb

What did she <u>write</u> ? [Wh Question]
       ↑1st form of Verb

3. **Verb 2nd form** can be used with **any 'Subject'**.
He played very well.
She played very well.
I played very well.
You played very well.
We played very well.
Ram played very well.
All the boys played very well.

EXERCISE NO. 20-Q

Change the verbs given below in the 2nd form and use them in your own sentences:

1. calculate   2. construct   3. collect   4. do   5. marry   6. prepare
7. drink   8. continue   9. spoil   10. manage   11. buy   12. sell
13. catch   14. remember

Uses of the Base (or) Original Form of Verb

1ST form	2nd form	3rd form	4th form	5th form
Go	Went	Gone	going	goes

Verb 1st form is called as present form of verb but I disagree with it because Verb 1st form can be used in **Present, Past, Future and Conditional tenses.**

1. I show you my photographs. [Present]
2. I did not show you my photographs. [Past]
3. I shall show you my photographs. [Future]
4. I can show you my photographs. [Conditional]

So we call **Verb 1st form as a 'Base form'** or **'Original form' of verb.**

USES

A. Verb 1st form is used with **Plural Subjects** and Pronoun = **I / We / You / They.**

1. **All the girls** sit in the class. [Plural Subject]
2. **I** sit in the class.
3. **You** sit in the class.
4. **They** sit in the class.

B. Verb 1st form is used with the **helping verbs** begin with **D** letter .

1. She **d**oes not **go** to meet her friend. **[Simple Present]**
   ↑**Verb 1ˢᵗ form**

2. You **d**id not **try** to understand me. **[Simple Past]**
   ↑**Verb 1ˢᵗ form**

3. I **d**o not **want** to see you. **[Simple Past]**
   ↑**Verb 1ˢᵗ form**

4. **D**oes my friend **try** to cheat you? **[Simple Present]**
   ↑**Verb 1ˢᵗ form**

5. **D**id Sana **fail** in the exam? **[Simple Past]**
   ↑**Verb 1ˢᵗ form**

EXERCISE NO. 20-R

Fill │**Do / Does / Did + not**│ in the blanks along with the correct form of 'Main Verbs' given in the brackets:

1. She ....(help) the poor people for such reasons. **[Simple Present]**
2. You .... (cheat) your friend for money. **[Simple Past]**
3. They............(do) anything for their friends in the time of need.

   [Simple Past]
4. I .... (catch) him red-handed while doing a crime. **[Simple Past]**
5. Merlin .... (want) to introduce me with his friends. **[Simple Past]**
6. Mr. James ....(help) you in the time of need. **[Simple Present]**
7. We.........(hurt) her sentiment in the party. **[Simple Past]**
8. You.........(inform) him in time about the accident. **[Simple Past]**
9. My friends .... (work) hard to pass the exam. **[Simple Present]**
10. Mr. Bob .... (buy) an old building. **[Simple Present]**

EXERCISE NO. 20-S

Use the verbs given below along with DO / DOES / DID + not in your sentences:

1. create   2. cheat   3. give   4. throw   5. accept   6. know
7. catch   8. trap   9. push   10. show   11. sing   12. believe
13. provide   14. break   15. crack

C.   Verb 1st form is used with [To]

1.   I want **to know** more about you.
       ↑**Verb 1st form**

2.   I live **to serve** my country.
       ↑**Verb 1st form**

D. Verb 1st form is used with [Order & Request]

1.   **Get** out from here right now. **[Order]**
      ↑**Verb 1st form**
       ↓

2.   **Return** my books to me. **[Order]**

3.   Please **give** me your money bag. **[Request]**

         ↑**Verb 1st form**
          ↓

4.   Please **tell** me the truth. **[Request]**

EXERCISE NO. 20- T

Use the verbs in your own sentences [Order (or) Request]:

1. cut   2. return   3. scold   4. suggest   5. study   6. buy
7. sell   8. do   9. marry   10. suggest   11. pray   12. receive
13. crack   14. produce   15. watch.

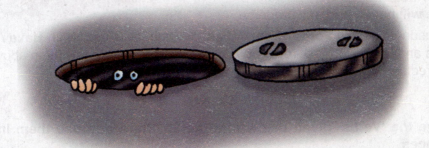

Five Forms of Helping Verbs

First form [or] Base form	Second form [or] Past form	Third form [or] Perfect form	Fourth form [or] Continuous form	Fifth form [or] Singular Present form
Be	Was	Been	Being	Is/Am
Do	Did	Done	Doing	Does
Have	Had	Had	Having	Has

Uses of Double Helping Verbs

Do / Does / Did

Helping Verb	Main Verb

1. She **does** not **do** her work in time.

2. He **did** not **do** the job properly.

3. They **do** not **do** anything for you.

Reason : **The First form of Verb** is used with Do / Does / Did and Do is the

First form of Verb so all the sentences written above are correct.

Have / Had / Has

Helping Verb	Main Verb

1. He **has** **had** his food.
2. You **have** **had** my gift.
3. They **had** **had** everything yesterday.
4. She **will have** **had** my property.

Reason : **The 3rd Form of Verb (Past Participle)** is used with **Have / Had / Has** and **Had** is the **3rd form of Verb** so all the sentences written above are correct.

EXERCISE NO. 20- U

Change the 'Verbs' given below into the 3rd form and use them in your sentences.

1. tell   2. find   3. change   4. capture   5. decorate   6. dye   7. divide
8. die   9. dare   10. love   11. live   12. move   13. tire   14. tie
15. trouble   16. hire   17. prove   18. starve   19. serve   20. save   21. wave
22. graze   23. invite   24. fire   25. leave.

Uses of Tenses

What is Tense ?

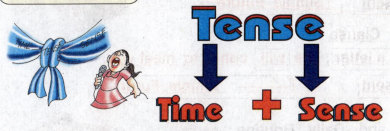

Tense

Time **+** Sense

Simple Present Tense

Subject + Verb + s/es ....[or] Subject + Verb 1ˢᵗ form .

1. She writes a good story for you .
   -Verb S/ES form

2. You sing to please everybody.
   -Verb 1ˢᵗ form

USES OF SIMPLE PRESENT TENSE

A. Simple Present can be used with the adverbials : **always, often, rarely, sometimes, never, seldom, frequently, generally, usually, occasionally, etc.**
   1.   He **always** **writes** a letter to his parents.
   2.   Your teachers **often** **try** to solve the questions.
   3.   I **usually** **study** in the morning.
   4.   You **occasionally** **go** to her house.
   5.   She **meets** me **once in a week**.

B. **Every + Point of time = Simple Present**

   She **goes** to garden **every** evening.
   They **visit** zoo **every** Saturday.

C. **General habits / bad or good habits** .

   He **drinks** wine after 10 o' clock. [**General habit**]
   She **smokes** in the garden. [**Bad habit**]
   I **like** music. [**Good habit**]

D. Exclamatory Sentences begin with **here / there**

There she weeps!

Here he cries !

E. Simple Present can be used in If Clauses with Simple Future .

↓ If Clause

If it rains , she will not come.

↑Simple Present   ↑Simple Future

↓——— If Clause

If you write a letter , he will come to meet you.

↑Simple Present   ↑——— Simple Future

F. Time Table and Daily Routine :

The train leaves at midnight.

My brother sleeps late at night.

I get up early for morning walk.

You advise everybody before leaving office.

G. Future Plans and Programmes :

My boss presents the budget tomorrow.

She leaves for America regarding a discussion with the President.

He thinks to prepare a project for your institution.

H. Universal and General Truth :

The Earth moves round the Sun.

Two and two makes four.

The Sun rises in the east.

The Moon shines brightly.

I. Quotation : Plato says : God is great.

J. Notice : The notice indicates : No talking.

Uses of Simple Past Tense

Subject + **Verb** [2nd form / Past Form] + ...

Verb [2nd form]

She **went** to Goa yesterday.

Verb [2nd form]

You **came** to meet my brother last night.

USES

A. In case of Story / History etc. [Other Tenses can also be used]

Akbar **was** a great king.

Long long ago there **was** a beautiful fairy who lived in a dream world.

B. **Incident / Accident etc**

A pilot **was killed** in a plane crash.

Yesterday, the bus **was hijacked** by terrorists.

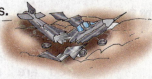

C. **Last + Point of time / Point of time + ago**

She met Phillips **last** Monday.

Last year, we were in London .

I met her a week **ago** .

D. **Yesterday / the previous day or any past time, Year / Month etc.**

In 1990, I was appointed as a Chief Justice .

She completed her work **yesterday** .

E. **Past habit =used to**

She **used to** go to temple. [**But now she does not go**]

My brother **used to** teach English. [**Not now**]

Uses of Simple Future Tense

Subject + shall / will + Verb [1st from]

I / We = Shall   Rest all Subjects = Will

I shall study properly for my future.

You will remember me for ever.

USES

A. Next + Point of time

Next Monday, she will solve the problem .

Next month, I shall pay you the rest amount .

B. In + Period

They will finish their duties **in** two hours.

My friend will return your book **in** a week.

C. Going to Future

She is going to do her duty.

You are going to help her.

Uses of Present Continuous Tense

Subject + is / am / are + Verb + ing

You **are making** me a fool.

They **are buying** vegetables from the market.

A. In case of Now, Still , At Present, At This Moment.

He **is still** waiting for you .

You **are creating** problem **at this moment** .

B. Any work that is continuously happening in present time.

Sheela **is driving** a car.

My father **is reading** Ramayana at home.

C. Present Tense + While + Present Continuous

She **is sleeping while** he is singing a song .

Uses of Past Continuous Tense

[Subject + Was / Were + Verb + ing]

She **was looking** forward to you.

My students **were studying** here.

A. Anything that was continuously happening in the 'Past'.

You were doing your home work.

I was swimming in the river.

He was correcting his mistakes.

B. Past Tense + While + Past Continuous.

My mother was cooking food while I was playing chess.

She was correcting her mistakes while you were laughing.

Uses of Future Continuous Tense

Subject + Shall / Will + be + Verb + ing

I / We + Shall

Rest all Subjects + will

I shall be going.

You will be writing.

USES

A. It is used when an action is likely to happen continuously in the Future.

It will be raining heavily.

The bus will be passing through a tunnel.

He will be studying for his exam.

B. Planned action for Future :

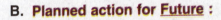

We shall be trying to get the contract.

You will be convincing him for the next project.

She will be returning back from her office.

Uses of Present Perfect Tense

Sub + has / have + Verb [3rd from]   (Past Participle)

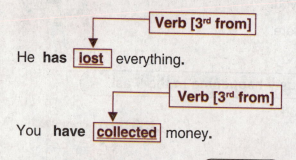

Verb [3rd from]

He **has** <u>lost</u> everything.

Verb [3rd from]

You **have** <u>collected</u> money.

USES

A. | It is used when the event has taken place a moment before or near <u>Past</u>.

The bus has arrived a few minutes before.

B. | Recently, Lately, Already, A few hours / Some minutes ago, etc.

indicate **Present Perfect tense.**

He has recently passed the I.A.S. exam.

You have already completed your work.

C. | Anything happened in the Past but it has a clear effect on Present.

In such cases Present Perfect tense is used.
He **has eaten** food. His stomach is paining.
She **has done** a crime. Now she is under police custody.

Uses of Past Perfect Tense

Subject + had + Verb [3rd form]

1. You had done so many mistakes.

2. I had met your brother.

USES

A. **When 2 incidents have taken place in Past then the 1st event that occurred should be in Past Perfect and the second one in Simple Past.**

Past Perfect   **Simple Past**

As she **had completed** her study, she **went** to the college.

When the book **had been published,** the writer was happy.

Uses of Future Perfect Tense

Subject + shall / will + have + Verb [3rd form] (Past Participle)

Verb [3rd form]

I **shall have** **completed** my job.

Verb [3rd form]

You **will have** **returned** back from America.

USES

A. **By + Point of time**

Point of time

Arthur **will have bought books for me** (**by**) **2 o' clock** .

Point of time

Sherlock **will have corrected the mistakes by** **next Sunday.**

B. **When it is certain that the action will be completed in future , Future Perfect is used.**

They **will have caught** the thief.

We **shall have written** so many stories.

Uses of Present Perfect Continuous Tense

Subject + has / have + been + Verb - ing

She has been watching TV for 2 hours.

You have been completing your work since **2 O' clock.**

USES

This tense is used when any action which is continued

in 'Present' will be continued till it will be completed.

Uses of Past Perfect Continuous Tense

Subject + had + been + Verb + ing

He had been sleeping in his house.

You had been playing the piano.

USES

This **tense** is used when action was started in past, continued and completed in the past.

Uses of Future Perfect Continuous Tense

Subject + shall / will + have + been + Verb - ing

I shall have been trying to meet you.

You will have been cracking jokes.

I shall have been crossing the road.

This **tense** is used when action will start in future and will be continued till the work will be completed.

EXERCISE NO. 21-A

Fill in the blanks with the correct tense:

1. She was unconscious while he _____[**play**] chess with friends.

2. He _____[**write**] a letter since 2 o' clock.

3. When he reached the platform, the train _____[**arrived**].

4. My clerk _____[**complete**] her work just now.

5. I _____[**meet**] you next week at the same place.

6. They _____ [study] English for two hours.

7. Your father _____ [eat] food by midnight .

8. Don't make noise. I _____ [do] a very important work.

9. She is still _____ [wait] for you at the bus stop.

10. The sun _____ [rise] in the east.

11. Two and two _____ [make] four.

12. She _____ [be] a very good teacher.

13. He _____ [have] a pen to write a letter.

14. Your daughter _____ [refuse] to give me some sugar yesterday.

15. Kalidas _____ [be] a great Sanskrit drama writer.

16. Taj Mahal _____ [build] by Shahjahan.

17. Sachin _____ [reach] home by 2 o' clock.

18. Mr. Brain _____ [watch] T.V. in the morning.

19. Miss Dona _____ [goes] to meet her father once in a year only.

20. Three strangers _____ [meet] the M.P. who had delivered his speech.

21. The President of U.S.A. _____ [appreciated] by the people of Asia last year.

22. Everyday , she _____ [take] medicine before going to bed.

23. Your cousin sister _____ [meet] you tomorrow after 7 o' clock.

24. Sam tried to dance while all the family members_____ [sleep] peacefully.

EXERCISE NO.21-B

Fill in the blanks with the correct form of verbs given in the brackets :

1. I .... (try) to achieve the goal of my life since 1994.

2. Being a friend of mine , he ....(returned) my money to my parents by 2 o' clock.

3. As the train ....(reached) the railway platform, the passengers ....(start) to fight for the seat.

4. Ashoka ....(be) a great ruler in the history of India.

5. Three and three ....(make) six.

6. Recently, I .... (write) a book for students of my college.

7. You .... already (lose) your book while returning back to home.

8. The aeroplane ....(fly) at 5 o' clock at its scheduled time.

9. Wisdom ....(be) better than strength .

10. Meghna ....still **(study)** in your classroom.

11. While Miss Joy ....(play) in the garden, **Miss Leech** ....
    (watch)her.

12. I ....(compose) a song at present for myself.

13. Rick ....(help) me next week because of my good nature.

14. You ....(buy) a car by next month.

15. Kanika ....(pass) the exam very soon.

PRONOUN

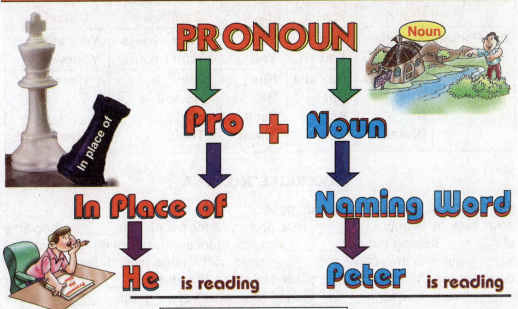

Noun

PRONOUN

Pro + Noun

In Place of   Naming Word

He is reading   Peter is reading

Kinds of Pronouns

1. Personal Pronoun
2. Relative Pronoun
3. Interrogative Pronoun
4. Demonstrative Pronoun
5. Distributive Pronoun
6. Indefinite Pronoun
7. Reflexive Pronoun
8. Emphatic Pronoun
9. Reciprocal Pronoun
10. Exclamatory Pronoun

Personal Pronoun

A **Pronoun** that indicates person is called a **Personal Pronoun**.
Example: – He, she, It, I, We, You, they, etc.

Person	Number	Subject	Object	Possessive	Reflexive
1st Person	Singular	I	Me	My/mine	Myself
	Plural	We	Us	Our/ours	Ourself
2nd Person	Singular	You	You	Your / yours	Yourself
	Plural	You	You	Your / yours	Yourself
3rd Person	Singular	He / she	Him	His	Himself
	It	Her	Her	Herself	
	It	Its	Itself		
	Plural	They	Them	Their	Themselves

EXERCISE NO. 22-A

Fill 'Personal Pronouns' in the gaps:

John lives in Mumbai. _____ is a doctor. All the people like _____ because of _____ helping nature. _____ hospital is located at Andheri and most of _____ patients are poor but _____ does not charge much money. _____ daughter goes to school. _____ studies in Vth Standard. _____ teachers love _____ very much. _____ friends are also very good. _____ always encourage _____. _____ have given _____ guidance in studies. _____ mother is also a teacher. _____ always encourages _____ to keep it up. I also like her as _____ often comes to _____ house. One day _____ told my mother that _____ wants to learn cooking. _____ mother taught _____ cooking. Now, _____ cooks food well.

Relative Pronoun

A **Pronoun** which shows relation is called a **Relative Pronoun**.
The girl, **whom** you met yesterday, was my sister.
The pen, **which** you have taken, is mine.
This is the lady **whom** everybody praises.

EXERCISE NO. 22- B

Fill 'Relative Pronouns' in the gaps:

Yesterday, I met a lady, _____ was an American. She was willing to see the Gateway of India _____ is located near the Taj Hotel _____ anybody can have a lovely view of sea. She was the lady _____ nobody knows in Mumbai but she was familiar to the people of Mumbai _____ she had to spend 1 month. She met a merchant _____ was very clever. She wanted to buy a pen _____ was imported from Japan. The merchant _____ everybody knows to be honest but the American lady proved him to be dishonest as the pen _____ he used to sell was made in India. His shop is located near Liberty Garden _____ people come for morning walk. She suggested him to remain honest and gives him 10 pens_____ were made in America.

EXERCISE NO. 22-C

Join the sentence using 'Relative Pronouns'.

1. She lives in a bungalow. A ghost lives there.
2. A man had been killed. He was taken to the graveyard yesterday.
3. I have a book. It is written by Rabindranath Tagore.
4. Give me a pen to write a letter. It was gifted to you on 16th birth anniversary.
5. Your daughter was very unhappy. She had lost her money.
6. This is the shop. It is bought by my uncle to sell garments.
7. Kavita hates Anne. Anne is a good teacher.
8. Rickey knows a cheat. The C .I .D. officers have arrested the cheat.
9. I have sold the hut. It was located at the bank of river.
10. Here is your gold watch. It has been found in the garden.
11. I have so many books to study. I bought these books from London.
12. Richa has created so many problems. Richa is my sister.
13. Some students had been waiting for the Principal. He used to guide them.
14. I have written a story. It is based on the real incidents of my life.
15. Sanjay wants to go to Delhi. Tamanna lives there.

Interrogative Pronoun

A Pronoun which asks a question is called an **Interrogative Pronoun.**

Who won the match**?**

Which is her pen**?**

Whom does he hate**?**

Which of these books do you like **?**

Interrogative Pronouns have been **underlined** above.

EXERCISE NO. 22-D

Fill in the gaps with appropriate 'Interrogative Pronouns'.

1. _____ bungalow is this?
2. _____ is her house?
3. _____ wants to meet me now ?
4. _____ does he want to help ?
5. _____ will create problems tomorrow?

6. _____ has she cheated to achieve the target?
7. _____ book has been taken by your class teacher?
8. _____ do you mean to say?
9. _____ does she expect from you?
10. _____ were you guiding about computer business?

Demonstrative Pronoun

A Pronoun which demonstrates **a Noun, an Object, a Complement,** etc. is called a **Demonstrative Pronoun.**

This is your result.

That was a silly mistake.

These are my books.

Those were my friend's books.

Distributive Pronoun

A Pronoun which distributes a group or a pair is called a **Distributive Pronoun.**

Each / Every / Either / Neither/ Any one / None / etc. are **Distributive Pronouns.**

1. **Each of** these pens will be sold.
2. **None of** the students can solve it , I shall be thankful to God .
3. **Either of** these students must have taken it.
4. **Neither of** your friends will come.

   Distributive Pronouns have been underlined.

   NOTE : [Of] is often found after **Distributive Pronoun** .

Indefinite Pronoun

A Pronoun, which is indefinite, is called an **Indefinite Pronoun.**

All , some , one , many, few , somebody , nobody , etc. are Indefinite Pronouns.

None have come to help you.

A few can build houses.

One should know one's job.

Many have been failed.

Reflexive Pronoun

A Pronoun which reflects the action towards the subject is called a **Reflexive Pronoun** .

Example:

She hurt **herself** while playing.

You have invented this machine **yourself.**

I shall do it **myself.**

He solved his problem **himself.**

Emphatic Pronoun

A Pronoun which is used for emphasis is called an **Emphatic Pronoun.**
Example:

I **myself** is enough to solve the problem.

You **yourself** will return my money.

He **himself** knows me very well.

They **themselves** will have to earn money.

A Reflexive Pronoun is used after the **Verb** but **Emphatic Pronoun** is used before the **Verb.**

Example:

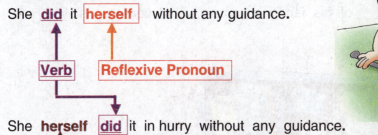

She **did** it **herself** without any guidance.

Verb   Reflexive Pronoun

She **herself** **did** it in hurry without any guidance.

Emphatic Pronoun

Reciprocal Pronoun

A Pronoun which shows relation with one another is called **a Reciprocal Pronoun.**

All the enemies kill **one another.**

The two girls hate **each other.**

Rule: **Each other** is used for **two persons** .

One another is used for **more than two persons.**

EXERCISE NO. 22- E

Fill in the gaps with appropriate Pronouns and tell their kinds :

1. _____ is an excellent opportunity.

2. _____ is my cock gifted by my father to me.

3. _____ should not praise about one's success.

4. _____ but fools try to cheat others.

5. _____ has taken my book without my permission.

6. _____ of these 2 students can solve this question.

7. _____ of those girls are allowed to enter before 5 o' clock.

8. _____ books have been written by a great Indian writer.

9. _____ have come to know the fact.

10. _____ of the students have passed the exam.

11. He _____ will accept the guilt.

12. The two sisters hate _____.

13. _____ have come to suggest us regarding this case.

14. She _____ did it in order to please her family members.

15. You have confused _____ watching a fowl in the nest.

16. _____ of your sisters will be able to justify the fact.

17. _____ of your friends can guide you.

18. _____ is your story based on your real life.

19. All your friends will misguide _____.

20. _____ of his family members would come to visit you.

ADJECTIVE

An **Adjective** is a word which qualifies a **Noun or a Pronoun.**
1. He is an **ordinary** man.
2. It is an **excellent** idea.
3. You are a **good** teacher.
4. **The** Earth is **round.**
5. **His** brother was a **foolish** man.

Kinds of Adjectives

1. **Adjective of Quantity**
2. **Adjective of Quality**
3. **Adjective of Number**
4. **Interrogative Adjective**
5. **Demonstrative Adjective**
6. **Possessive Adjective**
7. **Exclamatory Adjective**
8. **Emphatic Adjective**

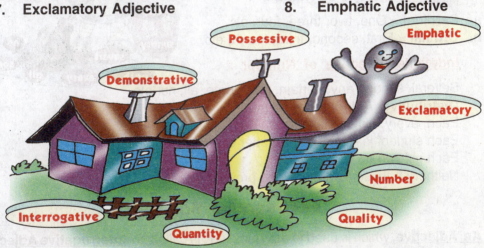

Adjective of Quantity

A word that shows the quantity of anything is called **an Adjective of Quantity.**
Example:
Sufficient , all, insufficient, whole, much, little, some, enough, any , etc.
1. I have **little** money to spend.
2. She has **much** patience to bear the loss.
3. He does not have **enough** time to study.
4. She is a lady of **great** courage.
5. I have done **enough** hard work.

Adjective of Quality

An **Adjective** which shows the **quality** of a **Noun or a Pronoun** is called **an Adjective of Quality.**

1. My grandfather has a **black** dog.
2. My daughter loves a **Japanese** doll.
3. The language is **difficult**.
4. The ground is **muddy**.
5. Phillips is a **careless** captain of our team.
6. Akbar was a **wise** king.

Adjective of Number

An **Adjective** which shows amount or number is called an **Adjective of Number.**
It has three kinds.

1. Definite Adjective of Number
2. Indefinite Adjective of Number
3. Distributive Adjective of Number

Definite Adjective of Number :

a. **Cardinal** = One, two, three, four, etc.
b. **Ordinal** = First, second, third, fourth, etc.

Indefinite Adjective of Number :

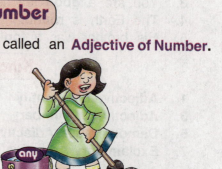

Several, sundry, any, certain, few, some, all, no, etc.

Distributive Adjective of Number :
Each, every, either, neither.
Each student is looking for a better chance.
Each girl can do it.
Neither of these evidences can prove the guilt.

Interrogative Adjective

An **Adjective,** which is used to ask question , is called an **Interrogative Adjective.**
e.g. whose, which , what, etc.

1. <u>**Whose**</u>   <u>book</u> is lost. **[After Wh word + Noun / Noun phrase etc.]**
   ↑ **Intro. Adj.** ↑**Noun**

2. <u>**Which**</u>   <u>bungalow</u> do you like **?**
   ↑ **Intro.Adj** ↑**Noun**

3. <u>**Whose**</u>   <u>purse</u> has been picked **?**
   ↑ **Intro.Adj** ↑**Noun**

Demonstrative Adjective

An **Adjective** which points out **a Noun** or **a Pronoun** is called **a Demonstrative Adjective**.

e.g. This, that, these, those, such, your, etc.

1. **These** **books** are very helpful to us.
   ↑Demo Adj ↑Noun

2. I like **such** **flowers.**
   ↑Demo. Adj ↑Noun

3. **Such** **people** have been very useful to them.
   ↑Demo. Adj ↑ Noun

4. **Those** **students** were not trying to solve the problem.
   ↑Demo. Adj ↑Noun

Possessive Adjective

An **Adjective** which shows possession is called a **Possessive Adjective**.

e.g. his, her, your, my, its, our, their, etc.

   ↓Noun
1. **Your** | bungalow | has been sold.
   Possessive Adj.

   ↓Noun
2. **My** | friend | had been to London.
   Possessive Adj.

   ↓Noun
3. **Their** | ideas | are impractical.
   Possessive Adj.

   ↓Noun
4. **Her** | husband | is a doctor.
   Possessive Adj.

Exclamatory Adjective

An Adjective which shows surprise is called an **Exclamatory Adjective**.

↓Noun
1. What a | mistake | !

↑
Exclamatory Adj.

↓Noun
2. What a | lady | she is !

↑
Exclamatory Adj

↓Noun
3. What a | snowfall | !

↑
Exclamatory

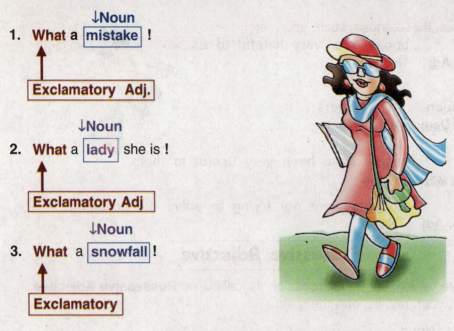

Emphatic Adjectives

An **Adjective** which emphasizes the idea , statement, etc is called an **Emphatic Adjective.**

↓Noun
1. It was your **own** idea.

↑
Emphatic Adj.

↓Noun
2. That is the **very** place where I met him.

↑
Emphatic Adj.

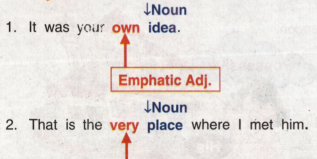

EXERCISE NO. 23-A

Find out the <u>Adjectives</u> from the sentences given below and tell their kinds also :

1. You should try to clear your confusion.
2. The great things are done when men and mountain meet.
3. It is my own mistake.
4. What a book it is !
5. Those people might have been waiting for you.
6. Every citizen should think about the future of country.
7. What type of lady is she?
8. Either of these boys must have stolen my money.
9. Birbal was a wise man.
10. The last train to Churchgate is very late.
11. I have enough money to survive in Mumbai.
12. She has spent all her money in shopping.
13. Undertaker was among the best wrestlers in the world.
14. It is a foolish mistake that you have done.
15. What a joke !
16. Whose wife is a C. I. D. inspector ?
17. Those buildings will be demolished soon by the order of court.
18. None of you can touch me.
19. Which type of people do you like?
20. I do not have any suggestion for you.
21. Nicky is a very punctual lady.
22. My views are totally different.
23. Such students are always having problems.
24. Those people, who work hard, always get success in life.
25. You are a very silly fellow.
26. What a high mountain !
27. His wife is a very kind lady.
28. Whose daughter has stolen your books ?
29. What a foolish idea !
30. You should not have bad blood with anyone.
31. I cannot disturb her in beauty sleep.
32. Intelligent people normally kill two birds with one stone.
33. After the failure, we are enjoying the blind man's holiday.
34. Tom, Dick and Harry are bosom friends.
35. After she kicked the bucket, I feel like broken-hearted.

ADVERB

ADVERB

↓   ↓

Add + Verb

A word that adds some meaning to a **Verb , Adjective** etc. is called **an Adverb.**

1. She walks **slowly** after the medical treatment.
2. You have solved the questions quite **correctly.**
3. He had completed his work **properly.**
4. I can do it **easily.**
5. She wept **bitterly.**
6. My brother works **hard** to pass the exam.

Kinds of Adverbs

1. Adverb of place
2. Adverb of time
3. Adverb of frequency
4. Adverb of manner
5. Adverb of reason or purpose
6. Adverb of degree or quantity or extent
7. Adverb of duration
8. Adverb of assertion
9. Relative Adverb

Manner
Time
Place
Frequency
Assertion
Relative
Purpose
Duration
Degree

Adverb of Place

An **Adverb** that indicates place is an **Adverb of Place**:
Ex: In, out, up, near, here, there, away, down.
1. She was looking <u>forward</u> to you.
2. He has kept your book <u>somewhere.</u>
3. Get <u>out.</u>
4. You can meet him <u>anywhere.</u>
5. Please sit <u>here.</u>

Adverb of Time

An **Adverb** which indicates something about the time of incident, state, etc. is called an **Adverb of Time. e.g.** – Before, now, soon, never, since, late, formerly, today, daily, already, yet etc.
Example:
1. He <u>will</u>   <u>never</u> help you.
   ↑Verb   ↑Adverb

2. She <u>has</u>   <u>already</u> paid money.
   ↑Helping Verb   ↑Adverb
3. They have <u>started</u> it <u>soon.</u>
               ↑Verb   ↑Adverb
4. I <u>got</u> up <u>early</u> in the morning.
   ↑Verb   ↑Adverb

Adverb of Frequency

An **Adverb** which shows how often the incident takes place is called an **Adverb of Frequency**.
1. She <u>never</u> goes to the temple.
2. meet him <u>occasionally.</u>
3. You <u>generally</u> fail in English.
4. Your brother <u>seldom</u> makes me fool.
5. They <u>often</u> create so many problems.

Adverb of Manner

An **Adverb** which shows how the work is done, is called an **Adverb of Manner.**
   Ex: thus, so, well, hard, slowly, quickly.
1. She had danced **thus.**
2. have been awarded **severally.**
3. He is approaching you **slowly.**
4. They did everything **carefully.**
5. They played **carelessly** so they lost the match.

Adverb of Reason

Adverb which shows reason is called an **Adverb of Reason.**

1. He was, **hence,** diverted towards other party.
2. She, **therefore,** will be happy to see you.

Adverb of Quantity / Degree

An **Adverb** which shows quantity, degree etc. is called an **Adverb of Quantity / degree**.

Example:

1. I am **extremely** sorry.
2. She is **rather** foolish.
3. You are **too** late.
4. Sachin is **well** set in his batting.

Adverb of Duration

An **Adverb** which shows duration is called an **Adverb of Duration**.

1. She has been studying **for** 2 hours.
2. You have been completing your work **since** morning.
3. I have been waiting **since** last October.

Adverb of Assertion

An **Adverb** which shows assertion is called an **Adverb of Assertion**.

1. I am **certainly** going ahead in my life.
2. She did not get **any** mistake.
3. He had **undoubtedly** been to London.

Relative Adverb

An **Adverb** which shows relation between the two **'Subjects'** is called a **Relative Adverb.**

1. She does not know the cause **why** he was killed.
2. It is the situation **when** you can help her.
3. This is the jungle **where** the lion was killed.

EXERCISE NO. 24-A

Find out 'Adverbs' from the sentences given below and tell their kinds also:

1. He could not tell the reason why he was punished.
2. This is the school where Dr. Abdul Kalam used to study during his childhood.
3. She had undoubtedly cleared the confusion.
4. Mr. Bruce is certainly using his forked tongue in order to prove his false statement.
5. He had been trying to get the fool's gold for 2 hours.
6. She is extremely sorry for building castles in the air.
7. Dick is slowly trying to understand the difference between chalk and cheese.
8. You have been playing devil's advocate since morning.
9. I see him occasionally behaving like a dog in manger.
10. He was rather innocent.
11. She, therefore, was drinking like a fish.
12. She was, hence, looking like a lame duck after her failure.
13. Mr. Ariel had undoubtedly been looking like a drowned rat.
14. He was, unintentionally, making his eyes in the party.
15. The judge, intentionally, turned a blind eye from the case.
16. Miss Bell is, therefore, crystal clear about her intentions.
17. She was never honoured as a crowning glory.
18. He is already dead to the world.
19. She is, undoubtedly, looking mad as an injured snake.
20. Shelly is, honestly, earning her honest penny.

CONJUNCTION

Conjunction

Con **+** Junc

Together Join

A Conjunction is a word that joins two **Words**, **Phrases**, **Clauses** or Sentences .

1. <u>Tom</u> and <u>Nicky</u> are writing letters. [Two Words]
   ↑Word   ↑Word

2. She is waiting for you <u>near the temple</u> & <u>under the tree</u>. [Two Phrases]
   ↑————Phrase   ↑———— Phrase

3. <u>You can not earn money</u>   <u>unless you get a job.</u> [Two Clauses]
   ↑————————Clause   ↑————————Clause

4. <u>I have stopped my car</u> .   <u>He did not do so</u>. [Two Sentences]
   ↑————————Sentence ↑————Sentence
   I have   stopped my car but he did not do so.
                            ↑ Conjunction

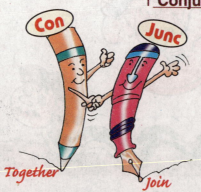

Kinds of Conjunctions

There are two kinds of **Conjunctions:**
1. **Co-ordinating** Conjunction
2. **Subordinating** Conjunction

Co-ordinating   Subordinating

Co-ordinating Conjunctions

Whether....... or, either......or, neither.......nor, nevertheless, as well as, both, or, nor, but, therefore, consequently, and, yet, still, otherwise, not only——— but also.

Subordinating Conjunctions

That, since, until, how, where, why, when, if, though, after, because, although, unless, till, before, as, etc.

Kinds of Co-ordinating Conjunctions

There are four kinds of **Co-ordinating Conjunctions:**
1. **Alternative** Conjunction
2. **Copulative** Conjunction
3. **Adversative** Conjunction
4. **Illative** Conjunction

Adversative
Illative
Alternative
Copulative

Alternative Conjunction

When there is choice between the two statements, **the Conjunction** which joins them is an **Alternative Conjunction.**

Example:
Either ......or, Neither.......nor, Whether.......or, otherwise, or, etc.
1. **Whether** he **or** she has stolen my money.
2. **Either** my brother **or** your sister will do the work.
3. **Neither** a pen **nor** a pencil is cheap.
4. Please return my book **otherwise** I shall complain to the Principal.
5. Give some instructions **or** help him.

Copulative Conjunction

A **Conjunction** which addresses one statement or fact to the other one is called a **Copulative Conjunction**.

Example:

1. She was **both** a cheat **and** a traitor.
2. Sita **as well as** Ram has to go to the forest.
3. Trust in God **and** speak the truth.
4. I am **not only** a teacher **but** a friend **also**.

Adversative Conjunction

When a **Conjunction** joins **two opposite statements**, it is called an **Adversative Conjunction**.

e.g. But, still, yet, nevertheless, etc.

1. She could pass the exam, **nevertheless** she worked hard.
2. I am studying hard **but** her brother is lazy.
3. Your brother is rich **yet** he is a miser.

Illative Conjunction

An **Illative Conjunction** joins two sentences to express inference.
e.g. therefore, consequently, for, etc.

1. He had done a crime **therefore** he was imprisoned.
2. She could not recognize his enemy **consequently** she lost everything .
3. My brother will get the target **for** he is studying day and night.

Subordinating Conjunction

A Conjunction that joins a **Principal** and a **Subordinate Clause** is called **a Subordinating Conjunction.**

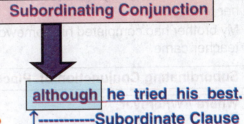

1. **He did not get success**
   ↑----------Principal Clause

   although he tried his best.
   ↑----------Subordinate Clause

2. **She is very unhappy**
   ↑--------Principal Clause

   however she has lots of money.
   ↑----------Subordinate Clause

3. **You are behaving**
   ↑--------Principal Clause

   as if you were a king.
   ↑----------Subordinate Clause

Kinds of Subordinating Conjunctions

A. **Subordinating Conjunction of Time :**

After / Since / Until / Till / Before / While / When.

a. He was playing **until** his parents came.
b. **While** she was studying, she was remembering her teacher.
c. My brother had completed his homework **after** the teacher came.

B. **Subordinating Conjunction of Place :**

Where / Wherever.

a. I shall come to meet you **wherever** you hide.
b. She knows well **where** he lives.
c. I do not know **where** he will continue the job.
d. He will get success **wherever** he goes.

C. **Subordinating Conjunction of Reason :**

That, Since, Because, As.

a. India won the match **because** they played well.
b. She will continue to eat **as** she is hungry.
c. The students could not meet the Principal **since** the school had been closed.

d. **Since** you re uneducated, you canno get a job.

D. **Subordinating Conjunction of Purpose :**

So that / Lest .

a. He dived **so that** he could catch the ball.
b. We should invite him **lest** he will feel insulted.

E. **Subordinating Conjunction of Concession:**

Though, Although, Even though, etc.

a. **Although** he is rich, he is not a miser.
b. **Though** she has no money, she will go to market.
c. **Even though** he is honest, he is blamed for cheating others.
d. **Although** Miss Dolly is a teacher, she cannot speak English.

F. | **Subordinating Conjunctions of Result:**

So

a. Australia played well **so** they won the World Cup.
b. He did not do the homework **so** he was punished.
c. You answered well **so** you were selected.
d. I was late **so** I could not meet him.

G. | **Subordinating Conjunctions of Manner :**

As if / As

a. He plays cricket **as if** he were Ricky.
b. His brother talks **as if** he were a fool.
c. She is eating **as** a hungry person eats.
d. You look **as if** you were a teacher.

H. | **Subordinating Conjunctions of Comparison :**

As / Than

a. My father is **as** intelligent **as** Mr. Lincoln.
b. The eyes are more beautiful **than** any gift of God.
c. His daughter is **as** white **as** snow.
d. This painting is more attractive **than** any other ones.

EXERCISE NO. 25-A

Pick out the Conjunctions from the following sentences and tell whether they are Co-ordinating or Subordinating Conjunctions:

1. She waited till the guest arrived.
2. They got into the bus before the rain started.
3. Carol will go to her mother's house if her mother invites her.
4. Unless you do the work, you will not be paid.
5. Neither you are mistaken nor I am.
6. They tried but did not succeed.
7. Undertaker is stronger than Johnsina .
8. I had been to Delhi because I wanted to meet the Prime Minister.
9. I do not know why he went.
10. The train was derailed by the mob but nobody was injured.

INTERJECTION & EXCLAMATION

A word which is used to express **emotion** or **sudden feeling** is called **an Interjection.**

Example: Hurrah ! I won the match.

Interjection for <u>Joy</u> **: Ha-Ha ! Hurrah!**

Interjection for <u>Sorrow</u> **: Alas ! Ah ! Ha! What!**

Interjection for <u>Surprise</u> **: Ha! What ! Ho!**

Interjection for <u>Contempt</u> **: For shame ! Pshaw ! Fie ! Pooh !**

Interjection for <u>Applause</u> **: Bravo ! Buck up !**

Interjection for <u>Invitation</u> **: Hear – Hear ! Hello ! Ho !**

Interjection for <u>Drawing Attention</u> **: Behold ! Listen ! Look !**

There are three types of **Exclamatory Sentences.**

Example:

1. <u>Alas !</u> She is dead. [<u>Interjection</u> & Simple Sentence]
2. What a foolish project ! [Exclamatory sentence <u>without a Verb</u>]
3. What a silly mistake it <u>is</u> ! [Exclamatory sentence <u>with a Verb</u> at the end]   ↑<u>Verb</u>

EXERCISE NO. 26- A

Write sentences by the help of the '<u>Interjections</u>' given below :

1. Behold !   2. Listen!   3. Look !   4. Ha-Ha !   5. Hurrah!
6. Ha!   7. What !   8.Ho!   9. Alas !   10. Ah!
11. For shame !   12. Pshaw !   13. Fie !   14. Pooh !
15. Hear – Hear !   16. Hello !   17. Bravo !   18. Buck up!

TRANSFORMATION OF SENTENCES II

Affirmative, Negative & Exclamatory Sentences

What is **Transformation of Sentence?**
When we change the form of a sentence without changing its meaning, it is called the ' **Transformation of a Sentence'.**

What is change according to the **'Formation of Sentence'?**
When we change the form of a sentence and the meaning changes, it is called change according to the ' **Formation of a Sentence'.**

Example :

She is a beautiful girl.
She is not an ugly girl. (transformation)
She is not a beautiful girl. (formation)

Affirmative to Negative Sentences

Sentences with a Helping Verb

Rules: Use 'not' after the helping verb and opposite form of Adjective / Verb etc.
Consider is / am /are / was / were always as a helping verb.
Example:

1. She is a literate lady. [Affirmative]

She is not an illiterate lady. [Negative]

2. They will remember us because of our hard work. [Affirmative]

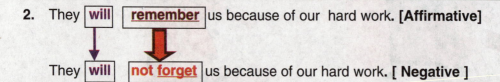

They will not forget us because of our hard work. [Negative]

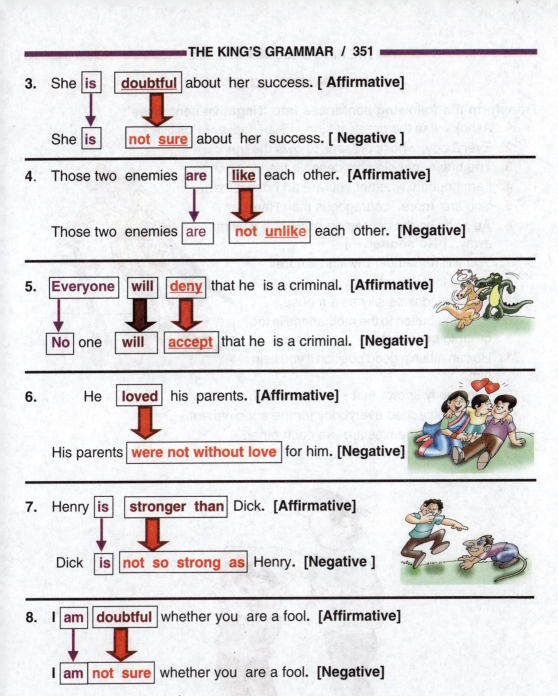

3. She **is** **doubtful** about her success. **[Affirmative]**

    She **is** **not sure** about her success. **[Negative]**

4. Those two enemies **are** **like** each other. **[Affirmative]**

    Those two enemies **are** **not unlike** each other. **[Negative]**

5. **Everyone** **will** **deny** that he is a criminal. **[Affirmative]**

    No one **will** **accept** that he is a criminal. **[Negative]**

6. He **loved** his parents. **[Affirmative]**

    His parents **were not without love** for him. **[Negative]**

7. Henry **is** **stronger than** Dick. **[Affirmative]**

    Dick **is** **not so strong as** Henry. **[Negative]**

8. I **am** **doubtful** whether you are a fool. **[Affirmative]**

    I **am** **not sure** whether you are a fool. **[Negative]**

9. Sachin **is** **the best** batsman in the history of Indian cricket.

    No other batsman **is** **as good as** Sachin in the history of Indian cricket.
    [Negative]

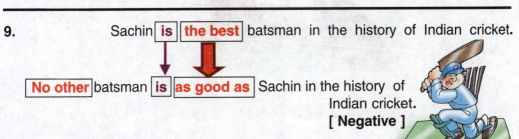

EXERCISE NO.27- A

Transform the following sentences into 'Negative sentences':

1. Ashoka was the greatest king. [Superlative = Positive]
2. Everybody, who is present, knows the truth.
3. The brave people only deserve the victory.
4. I am doubtful whether you are an honest man.
5. You are more courageous than Ram.
6. **As soon as** the policeman came, the thief ran away. [**No sooner —**]
7. You will remember my kind nature.
8. Only a fool will rely on you.
9. Your friend is as silly as a mouse.
10. His contribution to the motherland is too great to be ignored.
11. He can attain a good position if you help him.
12. Everybody knows that she is innocent.
13. She approached everybody for the appointment.
14. These two enemies are like each other.
15. She made a plan and succeeded.

Affirmative to Exclamatory Sentences

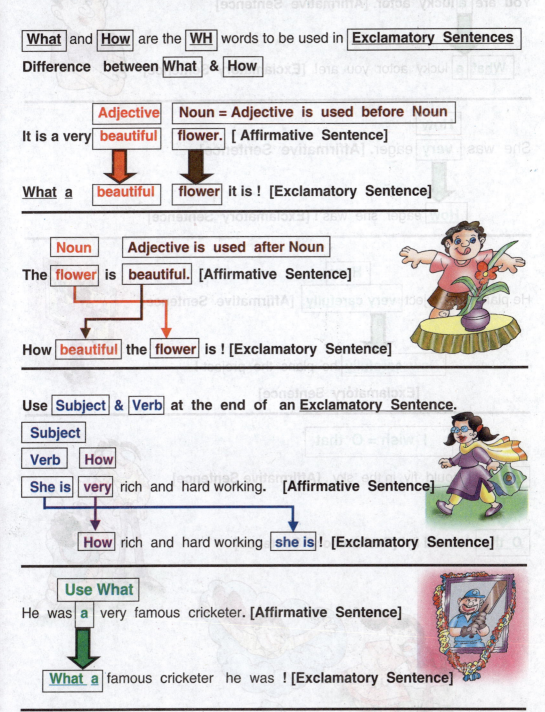

What and **How** are the **WH** words to be used in **Exclamatory Sentences**

Difference between **What** & **How**

Adjective

Noun = Adjective is used before Noun

It is a very **beautiful** **flower.** [Affirmative Sentence]

What a **beautiful** **flower** it is ! [Exclamatory Sentence]

Noun

Adjective is used after Noun

The **flower** is **beautiful.** [Affirmative Sentence]

How **beautiful** the **flower** is ! [Exclamatory Sentence]

Use **Subject** & **Verb** at the end of an **Exclamatory Sentence**.

Subject

Verb **How**

She is **very** rich and hard working. [Affirmative Sentence]

How rich and hard working **she is** ! [Exclamatory Sentence]

Use What

He was **a** very famous cricketer. [Affirmative Sentence]

What a famous cricketer he was ! [Exclamatory Sentence]

Use What

You are **a** lucky actor. [Affirmative Sentence]

What a lucky actor you are! [Exclamatory Sentence]

How

She was **very** eager. [Affirmative Sentence]

How eager she was ! [Exclamatory Sentence]

How

He plans the project **very carefully.** [Affirmative Sentence]

How carefully he plans the project !

[Exclamatory Sentence]

I wish = O that

I wish I could fly in the sky . [Affirmative Sentence]

O that I could fly! [Exclamatory Sentence]

EXERCISE NO. 27-B

Change the following sentences into 'Exclamatory Sentences':

1. It was a very wonderful idea.
2. She was truly noble.
3. It is very hot tea.
4. He had to suffer a horrible misfortune.
5. It is kind of you to guide me.
6. You answered very intelligently.
7. It is a stupid idea for this project.
8. My brother is a very mean fellow regarding money.
9. I wish, I could meet a fairy.
10. He is a very selfish fellow.
11. I wish that I could win the Nobel Prize.
12. He intensely desires to kill me.
13. It is a great surprise to see you walking in the morning.
14. Othello is a very popular tragic play .
15. Caesar was a very wise and religious king.

Interrogative Sentences (OR) Yes / No Question

When you transform the sentences into **Interrogative Sentences,** use 'not' in **Affirmative Sentences** and remove not from the **Negative Sentences .**

Example :

1. **She is a very cunning lady.**

   Is<u>n't</u> she a very cunning lady ?

2. **They were <u>not</u> waiting for a golden chance .**

   Were they waiting for a golden chance ?

Rules:

You will get two types of sentences .

1. Sentences with '**Helping & Main Verb**'
2. Sentences with only '**Main Verb.**'

Sentences with a Helping & a Main Verb

[Consider Is/ Am/ Are/ Was /Were etc. always as helping verbs]

Example:

She was trying to cheat me.

Use **Helping Verb** before the <u>**Subject**</u> with not.

Helping verb

not

She **was** trying to cheat me. **[Affirmative Sentence]**

Wasn't she trying to cheat me**?** **[Interrogative (or) Yes / No Question]**

Helping Verb

1. They **will** have been preparing for a better project . **[Affirmative Sentence]**

They **will** have been preparing a better project **.**

Won't they have been preparing a better project **?** **[Yes / No Question]**

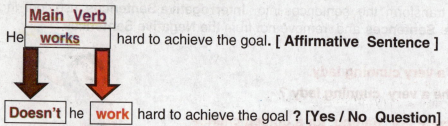

Sentences with only Main Verb

Use Do / Does / Did & Verb first form.

Main Verb

He **works** hard to achieve the goal. **[Affirmative Sentence]**

Doesn't he **work** hard to achieve the goal **?** **[Yes / No Question]**

Main Verb

You create**d** a landmark in sports . **[Affirmative Sentence]**

Didn't you create a landmark in sports? **[Yes / No Question]**

Main Verb

Your friends **wish** to snatch my popularity . **[Affirmative Sentence]**

Don't your friends **wish** to snatch my popularity **?** **[Yes / No Question]**

Negative Sentence

She **does** **not** try to understand me.

Does she try to understand me ? **[Yes / No Question]**

- -

They **do** **not** remember the lessons everyday.

Do they remember their lessons everyday? **[Yes / No Question]**

EXERCISE NO. 27-C

Transform the following sentences into 'Interrogative Sentences' (OR) 'Yes / No Questions'.

1. She was a notorious jewel thief.
2. You will have been trying to create the problems.
3. He does not have any idea about the robbery.
4. They are not waiting for anybody.
5. Sadhna writes a story for your magazine.
6. Hitler was a great tyrant.
7. Everybody knows the fact.
8. Money is as important as oxygen.
9. All the problems do not have their solutions.
10. You must get your son vaccinated.
11. Two and two does not make five.
12. We could have done something for you.
13. Jack is going to help my brother.
14. It is better to die than to live being lazy.
15. Fear is a universal weakness.
16. You must accept the fact of life.
27. He agrees that he has made a mistake.

Transformation: Imperative To Interrogative Sentences

Give me your book to study for the exam.

[Imperative Sentence]

Will you give me your book to study for the exam?
[Interrogative Sentence]

Please tell me the fact. **[Imperative Sentence]**

Will you please tell me the fact? **[Interrogative Sentence]**

EXERCISE NO. 27-D

Transform the following sentences into 'Imperative Sentences' :

1. Get out from here.
2. Write a letter to your friend.
3. Please sing a song for us.
4. Try to finish the work in time.
5. Please continue this project for one more year.
6. Catch him before he could meet your father.
7. Buy some vegetables and bring to me.
8. Teach him a lesson.
9. Push him out from this party.
10. Please call him here.

PARTICIPLE

A Participle is a form of **'Verb'** that does the work of **an Adjective.**

Example:

Go = Verb 1st form
Went = Verb 2nd form
Gone = Verb 3rd form

A.   **The stones are rolling.**
              ↑Verb

Adjective | **Noun**

B.   **Rolling**   **stone** **gathers no moss.**

Verb + Ing | **Participle** **(Present Participle)**

Adjective | **Noun**

C.   The **broken** **windows** need to be repaired.

Verb 3rd Form | **Participle**   (Past Participle)

Adjective | **Noun**

D.   **Having written** **letters,** she went to the post office.

Perfect Participle

Kinds of Participles

1. Present Participle   **2. Past Participle**   **3. Perfect Participle**

Present participle	Past participle	Perfect participle
Playing	Played	Having played
Speaking	Spoken	Having spoken
Closing	Closed	Having closed
Catching	Caught	Having caught
Practising	Practised	Having practised
Preaching	Preached	Having preached
Writing	Written	Having written
Clearing	Cleared	Having cleared

Verb 1st form	Verb 2nd form	Verb 3rd form	Verb 4th form	Verb 5th form
Go	went	gone	going	goes
Write	wrote	written	writing	writes

Present Participle

When **Ing form of a Verb** does the work of an **Adjective**, it is called **Present Participle**.

Ex : A boat is [**sinking**] (Verb) in the river.

1. Nobody can save a [**sinking**] (Adjective / Present Participle) [**boat .**] (Noun)

2. I saw your servant with a [**sleeping**] (Adjective / Present Participle) [**bag.**] (Noun)

3. Nobody can catch a [**running**] (Adjective / Present Participle) [**car.**] (Noun)

4. Saniya Mirza is trying to win a [**losing**] (Adjective / Present Participle) [**match.**] (Noun)

5. Krish is a [**rising**] (Adjective / Present Participle) [**star**] (Noun) of our country.

6. I want to buy a [**dancing**] (Adjective / Present Participle) [**doll**] (Noun) for my daughter.

7. You need a [**walking**] (Adjective / Present Participle) [**stick**] (Noun) to cross this road.

Past Participle

It is the third form of a **Verb** that does the work of an **Adjective.**

        I have **spoken** about you.
           ↑Verb

1. | **Adjective** | **Noun** |
   Spoken | **English** | is an important part of our daily life.
   ↑ **Past Participle.**

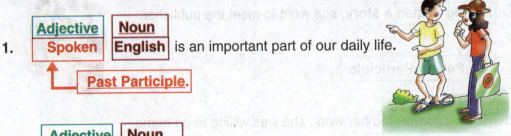

2. | **Adjective** | **Noun** |
   Written | **English** | must be grammatically correct .
   ↑ **Past Participle.**

3. | **Adjective** | **Noun** |
   Covered | **body** | was taken to the hospital .
   ↑ **Past Participle.**

4. He is fighting a | **Adjective** | **Noun** | of his life .
   lost | **battle**
   ↑ **Past Participle**

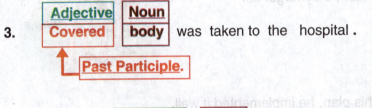

5. This is a | **Adjective** | **Noun** | for the next project.
   rewritten | **story**
   ↑ **Past Participle**

7. Nobody knows about the | **Adjective** | **Noun** |
   hidden | **truth.**
   ↑ **Past Participle**

8. Nobody can join a | **Adjective** | **Noun** |
   broken | **heart.**
   ↑ **Past Participle**

Perfect Participle

When **Having + Verb 3rd form** is used to show that an action is completed, it is 'Perfect Participle'.

1. **Having written** a **story**, she went to meet the publisher.

   Perfect Participle

2. **Having completed** her work, she was willing to go home.

   Perfect Participle
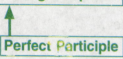

3. **Having been** to London, they forgot us.
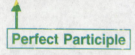

   Perfect Participle

4. **Having prepared** his plan, he implemented it well.

   Perfect Participle

5. **Having corrected** all the mistakes, she published her book.
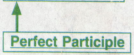

   Perfect Participle

6. **Having understood** the fact, they planned for a new project.

   Perfect Participle

7. **Having broken** all the records, he wrote his autobiography.
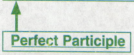

   Perfect Participle
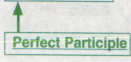

Gerund

When a 'Verb' acts like a 'Noun', it is a Gerund.

Example:

Verb

He is **swimming** in the pool .

Noun

1.   **Swim**ming is a good exercise.

        Gerund

Noun

2.   He likes **wal**king in the morning.

            Gerund

Noun

3.   **Dan**cing is a good exercise.

            Gerund

Noun   **Noun**

4.   **Dy**ing is better than **beg**ging.

       Gerund   **Ger**und

Noun

5.   She enjoys **sing**ing in the evening.

            Gerund

Noun

6.   Nobody is allowed for **smo**king.

            Gerund

Noun   **Noun**

7.   I feel that **talk**ing is **bor**ing.

            Gerund   **Ger**und

EXERCISE NO. 28-A

Find out 'Gerunds' & 'Participles'. Write about the kind of 'Participle' also.

1. Having taken medicine, he survived.
2. Hearing a noise, the child cried loudly.
3. Speaking in public is not easy.
4. Deserted by his friends, he lost his hope.
5. Smoking is not good for health.
6. Having eaten food, I feel better now.
7. He is the most promising staff in my office.
8. Do you see a moving bus in the market ?
9. We saw a young man who had lost his thinking power.
10. This sleeping fellow cannot continue the job.
11. Having eaten food, he ate medicine.
12. Having lost his money, he went to bank.
13. Jack and Rose died in a sinking ship.
14. A broken arrow cannot hit the target.
15. This writing pad is very cheap.
16. He has found the lost bag at his home.
17. I want a bottle of drinking water to quench my thirst.
18. The lost child was crying for his parents.
19. Having corrected all his mistakes, he can prove his innocence.
20. Having lost the battle, he was preparing for a war.
21. Having prepared his project, he went to bank for the finance.
22. I would like to have a written proposal from you.
23. You must repair the leaking pot immediately.
24. An ambition cannot be created with the pieces of broken dreams.
25. They need to buy a sleeping bag for the travelling purposes.
26. Having known about the accident, he wept bitterly.
27. The packed food is not good for health.
28. This is my drawing room where I listen music.
29. Having helped him, he can continue his social work.
30. She is the rising star of this college.

UNFULFILLED CONDITION

IF CLAUSE

IF CLAUSE	**PRINCIPAL CLAUSE**
1. Simple Present ⟶	Simple Future
2. Simple Past ⟶	Would / Should
3. Present Perfect ⟶	Future Perfect
4. Past Perfect ⟶	Should / Would have

Example:

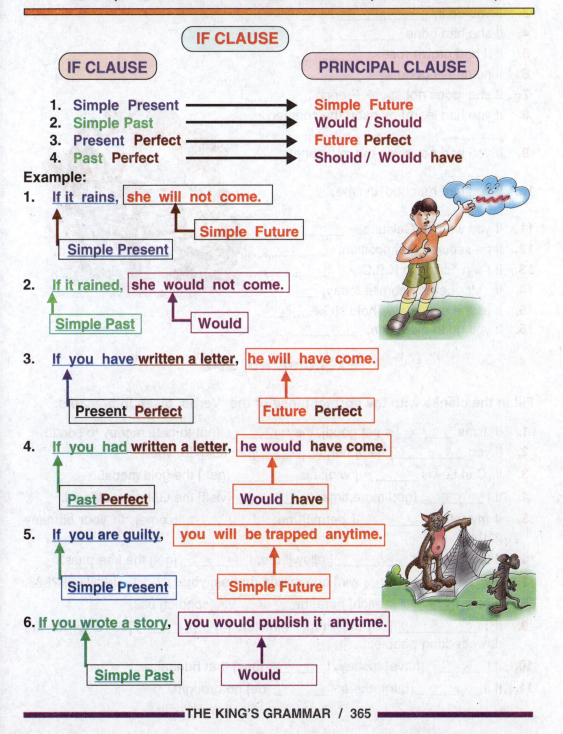

1. If it rains, she will not come.
   Simple Present → Simple Future

2. If it rained, she would not come.
   Simple Past → Would

3. If you have written a letter, he will have come.
   Present Perfect → Future Perfect

4. If you had written a letter, he would have come.
   Past Perfect → Would have

5. If you are guilty, you will be trapped anytime.
   Simple Present → Simple Future

6. If you wrote a story, you would publish it anytime.
   Simple Past → Would

EXERCISE NO. 29-A

Complete the following sentences, keeping in mind the tenses to be used:

1. If they do not obey us, _____.
2. If the criminal had not pleaded guilty, _____.
3. If you do it, _____.
4. If she had gone, _____.
5. If I had grown roses, _____.
6. If he does not do well, _____.
7. If she does not speak French ,_ _____.
8. If you had learnt by heart the chapter, _____.
9. If you had not given me my money,_ _____.
10. If you had reached in time, _____.
11. If you went to Calcutta, _____.
12. If he secures first position, _____.
13. If I win 1crore in K.B.C., _____.
14. If Mr. Lewis comes today, _____.
15. If all the employees held strike,_____.
16. If you go to meet him, _____.

EXERCISE NO. 29-B

Fill in the blanks with the correct tense of the 'Verbs' given in brackets:

1. If films _____[is not good], they _____[not to get] money to see it.
2. If you _____[help] her, I _____ [not talk] to you.
3. If Carl Lewis _____ [win], he _____ [get] the gold medal.
4. If I _____ [get] more time, I _____ [visit] the Gateway of India.
5. If my father _____ [permit] me, I _____ [come] to your birthday party.
6. If the manager _____ [allow] me, I _____ [get] the free pass.
7. If you want _____ [win] one million rupees, you _____ [dial] 6352888.
8. If he _____ [reach] here, he _____ [contact] us.
9. If I _____ [be] the Prime Minister, I_____ [do] a lot for the downtrodden people.
10. If I _____ [have] money, I _____ [buy] that bungalow.
11. If it _____ [rain], there _____ [be] no drought.

12. If she _____ [sign] the agreement, her father _____ [be] happy.

13. If he _____ [cure], he _____ [come] to meet you.

14. If two or three persons_____ [come] with a high spiritual aim, the world _____ [fall] into their hands like a ripe peach.

15. If a sense of duty _____ [torture] a man, it also _____ [enable] him to achieve prodigies.

16. If the judge_____ [punish] Jack, he _____ [be] more furious.

17. If the lion _____ [see] me, he _____ [move] towards his cave.

18. If the Board _____ [test] my potential, I_____ [selected] easily.

PREPOSITION

Preposition = **Pre** + **Position**

Pre = **Before** (or) **Beginning**

Subject

Subject is used in the beginning of a sentence.

Preposition tells us about the position of a subject / agent in a sentence.

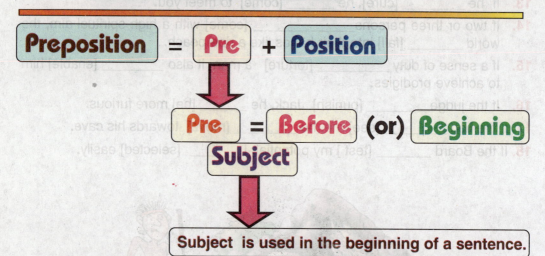

Example:

Subject

Miss Oak is sitting **under** **the tree**.

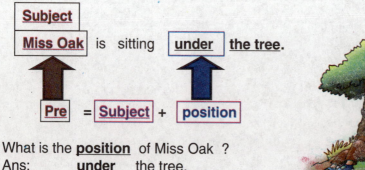

Pre = **Subject** + **position**

What is the **position** of Miss Oak ?
Ans: **under**   the tree.

Ex:

Subject	Preposition

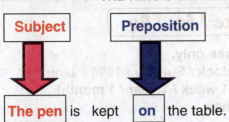

The pen is kept **on** the table.

What is the **position** of the pen?

Ans: **On** the table.

Ex:

You have kept your money in the bank.

What is the **position** of your money?

Ans: **In** the bank.

Uses of Preposition

Preposition of motion

To – Indicates motion.

1. She goes to school every day.
2. He returns back **to** his house.

In + **to** = **Into**

In = Inside | to = Motion

The tiger enters into the jungle. (Inside with motion)

On + To = Onto

Anybody [or] anything with motion comes and stays.

1. The mouse jumped <u>onto</u> the table [one table to other one]

Up + To = Upto

[In motion from down to up and then stay at a place.]
The cat climbed <u>upto</u> the tree.

Since / For / By

Both are used in Perfect Tenses only.
Since = Point of time. [5 O' clock / Sunday / 1996 / January]
For = Period of time [1 hour / 1 week / 1 year / 1 month]
by + time = Future Perfect Tense

1. She **had started** creating problems since   **last** Monday.
      ↑**Past Perfect**   ↑**Point of time.**

2. You **have been writing** a letter   **for** 2 hours.
      ↑**Present Perfect Continuous**   ↑**Period of time.**

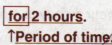

3. They **will have completed** the work **by** 1999.
       Future Perfect Tense↑   ↑**Point of time**

4. My brother **has solved** his problem **since** January.
       Present Perfect↑   **Point of time**↑

5. You **had been singing** a song   **for** 10 minutes.
      ↑**Past Perfect Continuous**   ↑**Period**

Between & Among

Between = In the middle of two persons, things etc..
Among = More than two persons, things etc..
1. Radha is sitting between **Sita & Gita** [two persons]
                        [1]   [2]

2. The politician is standing among **the crowd.** [more than 2 persons]
3. My bungalow is located between **the hospital** and **the school**. [Two]
4. The chair is kept among **so many tables**. [Many]

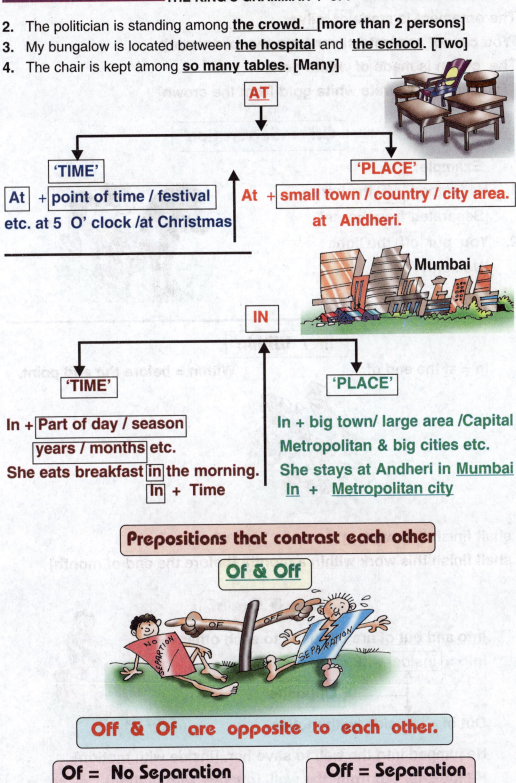

AT

'TIME'

At + point of time / festival
etc. at 5 O' clock /at Christmas

'PLACE'

At + small town / country / city area.
at Andheri.

Mumbai

IN

'TIME'

In + Part of day / season
years / months etc.
She eats breakfast in the morning.
In + Time

'PLACE'

In + big town/ large area /Capital
Metropolitan & big cities etc.
She stays at Andheri in Mumbai
In + Metropolitan city

Prepositions that contrast each other

Of & Off

Off & Of are opposite to each other.

Of = No Separation   **Off = Separation**

The ornament is made of silver.

[You cannot separate silver from the ornament]

The crown is made of white gold.

[You cannot separate white gold from the crown]

Off : Separation

Example:

1. He jumped off the horse.

    [Separated from horse]

2. You put off the light.

    [No light]

In / Within

In = at the end of   **Within = before the end point.**

I shall finish this work <u>in</u> a month. [end of month]

I shall finish this work <u>within</u> a month. [before the end of month]

Into & Out of

<u>Into</u> and <u>out of</u> are opposite to each other.

Into = inside with motion.

Opposite

Out of = outside with motion.

He jumped into the well to save her. [inside with motion]

He took her out from the well. [outside with motion]

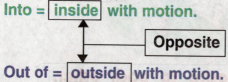

Under & Over

They are opposite to each other.

Under = down = without touching (upper) part.

Opposite

Over = up = without touching (lower) part.

1. The book is lying under the table.

   [Book is not in touch with the table]

2. The bridge is over the river.

For / Against

They have opposite meanings

For = In favour of / Support

She has kept fish for you.

Against = Oppose.

He is always against his friends.
[Oppose]

Similar Types of Prepositions

Differences

Below

Below = **Lower than**. [anywhere]

His leg is defective <u>below</u> the knees.

Under

Under = **Vertically lower**.

She is sitting <u>under</u> the tree.

To

<u>To</u> = <u>destination</u>

She goes to school.

Towards

<u>Towards</u> = <u>direction</u>

She goes towards school and met his friend on the way.
[She does not reach the school]

Above

Above = Higher than. [Anywhere]
There is a camp at the hilltop above the valley.

Over [Both indicate higher than]

Over = Vertically higher.
If you stand under this tree you will find a bunch of mangoes over your head.

Beside

Beside = near.

My house is located beside the school. [near the school].

Besides

Besides = in addition to.
She wants to buy pens besides pencils.

By

By = Passive voice for person.
The lion is killed by Harry.
[Passive Voice]

With

With = instrument.
He killed a tiger with a gun.
[instrument].

Behind

Behind = Place

She always stands <u>behind</u> Carol in the house. [Place]

After

After = time.

My brother will come after <u>5 O' clock</u>. [time]

Opposite

Opposite = Facing each other.

Peter is standing <u>opposite</u> to James. (Facing each other) [Opposite direction]

In front of

In front of = Same direction

Peter is standing <u>in front of</u> James. [Both are facing same direction].

During

During + Noun or Adjective

Noun

I was sleeping during the match.

While (Conjunction)

While + Subject & Verb

Subject | Verb

I did not say anything <u>while</u> I was playing.

Along

She is walking along the seashore.
[Parallel]

Across

The old man swam across the river.
[From one side to another]

By   [Nearness]   About

Hick sits <u>by</u> the fire.   She is <u>about</u> to catch the bus.

Than = Comparison

Sony is more intelligent than Dick.

Through = Across /in the interior of

You went <u>through</u> sufferings.
The bus is passing <u>through</u> the tunnel. [From one side to the another]

Beyond

This work is <u>beyond</u> my capacity.
Your English is <u>beyond</u> his understanding.

Up to

Up = 'Higher' To = Motion
My brother climbs <u>up to</u> the top of the hill.

Day

On + day = on Monday / on Friday / on Friday morning.

[in = number + period]

Ex : in + number + day / week / month / year etc. / hours.

1. I shall write a letter <u>in</u> 4 days.

2. He will finish his project <u>in</u> 2 years.

3. You have to solve the problem <u>in</u> a month.

'For' shows the meaning of :

1. In spite of — | For | your silly mistakes, I have forgiven you.

2. Exchange — I would like to have oranges | for | mangoes.

3. Reason — Your brother is imprisoned | for | a crime.

4. Devotion — I have born to die | for | my country.

5. Purpose — She works hard | for | exam.

6. Distance — They had run | for | 6 kilometres to win the gold medal.

7. In support to — I shall collect money | for | you.

8. | Abstract Noun |

Nehruji is well known for | his honesty. |

She has paid fine for | her carelessness. |

By + Automobile

[In course of going or travelling]

by bus / by car / by auto-rickshaw / by plane / by bike etc.

She travelled by a car to Delhi.

From.............to

[start to end point]

They stayed in New York from 1960 to 1966.

With + Instrument'

He repairs it with a screw driver.

She has cut vegetables with a knife.

By / with = Manners

You have to complete your work with courage.

My brother knows the whole story by heart.

From + Source

We get more energy <u>from</u> green vegetables.

I have received your letter <u>from</u> the post office.

By + Measurement

My brother is shorter than her   <u>by 2 inches</u>.

She could not win the race   <u>by 3 metres</u>.

An Easy Approach To Preposition

Preposition relating to Person

Noun + Preposition + Person

1. **Authority over a person.**
   The Principal has an **authority over his staff** .
   ↑a person

2. **Bargain with a person.**
   She bargains **with a shopkeeper** .
   ↑a person

3. **Complaint against a person.**
   The society members have **a complaint against John** .
   ↑a person

4. **Confidence in a person.**
   We have **confidence in Mr. Murphy.**
   ↑a person

5. **Disgrace to a person.**
   My son is a **disgrace to me.**
   ↑a person

6. **Duty to a person.**
   You should work hard. It is a **duty to God.**
   ↑a person

7. **Quarrel between two persons.**
   There was an unnecessary **quarrel between Peter & Paul.**
   ↑a person

8. **Quarrel with a person.**
   I had **a quarrel with my brother** regarding this project.
   ↑a person

9. **Power over a person.**
   The director has **a power over a staff** to take action any time.
   ↑a person

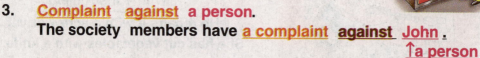

10. **Hatred** **for** a person.
Hitler had **hatred** **for** a **Yahoodi** named Britanicus.
↑a person

11. **Love** **for** a person.
I have deep **love** **for** **my colleague**.
↑ a person

12. **Enmity** **with** a person.
You must maintain **the enmity** **with** your enemy .
↑ a person

13. **Correspondence** **with** a person.
John Keats has a **correspondence** **with** Peter.
↑ a person

14. **Connection** **with** a person.
The capital punishment has a straight **connection** **with** the President.
↑ a person

Verb + Preposition + Person.

15. **Apply** **to** a person.
I have **applied** **to** the Principal for this post.
Verb ↑   ↑ a person

16. **Belongs** **to** a person.
This house **belongs** **to** William Wordsworth.
Verb ↑   ↑ a person

17. **Plot** **against** a person.
Macduff **plotted** **against** Macbeth in order to kill him.
Verb ↑   ↑ a person

18. **Demand** something **from** a person.
You should **demand** your salary **from** your boss .
Verb ↑   ↑ a person

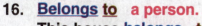
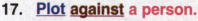

19. **Buy** something <u>from</u> a person.
We can <u>buy</u> a car <u>from</u> Mr. Lara
    <u>Verb</u> ↑   ↑ <u>a person</u>

20. **Agree** <u>with</u> a person.
The staff members were <u>agreed</u> <u>with</u> Paul.
                  <u>Verb</u> ↑   ↑ <u>a person</u>

21. **Talk** <u>to</u> a person.
The candidates can <u>talk</u> <u>to</u> <u>the examiner</u>.
            <u>Verb</u> ↑ ·↑ <u>a person</u>

22. **Interfere** <u>with</u> a person.
You should not <u>interfere</u> <u>with</u> <u>him</u> regarding Philosophy.
            <u>Verb</u> ↑   ↑ <u>a person</u>

23. **Enquire** <u>about</u> a person.
Anybody can <u>enquire</u> <u>about</u> <u>your lost friend</u>.
          <u>Verb</u> ↑   ↑ <u>a person</u>

24. **Hide** something <u>from</u> a person.
You cannot <u>hide</u> this fact <u>from</u> <u>me</u>.
         <u>Verb</u> ↑   ↑ <u>a person</u>

Adjective + Preposition + Person.

25. **Angry** <u>with</u> a person.
Mr. Baker was <u>angry</u> <u>with</u> Simon regarding his behaviour.
      <u>Adjective</u> ↑   ↑ <u>a person</u>

26. **Responsible** <u>to</u> a person.
You must be <u>responsible</u> <u>to</u> <u>your family members</u>.
         <u>Adjective</u> ↑   ↑ <u>a person</u>

27. Related <u>to</u> a person
These social workers are <u>related</u> <u>to</u> Mrs. Anne .
               <u>Adjective</u> ↑   ↑ <u>a person</u>

Preposition relating to thing

Noun + Preposition + thing

Thing = All that you can think about.

28. Decision on something.
The Jury has got the final <u>decision</u> <u>on</u> <u>bank robbery</u>.
↑Noun ↑thing (incident)

29. Experience in a thing.
I have three years of <u>experience</u> <u>in</u> <u>teaching</u>.
Noun↑

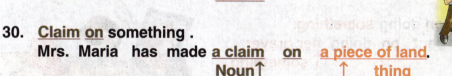

30. Claim on something .
Mrs. Maria has made <u>a claim</u> <u>on</u> <u>a piece of land</u>.
Noun↑ ↑ thing

31. Doubt about a thing.
Caesar had <u>a doubt</u> <u>about</u> <u>the murder conspiracy</u>.
Noun↑ ↑ thing

32. Complaint about a thing.
I have <u>a complaint</u> <u>about</u> <u>your old car</u>.
Noun↑ ↑ thing

Verb + Preposition + Thing

33. Search for something.
Maria is <u>searching</u> <u>for</u> <u>her books</u> in the library.
Verb ↑ ↑something

34. Quarrel over something.
The football team <u>quarrelled</u> <u>over</u> <u>the football</u> to be used for the match.
Verb ↑ ↑ something

35. Hope for something.
My teachers have <u>hoped</u> <u>for</u> <u>my success</u>.
Verb↑ ↑something

36. Blame somebody for something.
Peter cannot <u>blame</u> <u>Joy</u> <u>for</u> <u>his failure</u>.
Verb ↑ ↑something

37. **Ask for a thing.**
    Miss Oak is <u>asking</u> **for** <u>a drink</u> in the party.
          <u>Verb</u> ↑   ↑something

38. **Long for anything.**
    Miss Batra is <u>longing</u> **for** <u>a world record</u>.
          <u>Verb</u> ↑   ↑ something

Preposition + thing.

39. **Bent <u>on</u> doing something.**
    She <u>bent</u> <u>on</u> <u>doing</u> <u>her prayer</u>.
                ↑ something

40. **Determined <u>on</u> doing something.**
    Kika is <u>determined</u> <u>on</u> <u>getting</u> <u>her crown</u>.
               ↑ something

41. **Angry <u>at</u> a thing.**
    My teacher is <u>angry</u> <u>at</u> <u>my behaviour</u>.
               ↑ something

42. **Amazed <u>at</u> anything.**
    George was <u>amazed</u> <u>at</u> <u>my performance</u>.
               ↑ something

43. **Responsible <u>for</u> a thing.**
    The driver is <u>responsible</u> <u>for</u> <u>the accident</u>.
               ↑ something

44. **Tired <u>of</u> doing something.**
    Mr. Newbolt is tired <u>of</u> getting <u>his goal</u>.
               ↑ something

PERSON / THING / PLACE

45. Attack <u>on</u> a place.
The terrorists had <u>attacked</u> <u>on</u> the World Trade Centre.
                       ↑   a place

46. Control <u>over</u> a person or a thing.
The commander should have <u>control</u> <u>over</u>   his soldiers.
                       ↑ person

47. Reference <u>to</u> <u>a thing</u>.
This is the reference <u>to</u>   the context of the poem.
                ↑ thing (anything)

48. Compete <u>with</u> a person or a thing.
John Sina can <u>compete</u> <u>with</u>   any wrestler.
                   ↑ person

49. Attach <u>with</u> a person or a thing.
Ann was <u>attached</u> <u>with</u> <u>her friends</u> in the time of need.
                    ↑ person

50. Laugh <u>at</u> a person or a thing.
She <u>laughed</u> <u>at</u> <u>him</u> because of his foolish habits.
          ↑ person

51. Apply <u>to</u> a person or a thing.
The candidate will have to <u>apply</u> <u>to</u>   the principal for the post.
                         ↑ person

52. Acquainted <u>to</u> a person or a thing.
She is <u>acquainted</u>   <u>to</u>   my mother.
                  ↑ person

53. Accountable <u>to</u> a person or a thing.
You must be <u>accountable</u> <u>to</u>   the judge regarding this case.
                     ↑ person

54. Send <u>for</u> a person or a thing.
Robby has to <u>send</u> an invitation card <u>for</u> Rick.
                                 ↑ person

ABSTRACT NOUN

55. Pity for the weak.
My teacher is pity for the weak students.
   Abstract Noun↑

56. Accusation of theft.
There is an accusation of theft against you.
        Abstract Noun ↑

57. Exception to a rule.
There is no exception to this rule in any book.
Abstract Noun ↑

58. Fine for an offence.
Dick will be fined for this offence anytime.
      Abstract Noun ↑

59. Obedience to order.
The students must have obedience to the order passed by the authorities.
      Abstract Noun ↑

60. Trust in honesty.
Mr. M. K. Gandhi used to trust in honesty.
     Abstract Noun ↑

61. Apologise for mistakes.
According to Plato one must apologise for the mistakes.
     Abstract Noun ↑

62. Candidate for election.
Mr. Batra is the most suitable candidate for the election .
     Abstract Noun ↑

63. Desire for happiness.
I would prefer to go to heaven as I have desire for happiness.
     Abstract Noun ↑

64. Excuse for a mistake.
Each culprit has an excuse for a mistake.
    Abstract Noun ↑

65. <u>Invitation</u> **for** a party.
Jesus had <u>an invitation</u> **for** a party in the evening.
Abstract Noun ↑

66. <u>Warning</u> **of** a <u>danger</u>.
There is a <u>warning</u> **of** danger near the checkpost.
Abstract Noun ↑

67. <u>Struggle</u> **against** <u>obstacles</u>.
Hercules struggled **against** all the <u>obstacles</u>.
Abstract Noun ↑

68. **Satisfied** <u>with</u> <u>an achievement</u>.
I am not **satisfied** <u>with</u> my <u>achievement</u>.
Abstract Noun ↑

69. **Qualified** <u>for</u> <u>a job</u>.
Martin is well qualified for <u>the job</u>.
Abstract Noun ↑

EXERCISE NO. 30-A

Fill in the blanks with suitable <u>Prepositions</u> :

1. Jack acted _____ my advice.
2. We should act _____ our conscience.
3. Consistent hard work and patience are the key _____ success.
4. This road leads _____ Cuttack.
5. We should not look _____ the things that belong to others.
6. The girl laughed _____ the joker.
7. Think _____ the devil and the devil is here.
8. He was run down _____ a car.
9. The file was lying _____ the table.
10. The mouse was jumping _____ the table.
11. There is a forecast _____ rain.
12. He is like a frog _____ the well.
13. Robin died _____ Diarrhea.
14. They sacrificed their life _____ their country.
15. I have no taste _____ Gazal.
16. The girl is afraid _____ the cockroach.
17. Deepa is fond _____ landscape painting.

18. This building was built _____ the Raheja group.
19. The black dog jumped _____ the well.
20. The thief jumped _____ the low wall of the compound.
21. She took offence _____ his brother's remark.
22. The teacher objected _____ your words.
23. Rick came _____ our house _____ a discussion.
24. Mr. Rao went _____ the airport _____ see his friend.
25. Tomorrow the guest will arrive _____ 5 o'clock.
26. The final exam is going _____ be held _____ Monday.
27. Mr.Pradhan hails _____ Orissa.
28. Mrs. Tony belongs _____ a noble family _____ Madhya Pradesh.
29. My boss will return _____ a month.
30. Please listen _____ me.
31. You are requested _____ listen what the speaker says.
32. The boys did not pay attention _____ what the supervisor said.
33. Everybody must be loyal _____ their motherland.
34. An ideal citizen abides _____ the rules of the constitution.
35. Papers are sold _____ the dozen.
36. The beggar died _____ Aids.
37. Surya Babu is _____ debt _____ head _____ tail.
38. I can make neither head nor tail _____ what you say.
39. They went _____ after adopting the other way.
40. Utkarsha made _____ her mind _____ become a writer.
41. Mr Greg has made _____ his deficiency in English.
42. Miss Dolly is always busy _____ reading her books.
43. The young man killed the lion _____ a rod.
44. Berhampur is not very far _____ the sea.
45. I have made a contract _____ him.
46. What are you looking _____ ?
47. They are slaves who fear _____ speak.
48. She is well versed _____ psychology.
49. The Mughals often quarrelled _____ themselves.
50. Look _____ his face.

EXERCISE NO. 30-B

Fill in the blanks with suitable Prepositions :

1. Distribute these sweets _____ the children.
2. She married him _____ money.
3. Never work _____ your capacity.

4. We should try _____ live _____ our means.

5. It is not true that the study of science tends _____ atheism.

6. I am sick _____ the whole business.

7. _____ the history of mankind, there has hardly been an era _____ total peace.

8. He complained _____ the Principal _____ me.

9. Cut your coat according _____ your cloth.

10. We live _____ deeds, not _____ years.

11. She stood ___ the window.

12. The art of photography was invented_____ Louis Jacquos.

13. A man is known _____ the company he keeps.

14. The collector is the chief officer_____ the district.

15. Nothing will come out _____ this project .

16. Helen is no match _____ Simron.

17. People _____ different castes live in India.

18. He was born _____ Solapur, _____ Maharashtra.

19. Dick lives _____ Ahmedabad.

20. My parents live _____ Washington D.C.

21. She should be able _____settle your disputes.

22. The tiger pounced _____ the fox.

23. This way, you can kill two birds _____ one stone.

24. The robber was killed _____ a sword.

25. The summer vacation will commence _____ next month.

26. There is a wide economic gulf _____ the rich and poor people.

27. Our building is located _____ the riverside.

28. _____ me, four other travellers were there _____ the inn.

29. The English established 13 colonies _____ North America.

30. My house is infested _____ cockroach.

31. His remarks are nothing but only a conspiracy _____ get political mileage.

32. The path _____ glory is beset _____ uncountable difficulties.

33. Sweet music is beneficial _____ brain.

34. The king was wondered _____ the answer of the courtier.

35. All of us are dedicated_____ God.

36. Anne believes that her husband's death was caused _____malaria.

37. Totto-chan called the street musicians _____ the windows _____her classroom.

38. A flower is given _____ her as a reward _____her hard work.

39. Give _____ your bad habits.
40. Smoking is injurious _____ health.
41. My brother is addicted _____ brown sugar.
42. As a consequence _____ his misbehaviour, he was put _____ the bars.
43. Every worker will be entitled _____ extra salary for working overtime.
44. Anamika is blind _____ one eye.
45. Her mother was unaware _____ his deeds.
46. Her parents repent_____ his son's misdeeds.
47. She has no aptitude _____ maths.
48. Gandhiji was indifferent _____ praise.
49. Andrew is _____lazy _____ complete her work in time.
50. His greediness _____ money will never come to an end.

EXERCISE NO. 30-C.

Fill in the blanks with suitable <u>Prepositions</u> :

1. They took the old man _____ his house.
2. He has acted _____ confidence _____ your wishes.
3. I have no contact _____ the Chief Minister.
4. This medicine is an antidote _____ poison.
5. Beware _____ pickpockets.
6. He was disgusted _____ life.
7. The committee disapproves your ways _____ behaving _____ others.
8. Ravindra had _____ accept his foolishness.
9. The labourers were demanding _____ increase the salary.
10. The young man is busy _____ discussion.
11. Whom are you canvassing _____?
12. The magician showed magic _____ the audience.
13. My friend has got admission _____ the National Defence Academy.
14. Abha was absent _____ the office.
15. He has embarked _____ a new career.
16. My students are greatly devoted _____me.
17. The shopkeeper has accused me _____ theft.
18. Sam arrived ___the station just in time.
19. I have no pen ___write with.
20. They promised us ___supply paper___ the company.

21. Joseph was not invited_____ the party.

22. He has a complete trust_____ my brother.

23. She smiled ____my words.

24. I must insist ____a thorough inquiry.

25. Carol's passion _____dancing is well known.

26. The Red Fort is famous _____ its beauty.

27. I found a bird sitting _____ the branch _____a tree.

28. Trespassers are liable _____ be prosecuted.

29. You are liable _____ your brother's debts.

30. The scientist was distinguished _____ his great research works.

31. I am grateful _____ you _____ your kind help.

32. He was not concerned _____ what his mother had to say.

33. The Prime Minister is greatly concerned _____ the killing of more than 100 people in the accident.

34. The patient is now out _____ danger.

35. Illtutmish succeeded _____ getting the throne of Qutab-ud-din.

36. My father deals _____ gold.

37. I shall talk _____ him at the appropriate time.

38. The police entrusted the task____ finding out my daughter.

39. He is confident_____ his success.

40. The cricket control board took a strong step _____ the remarks____ Tony.

41. My father has invested all his money _____ shares.

42. He has been provided _____ the powers of a magistrate.

43. I shall talk _____ him _____ this matter.

44. His reputation, as a good teacher, is well known _____ all the people.

45. He is ignorant ____ the customs prevailing there.

46. The government has shabbily treated _____the victims ____cyclone.

47. After this, we will proceed _____ Paris .

48. He donates food and clothing _____ the poor people.

49. Mr. Barry has invested all his money _____ I.T. sector.

50. Miss Dolly is very honest _____ her dealings.

EXERCISE NO. 30-D

Fill in the blanks with the suitable Prepositions :

1. He has no ill will____ your friends.
2. The teacher cannot permit you _____ go with him.
3. She is bound _____ come.
4. She is not depending _____others.
5. He is a native _____ America.
6. Mr. Paul has insisted me _____provide suggestion _____her next project.
7. Peter had been teaching me _____ the last two years.
8. The police charged him_____theft.
9. She is pleased_____ know the truth.
10. Taruna expects me _____ return soon.
11. She felt ashamed _____his conduct.
12. The parents are very glad to know _____the success story ____ their children.
13. She had died ____ the age of sixty.
14. Am I eligible _____this post?
15. Let us wait _____him.
16. Beware _____pickpockets.
17. Rome was not built _____a day.
18. Do not cry _____spilt milk.
19. Her opinion is indifferent _____me.
20. The ball fell _____the well.
21. The mouse jumped _____the table.
22. The seminar will be over_____ 5 :00 p.m.
23. The church is located _____the library.
24. Would you like _____read this magazine?
25. Have you ever contributed an article _____any newspaper?
26. Do not be angry _____anybody.
27. Your attitude is hostile _____ me.
28. Please look _____the matter.
29. The industrialist's carelessness resulted _____his failure.
30. The building has been reconstructed _____its legitimate owner.
31. She has no inclination _____ study.
32. I intended _____help him.
33. Do not stare _____ women.
34. He withdraws his name _____the contest.
35. Do not argue _____ me _____this matter.
36. They requested me _____ justify his idea.

37. What do you think _____ yourself?
38. He fell a prey _____ the enemy's net.
39. He began to interfere _____ this matter.
40. What can you do _____ me?
41. He is confident _____ his success.
42. The Chief Guest conferred him _____ the title _____ "The King's Grammar."
43. Lack of unity is a threat _____ freedom.
44. All system _____ government is imperfect.
45. It is not easy _____ tell you what our culture is.
46. She is fond _____ singing.
47. Do you have any interest _____ history?
48. You cannot find any exception _____ this rule.
49. Gandhiji is remembered _____ his ideology.

COMPOSITION

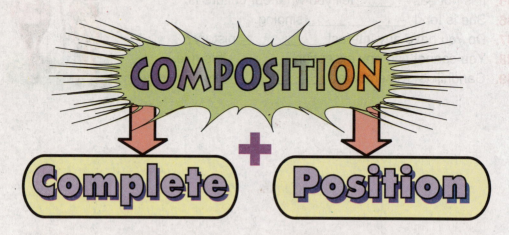

Composition tells about the complete position of a topic

(A) ESSAY WRITING

Most of the students think that writing an essay is a very boring task as well as difficult. The weak impression of the students regarding essay writing makes them away from creativity. So cultivation of the importance of essay writing among the students is highly viable now-a-days. Writing an essay is like the construction of a building, step by step on a firm foundation.

Lexically, essay means to make an attempt or to try. Essay writing means an attempt to put your ideas and thoughts in the form of · words on a given topic. Essay writing is designed in the school and college curriculum and also in competitive examination to test the students' stock of ideas, his thoughts, opinions, beliefs, and proficiency in current events and secondly his ability in the language, presentation, grammar, word power etc. A student can secure more marks in an essay if his presentation is systematic, free from errors and mistakes and a thorough knowledge of the topic. Now-a-days most of the students, those who are from vernacular schools, lag behind in English Grammar. Though they have the ability to conceptualize the matter, fet lack of sufficient knowledge in English debarrs them in presenting the essay in a beautiful style.

Essay being defined as a loose sally of the mind, an irregular and undigested piece, not a regular and orderly composition, according to Dr. Johnson. There is no concrete definition so far as essay is concerned but after collecting all the facts of different essayists together, we can define essay in the following way:

"An essay is a thought of the heart, creation of the mind and presentation of the language. It should be original, free from bias and presented in a systematic manner."

No doubt, there are diverse subjects. Students may not be proficient in every subjects. Average students are not expected to know much. There are some essays which need technical knowledge or some factual information. During every exam, the examiner always offers a list of subjects of varied interests. The students can choose their favourite topics which suit them according to their interest. It is necessary to have lots of exercises on diverse topics to write a satisfactory essay on any subject. Let us have a classification of essays.

Essays can be classified as follows:

1. Descriptive Essays:

The simplest type of essay, which consists of a description of a place, person thing etc., is called a descriptive essay.

Ex: A River, A Football Match, An Excursion, etc.

2. Narrative Essays:

These essays consist of narrations during : a journey, an incident, a natural calamity, an accident you have witnessed, story, etc.

Ex: A journey by train, A cyclone you have witnessed, etc.

3. Reflective Essays:

Reflective essays are those essays which express the writer's thought or reflection on various aspects of life :

(a) Social and domestic aspects, e.g. Friendship,Education and educational problems., Social and cultural, Customs and tradition.

(b) Political aspects, e.g., Democracy, Elections, War, World Peace, Liberalism.

(c) Scientific and religious aspects, e.g., Science and war, Atoms for peace, The Purpose of life, Science and religion, Religion in life.

4. Imaginative Essays:

Imaginary essays are those essays where the writer has to represent a situation or think himself in which he has never been before and describe what he would do in such circumstances,

Ex: 'If I were the Prime Minister of India', 'If there is no Electricity', 'Life without Newspapers', 'An Autobiography of a Pen'.

5. Biographical Essays:

Essays based on life of eminent personalities excelled in fields like politics, social services, culture, science, art, economy, etc are included in biographical essays.

6. Expository Essays:

Expository Essays are based on a theory or doctrine.

Ex: Evolution of man, Karma, Birth and Death or topics on literature etc.

How to Begin an Essay:

1. Introduction

2. With a Definition

3. With a Quotation

4. With a Question

5. With a Proverb or a Striking Statement

6. With a Piece of Vivid Description

Some useful hints on essay writing:

1. Choose the essay which, according to you, is easier to write and have a clear idea.

2. Try to understand the scope of the selected essay like " The Evils of Dowry." Here you are asked to write about the evils of dowry only therefore it would be better to concentrate on its evil aspects only. You should not include the origin, its sanctity or the government's bid to control it.

3. Think over the topic again and again, concentrate your mind and try to conceptualize your thoughts and ideas. Then jot down all the points that come to your mind in connection with the subject. You can also cite any story, examples, incidents or illustrations to write at first. It will arouse interest and curiosity to the examiner.

4. Arrange the facts in a logical manner, divide the entire topic into paragraphs. Do not write in a haphazard manner. In each paragraph, explain the point as you divide the whole subject into points.

5. Your sentences should be not too long. It may result in losing the connection and make the construction of the sentence.

6. Pay enough attention to grammar, punctuation and style. Slang and colloquial expressions should be avoided.

7. Keep in mind, the paragraphs should not be numbered and the heading must not be inserted within the body of the essay.

8. After the writing is over, revise thoroughly.

Here, we are only giving the outlines of a few essays. Follow them and write accordingly:

1. Your best friend.

i. Introduction **ii.** His habits   **iii.** His qualities you like the most

iv. His achievements **v.** Conclusion

2. **The Television**.

   i. Introduction **ii.** Invention   **iii.** Importance in our daily life

   iv. Its disadvantages **v.** Conclusion

3. **An Election Scene**.

   i. Introduction **ii.** Date and Time **iii.** Polling Station

   iv. Scene outside the polling station **v.** Casting votes **vi.** Conclusion

4. **Visit to a Historical Place**.

   i. Introduction – importance of historical places

   ii. Place you visited – its location, your passage to the location

   iii. Its historical importance

   iv. Description of the place

   v. Description of the monuments

   vi. Conditions at present

   vii. Conclusion

5. **A Journey by Train**.

   i. Introduction **ii.** Scene at the booking office **iii.** Scene at the platform
   iv. Description of the journey **v.** Conclusion

6. **Rabindra Nath Tagore**.

   i. Birth and parentage **ii.** Education   **iii.** Work as a poet **iv.** Work as a freedom fighter **v.** As an educationist **vi.** His qualities

   vii. Conclusion.

7. **The Role of Students in Modern India**

   a. Introduction **b.** Role of students in the freedom struggle **c.** Comparison of students with foreign students **d.** Becoming a true nationalist **e.** Bring national integration **f.** Take part in social services **g.** Raise the educational standard. **h.** Keep yourself away from corrupt politicians **i.** Conclusion.

8. **The Importance of Discipline**

   a. Introduction **b.** Importance of discipline in our life **c.** In armed forces **d.** In educational institutions **e.** In offices **f.** In social and political field **g.** Conclusion

9. **The Status of Women in India**

   a. Introduction **b.** Position in social sphere **c.** in education field **d.** in political field **e.** in industry & service sector **f.** Govt. schemes to raise the status of women **g.** Conclusion.

(B) LETTER WRITING

Letter writing is an art. All of us write letters. We write personal letters to friends and relatives, business letters, invitation, applications and so on. That is why, it is highly essential to cultivate the art of writing different kinds of letters.

There are different kinds of letters but certain common features are important:

1. The Heading

2. Greeting or Salutation

3. The body of the letter

4. Leave taking or subscription

5. The Address

1. The Heading: The heading can be written at the top left hand corner of the letter because of the vast use of computers . This consists of the writer's address and the date.

24,Monali Appt.,

Mumbai Central,

Mumbai-10.

April 17, 2000.

2. Greeting or Salutation: The form of salutation should be written according to the type of letter you write. It should be written below the address and date, beginning from the left hand side of the page and should be followed by a comma.

Example:

A. Father, mother, brother, sister, uncle, aunt, cousin –Here we can use only. "My dear" before the above words: "My dear Father", "My dear Uncle", "My dear Brother", etc.

B. The salutation to friends will be:

If he is not very intimate—Dear Mr. Suresh;

If he is more intimate—Dear Suresh;

If he is more intimate and affectionate— My Dear Suresh

C. The salutation to strangers will be : Dear Sir, Dear Madam

D. The salutation to superiors will be : Dear Sir or Sir

3. The Body of the letter : This is the main part of the letter. The language of the letter should be simple and in a natural style. It should be presented systematically. **Long letters should be divided into paragraphs. Write all what you want to say. Follow a formal manner in official correspondence but you may follow a familiar and colloquial style in personal letters.**

4. Leave taking or Subscription: After completing the body of the letter, one should write the leave taking phrase to the left side of the page and sign below it.

Example:

Yours ever,

Tom

A few examples of start and conclusion of private letters:

Start	End
My dear father	Yours affectionately
My dear mother	Your loving son
My dear brother	Your loving brother
My dear Hari	Your loving sister
Dear Ramesh	Your sincere friend

Close Your Letter with:

With love

Best regards

Best wishes

Cordially

Respectfully yours

Yours truly

Respectfully

Thanks

Take care

Sincerely yours

With oceans of honour

Thank you

Thanks

Regards

Sincerely

Important Note

1. While writing the address:

   a. Write Mr. before the name in case of a male

   b. Mrs. is used in case of a married woman

   c. Miss is used in case of an unmarried woman

   d. Messrs is used in case of a firm or company

Classification of Letters:

Personal letters
Invitations
Application
Letter to Newspaper

Personal letters

1. Write a letter to your mother telling her how you have fared in the annual examination.

705,Ram Darshan,
Lenin Sarani,
Kolkata-45.
April 20 1999

My dear mother,

I received your letter full of your soul touching love this morning. It has added a glory to my heart. Now I would like to tell you about my performance in the annual examination which is over. I have attempted all my papers very well.

I was not confident in English paper but the English paper was very easy. I hope to get 70% in it. Besides my better performance in Social Studies & Science, I have attempted Grammar very well. In the Science paper questions were not asked according to the syllabus but I have answered in a fairly and satisfactory manner.

Hoping that I would get your guidance and make my dream come true in my life, I would like to conclude my letter with an ocean of love and regards to you.

Your loving son,

Sunil

2. Write a letter to your friend congratulating him on his birthday.

08,Ekta Apts.
Malabar Hill,
Mumbai-6.
April 26, 2000.

Dear Monalisa,

Please accept my heartiest congratulation on your birthday and wish you many happy returns of the day. I wish this day to be as happy and gay as lily in May.

I didn't know what to send you as a present, but I have decided to gift you complete works of Shakespeare. I know your great veneration for literature. I hope you like the small gift I sent you today to convey my warm feelings.

Once again I convey my sincere greeting on this auspicious occasion.

Your sincere friend,

XYZ

3. Write a letter to your younger brother, who is a bookworm advising him to take part in games.

105 Government
Colony, Bandra,
Mumbai-54.

June 8, 2000
Dear Symonds,

     I received your letter yesterday with your progress report and came to know that you always keep yourself busy in your studies, sparing no time for games and other extra-curricular activities. It is not fair. You know it very well "All work and no play makes Jack a dull boy." I agree with you that study is very essential and should indeed be the main concern of the students' life, but study at the cost of health is not at all desirable. You should keep in mind that a sound mind in a healthy body can only act towards the positive direction.

     In school, equal importance has been given to the games and exercises as they are helpful to improve our health, develop our character and bring about an all-round development in our body and mind. We can develop our sportsman's spirit. It also teaches us to achieve the victory and defeat alike. We learn team spirit, discipline and quality of leadership from games and sports.

     So you are advised to take part in games as well as in studies and develop a balanced personality. I do hope you think seriously and adopt my advice positively in your life. It will glitter your life with the glory of achievements.

     Wishing you all the best.

     Yours lovingly,
     K. Shailja Rao

4. Reply to above:

M.G. Road,
Ahmedabad.
April, 27, 2000.

My dear Renu,

    Thanks for your birthday invitation reply card, your warm wishes and your small but splendid present. It is a book that everyone should read. I am very proud of it. You know that I am interested in literature and I am very eager to know more and more. Your presentation is a flame which lit fire in my heart regarding my literary feelings.

            Thanking you again with lots of best wishes.

  Your affectionate friend,
    Monalisa

5. Write a sympathizing letter to a friend on the death of his father.

111, Hi-Tech Appt,
Garodia Nagar,
Ghatkopar (E)
Mumbai-85

August 5, 1999.

My dear Kunal,

    I am grieved to hear the sad news about the death of your loving father. Your loss is immense and I do not know how to express myself in such a grief occasion. His death was an irreparable loss to you and your family. He has left responsibilities for you. May God give peace to his soul and courage to you in performing your duties and carrying out the ideals of your father.

    Kunal, I am always with you. If you need any kind of help from me, please do not hesitate in telling me.

With deepest sympathy.

Yours sincerely,
  XYZ

INVITATION

6. Write a letter of invitation to your marriage anniversary.

Mr. & Mrs. Mahapatra cordially invite Mr. & Mrs. Smith on the occasion of their marriage anniversary on Thursday, the 26th day of July, 2000 at 7 o' clock.

Mount Mary Road,

Hyderabad

20th July, 2000

7. Note of acceptance:

Mr. & Mrs. Smith have great pleasure in accepting the invitation of Mr. & Mrs. Mahapatra' s marriage anniversary celebration on Thursday, the 26th day of

July, at 7 o' clock.

12, Garden View Apartment
Begumpet
Hyderabad
20th July, 2000

8. Write a letter of invitation, inviting your friend and his family to a dinner.

Sharada Bhavan
Aarey Colony,
Mumbai-87.
June 18, 2000

My dear Sunetra,

    I have invited a few friends at dinner on next Sunday at 8.00 p.m. We' ll be very happy if you and your family join us. After dinner, we shall have a programme of antakshari competition. I do hope both of you will grace the occasion.

Yours very sincerely,
Pallavi

9. Note of acceptance

120, Oshiwara,
Mumbai-89.
18 June 2000

My dear Pallavi,

Thank you so much for your very kind invitation. My family will be very happy to attend the dinner. We look forward to a joyous gathering.

Very sincerely yours,

Sunetra

APPLICATION

1. Your college is situated very close to a busy street. The students and their parents find it difficult to cross due to the bad condition of the street and heavy traffic. Write a letter to the corporator in your area.

B/407, Sai Colony,
8, Worli Naka,
Mumbai-400 011.
18th Aug 2000

To,

The Municipal Corporator,
'D' Ward Office,
Brihanmumbai Municipal Corporation,
Worli Naka,
Mumbai-400011.

Dear Sir,

Worli Naka is the centre of all business activities and a number of schools and colleges are there. In the vicinity, a large number of people gather here for business purpose. It has become an area of heavy traffic. Besides this, the main road has been crumbled with potholes, cracks and bumps. Plying on this road has become very difficult. Crossing the road to reach St.George School and Wadia College has become almost impossible. Last July, a terrible accident had occurred in which five school boys died on the spot. I am sure, you are well aware of this incident.

I am sure, you will, with the help of the BMC, come up with solution. Kindly consider the matter and take immediate steps to overcome this problem.

Thanking You.

Yours sincerely,

Nom-de-plume

2. Read the following advertisement and prepare a letter of application for it. You do not have to prepare your bio-data.

SITUATION VACANT

Wanted Secondary Teachers for various schools run by Borivali Shikshana Prasaraka Mandal, Mumbai. Candidates must have passed B.Ed. The candidate must have a flair for teaching with fluency in English. Write giving details to **The Secretary, Borivali Shikshana Prasaraka Mandal, Borivali, Mumbai-85**

Bindu Darsan,
Niranjan Nagar,
Sishirakanta Marg,
Borivali-400085.
12th November 1999.

To,

The Secretary,
Borivali Shikshana Prasaraka Mandal, Borivali, Mumbai.

Ref: Your advertisement in " The Times of India" dated 11th November 1999.
Sub: Application for the post of a secondary teacher.

Dear Sir,

With reference to your advertisement in "The Times of India" dated 11th November 1999, I offer my candidature for the post of a secondary teacher in the school run by your esteemed trust.

I am an arts graduate from the University of Mumbai. I did my B.Ed. course from Indira Gandhi National Open University, New Delhi. I passed with a first class and an 'A' grade in practicals. I have completed my entire schooling through English medium. I can fluently speak English. My favourite hobbies are music and reading autobiographies. I have participated in a number of curricular and extra-curricular activities during my school and college days.

I have enclosed the copies of my testimonials with this application. I shall be happy if you give me an opportunity of an interview so that I may furnish you with more details.

Thanking You,

Yours sincerely,
  XYZ

Encl.: Five testimonials

3. Write a letter to the Deputy Superintendent of Police complaining about the anti-social activities in your area because of two bars in your area.

184, Govt. Colony,
Bandra,
Mumbai-400045.
30th June 2000.

To,
      The Deputy Superintendent of Police,
      Bandra Police Station,
      Mumbai-400045.

Dear Sir,

      Sub: Anti-social activities

      I, on behalf of the residents of Government Colony, Bandra, attract your attention that some anti-social elements in our area have increased to a great extent since last 15 days. You know that ours is a residential area. Because of the two bars, the atmosphere has been changed so much that people of our locality are unable to carry on their daily activities safely.

      Our society has become a centre of undesirable and anti-social activities. We also came to know that some people are engaged in smuggling drugs and it may addict many people in our locality. Women feel insecure to move about after it is dark. The bar owners have warned the people of serious consequences if they complain to the police.

      On behalf of all the residents, I appeal you to take immediate steps to curb these undesirable elements. We also request you to cancel the licence so that the residents can live peacefully.

Yours faithfully,
XYZ

4. Draft a letter to a social welfare organization seeking financial help for continuing further studies.

26,Azad Wadi,
Girgaon,
Mumbai-400 020.
26th June 2000.

To,
 The Secretary,
 The Bal Ashram Charitable Trust,
 N.G. Road,
 Chembur,
 Mumbai-400 071.

 Sub: Financial help

Dear Sir,

 I have passed my SSC examination this year, the result was declared on 7th June 2000. I have scored 90 % marks. I have secured 18th position in Mumbai Board. It is my long cherished desire to continue my studies in the Science stream to become a doctor. But my father, who is labourer, is unable to afford the high fees.

 I have come to know from the reliable sources that your 'Charitable Trust' helps needy students to continue their higher studies. May I request you to help me financially for pursuing my studies in Science? I need a form to apply for the financial help. I am enclosing a xerox copy of my SSC examination mark sheet and a letter from my headmaster recommending my case for financial help. I request you to help me financially on the basis of a loan or a scholarship, which will be refunded by me after I finish my studies and become self-reliant.

 Eagerly waiting for an early, favourable and positive reply from you.

Yours faithfully,
 XYZ
Encl. **1.** Copy of SSC mark sheet

 2. Headmaster's letter of recommendation

5. Write an application for the post of a clerk.

Sun view

Begumpet,

Hyderabad-45

2nd Oct, 1998.

To

      The Manager, (H.R)

      Datamatics Pvt. Ltd,

      Begumpet,

      Hyderabad-2.

Sub: For the post of a clerk .

Dear Sir,

    I have come to know through a reliable source that you have a vacancy for the post of a clerk in your esteemed organization. I want to apply for the same and prove my eligibility. Being a graduate in arts, I have computer knowledge also. I have been working in Pink Packaging Pvt. Ltd. for the last two years.

    Hoping that I shall get a chance to work under your kind control, I have enclosed my bio-data with this application.

Thanking you.

Yours faithfully,

XYZ

6. Write an application to get free studentship.

To,

        The Principal,

        Ruia College,

        Matunga,

        Mumbai-12.

Sub: For free studentship.

Respected Sir,

     I am a dedicated student of X std. I have got 88% in my previous examination but my poor financial condition is trying to snatch me away from the gift of education. My father is a farmer and his income is hardly enough to fulfil our basic needs.

     Most respectfully, I would like to request you to grant me free student, ship so that I can continue my study with zeal. Keeping in view the reason mentioned above, I am hoping for a positive response as an act of kindness to me.

Thanking you with the best regards.

Yours faithfully,

XYZ

7. Read the advertisement given below and write a letter in response to the advertisement published in "The Times of India."

<u>Accomodation Available</u>

For Bachelors 1 Room Kitchen Rs.1000, 2 Room Kitchen Rs. 2000,

3 Room Kitchen Rs. 3000 near Borivali Railway Station.

Contact – Bina Rao, B.R. Consultancy, Shan Appt.

Navghar Rd., Bhayander [E] Ph # 816 1112.

410, Megha Apt.,
Chandikala Road,
MHADA Colony,
Andheri [W].
2nd Dec 1999

To,

     The Proprietor,
     B.R.Consultancy,
     Shan Appt, Navghar Road,
     Bhayander [E]

Sub: For accommodation.

Dear Madam,

    Through the advertisement published in the "Times of India", I have come to know about the accommodation facilities. Being a bachelor, I am looking for a one-room kitchen and the quotation which has been mentioned in your advertisement suits me.

    I am a computer engineer, working for Sai-Mag Computers, located at Bhayander. It will be quite comfortable for me. I hope that you will provide me one room kitchen flat as soon as possible.

Thanking You,

Yours faithfully,

XYZ

8. Write a letter to your Principal for granting 7 day's leave, as you had been ill.

402, Reema Nagar,

Surabhi Rd,

Bandra [W]

Mumbai-57

4th Oct 1999

To,

The Principal,

Bhavan's College,

Andheri [W]

Mumbai-20

Sub: For Leave.

Respected Sir,

I am a regular student of X std, studying in your esteemed institution. My roll No. is 49. My achievement in the field of studies and my regularity in my classes is well known to my class teacher. Unfortunately, I had been ill and our family doctor had suggested for a complete bed rest.

So, I could not come to attend my lectures during 6th Oct.1999 to 12th Oct 1999. I shall be highly obliged if you grant me leave for my absence.

Date ....

Yours faithfully,

XYZ

9. Write a letter to the Zonal Secretary, B.S.E.S., complaining about frequent instances of power failure during examinations. Request him to restore normalcy in power supply.

78 Sahakar Complex,
Naigaon Cross Road,
Dadar-400 014.
18th March 2000

To,

The Zonal Secretary,
B.S.E.S.,
Dadar-400 014.

Dear Sir,

Sub : Frequent power failure in Naigaon Cross Road area.

I am a resident of Sahakar Complex, Naigaon Cross Road. My annual examination will be held on 20th March. I am finding it very difficult to prepare for my forthcoming exams as the power supply in our locality is frequently disturbed. Besides usual power cut, there is frequent power cut every day, so studying in the night is a nightmare.

Nobody understands that this way we cannot attempt well in the examination. None seems to be serious. Even MSEB is indifferent regarding this matter.

Ultimately, I request you to take immediate steps in order to deal with the problem and come to its solution as earliest as possible.

Kindly consider the matter treating it with utmost urgency. We shall be thankful to you.

Yours faithfully,
XYZ

10. Write a letter to the postmaster regarding the change of your address.

Sai Sadan CHS,
407, MHADA Colony,
Andheri East,
Mumbai-72.
5th Sept 1999

To,
        The Postmaster,
        Saki Naka Post Office,
        Andheri [E].
        Mumbai.

Sub: For the change of address.

Dear Sir,

      With due respect, I would like to inform you that my address has been changed. I was living in 407 MHADA Colony but now I have changed my room at the above mentioned address. I have already informed all the people concerned, still in case of any correspondence in my name at the previous address, please send it to my new address.

      Kindly inform the staff concerned regarding this matter.

Thanking you with the best regards,

Yours faithfully,
XYZ

11. Write an application for the post of an Asst. Marketing Manager in an upcoming organization. Address your letter to Box No.WSE8758YY56, The Times of India, Mumbai-400 001.

85, L.B.S., Marg,
Vikhroli [East],
Mumbai-400 089.
12th October 2000

To,

      The Advertiser,
      Box No.WSE8758YY56,
      The Times of India,
      Mumbai-400 001.

Ref : Your advertisement in 'The Times of India' dated 10th Oct, 2000.

Sub : Application for the post of Asst. Marketing Manager.

Sir,

      With reference to your advertisement dated 10th Oct of "The Times of India" for the post of Asst. Marketing Manager, I would like to offer my candidature for the same and I furnish the particulars required for your kind perusal. I am confident that I have the required qualification and experience that you need.

      I have an MBA degree in Marketing. I did my graduation from the K.C. College of Management, Fort, Mumbai in 1998. I have worked as an Assistant Marketing Manager in Trishul Pharma Products, Kandivali. Prior to this, I was working as a sales officer in Sarathi Automation Pvt. Ltd. on part-time basis which has enabled me to acquire the knowledge about the different aspects of marketing administration.

      Regarding my abilities you may refer to the following:

1. Prof. Atul Mathur

    K.C College of Management
    Fort, Mumbai-400002

(ii) Mrs.Sunayana Chatterji, Director
     Trishul Pharma Products,
     Kandivali (W), Mumbai-82.

I shall be happy to come for an interview at any time convenient to you.
Thanking you with the best regards,

Yours faithfully,

XYZ

12. Write a letter complaining to the Health Officer, New Mumbai Municipal Corporation, regarding the removal of accumulated garbage.

8, "Sahyadri",
Sector-18,
Nerul,
New Mumbai- 400108
17th July 2000.

To,

The Health Officer,
New Mumbai Municipal Corporation,
Nerul Ward Office, Nerul,
Mumbai- 400 108.

Sub : Removal of accumulated garbage.

Dear Sir,

Since last week, the dustbins near the Nerul Post Office building have not been cleared and the filth has been on the road. The dirty smell emanating from the accumulated garbage has become unbearable and is causing great inconvenience to us. It has caused various diseases to the residents and people are suffering. Please take proper action against the responsible people and act accordingly to solve this problem as soon as possible.

I hope you will take action in this regard as soon as possible.

Yours faithfully,
XYZ

13. Write an application to the Principal of a Degree College asking for admission.

Hill View Apartment,
Turner Road,
Bandra (East),
Mumbai - 55
26th Nov.1999

To,

       The Principal,
       National College,
       Bandra (West)
       Mumbai- 400055.

Sub: Application for admission.

Respected Sir,

      I am a student of HSC Science in Patkar College, Goregaon, and have just received my results. I have secured 78% marks. I wish to join your reputed institution in F.Y. Science in order to pursue a career in Biology.

      Kindly send me your prospectus, admission form and other necessary details as early as possible.

      Thanking you with the best regards,

Yours sincerely,
XYZ

14. Given below is a format of bio-data in response to an advertisement for a job published in 'The Indian Express'. Fill in the Bio-data.

The advertisement is as follows:

Brainswave Technologies Pvt.Ltd requires Data Entry Operators preferably with about 2 years experience. Only persons with good command in English and typing 60 W.P.M. should apply.

Box No. ZXE 875UJ25, The Times of India', Mumbai - 400 001.

Bio-data:

1. Name [in block letters]
2. Address :
3. Marital status :
4. Academic Qualifications :
5. Other Qualifications :
6. Experience :
7. Reference :

Bio-data

| 1. | Name [In block letters] | : | ABC |

| 2. | Address | : | 24-A-407 Monalisha Apts.Sector-18. Nerul,   New Mumbai-400 108 |

| 3. | Marital Status | : | Single |

| 4. | Academic Qualifications | : | |

Sr No.	Exam passed	Institution	Year of passing	Percentage
(i)	SSC	M.S.B.S.E.	1995	72 %
(ii)	HSC	Mumbai University	1997	65 %
(iii)	B.A.	Mumbai University	2000	67 %

5. Experience : 2 years as a typist in Shahaji Estate Agent Co.,
   Typing Speed : 60 w.p.m. Shorthand : 90 w.p.m.

6. Other Qualification : 6-month diploma course in
   Computer Programming.

LETTERS TO NEWSPAPERS

1. Write a letter to the editor of "The Indian Express" in order to protest against the school fees.

50, Kalba Road,

Calcutta-700 004,

7th July 1998

To,

> The Editor,
>
> The Indian Express,
>
> Calcutta-24.

Dear Sir,

The schools, temples of deity Saraswati, are being turned into business centres of education nowadays. The education has become so expensive that it is very difficult to afford it by the poor people. Education, which is a birthright, has become an impossible dream for the students who are from lower class or middle class families.

Thus I would like to request the authorities concerned and draw attention of Education Ministry in order to look into this matter to make such plans for implementation so that most of the Indians can be equally educated.

Yours faithfully,

Desmukh

2. Write a letter to the editor of a newspaper protesting against the roads and traffic problems.

12, Primrose Apt.

Lall Street, Khar,

Mumbai-48,

16th Jan 1998.

To,

> The Editor,
>
> Indian Express,
>
> Mumbai.

Sir,

The increasing numbers of vehicles have made the roads of Mumbai an ocean of cars, lorries, etc. Traffic signals are not enough to control them. Most of the flyovers are under construction for a very long time. The speed breakers are either broken or not at the required place. Garbage and rubbish can be seen anywhere. Street hawkers are seen packed anywhere selling their products.

I would like to draw attention of the authorities concerned to take immediate step and make the traffic facility more comfortable so that our city would become a better place to live in.

Yours faithfully,

XYZ

3. Write a letter to the editor of "The Times of India" regarding the cable operators showing pirated movies.

184, Jack House,

Malad [E], Mumbai-42,

12th May 1999

To,

        The Editor,

        The Times of India,

        Mumbai-1

Sir,

      A movie is a mirror of society. It is a treasure house of our rich culture and heritage. Now-a- days, the film industry is also a source of great revenue to our government. The production value of movies can be seen rising up to the pinnacle. A movie costs about 7 to 8 crores and about 3 to 5 years for its completion. As movies are released, the cable operators buy pirated video cassettes from abroad and show them on the cable which causes a great harm to the film industry as well as to the government revenue.

      The intention of my letter is to expose the truth and request the authority concerned to save the film industry.

Yours faithfully,

XYZ

4. Write a letter to the editor of the "Times of India", regarding the patients facing problems in the hospitals of Mumbai.

2 Sea Princes Appt.

Lokhandwala Complex,

Andheri [W], Mumbai-52,

3rd March 1999

To,

      The Editor,

      The Times of India,

      Mumbai-1

Sir,

      Mumbai is a centre of medical treatment. People from different parts of the country come with the hope to get proper medical facility but as they see the filthy condition of hospitals, they find their hopes broken into pieces. Most of the hospitals have fewer beds for the patient. The rooms, passages, toilets, etc. are looking shabby and stinking for many weeks. The empty and fake medicine bottles can be seen thrown here and there. The patients are often found crying with pain and nobody is there to look after them. The environment is too unhealthy to survive there for a long time.

      The aim of my letter is to convey the above-mentioned problems to the authority concerned so that the people can get proper medical facilities and live a healthy life.

Yours faithfully,

XYZ

5. Write a letter to the editor of The "Times of India" regarding the problems of street dogs.

203, Eklavya,
Andheri (East),
Mumbai- 72.
2nd May 2000

To,

     The Editor,
     The Times of India,
     Mumbai-1.

Sir,

     The increasing number of stray dogs in the streets of Chandivali is a horrible problem to the people who are staying in this area. Mostly, people return back home late night. Dogs attack them and injure them. In case of injury, they have to go for a medical treatment which is very expensive. Last week a pack of dogs attacked and horribly injured my 5-years-old daughter. She is getting medical treatment in Mukunda Hospital and her nose needs plastic surgery. Neither we can complain to any owner nor we can kill the dogs or hurt them as the dog lovers feed them and threaten to take legal action against it.

     I would like to request the authority concerned to take action and solve this problem in order to save us from the stray dogs.

Yours faithfully,

XYZ

6. Write a letter to a publisher to send some books through VPP.

408, D.S.Phalke
Road, Dadar (East),
Mumbai-400014.
12th January, 2000

To,

     The Publisher,
     S. Chand & Co Ltd.,
     Ram Nagar,
     New Delhi – 110 055.

Dear Sir,

     I shall be thankful if you send me the following books by VPP at the earliest as our examination is at the doorstep:

     a. Modern History of India   **V.D. Mahajan**
     b. History of Europe   **C.D. Hazan**
     c. English Grammar & Composition   **Wren & Martin**

                   Yours faithfully,

                      Sam

7. Write a letter to the editor of a newspaper regarding slums in your city.

263 -A, Panchavati,
Tardeo,
Mumbai-400 008.
05th August 2000

To,

      The Editor,
      The Free Press Journal,
      Mumbai-400004

Dear Sir,

Sub : Control the slums

      I would like to attract your kind attention that the slum can not be an ideal place for the survival of common people. It has become almost impossible for a common man to get a proper accommodation in Mumbai.

      The approach to the problems of slum lies in making suitable amendment in "Shops and Establishment Act" and "Factory Act" to make it obligatory that all traders and factory owners provide suitable accommodation to their employees in a phased manner. Such shelters should provide community kitchens, lockers, and toilet facilities. Such accommodations could be made more attractive than living in slums by providing common rooms with library, reading rooms, TV, telephone facilities, etc. Such accommodations should be offered to slum dwellers on hire with a nominal deposit.

      The step mentioned above and review of other relevant tax laws can only encourage the availability of housing in urban areas and control slums.

Yours faithfully,
PQR.

(C) REPORT WRITING

1. Write a report on the beauty contest held at Nikosia and selection of Miss India Lara Dutta as Miss Universe.

Miss Universe Pageant—Indian Beauty at the top

23 May, Nikosia, Cyprus

21-year old Indian model Lara Dutta was crowned as Miss Universe 2000. She is the second Indian model to be crowned as Miss Universe after Shushmita Sen. Since previous decade, Indian beautiful models have proved themselves to be the most beautiful model in all over the world. She is the 49th Miss Universe. She was crowned by Miss Quelagobe, the Miss Universe of previous year from Botswana. After conquering the title of Miss Universe, she said that it was the greatest gift to her father who was celebrating his birthday on the same day. All the participants participated in the contest with discipline and zeal. 22-years old Miss Clydia Morona [Miss Venezuela] was the 1st runners-up and the second runners-up was 18-year old Miss Helen Lendis [Miss Spain]. Indian Prime Minister Shri. Atal Bihari Vajpayee congratulated her and blessed her to reach the culmination of life.

2. Prepare a report on the cancellation of trains due to derailment of Howrah Express.

Train Cancelled

28 Aug, Mumbai

The Western Railway has announced that the Gorakhpur- Mumbai Express, Gitanjali Express and Coachi-Mumbai Express have been cancelled because of the derailment of Howrah Express at Pune. According to the railway authority, 3 bogies have been derailed. The cause of derailment is still unknown. The rescue and repair work is under progress and it is hoped that the railway service will be continued soon. All the passengers have been requested to reschedule their journey.

3. Prepare a report on the sufferings of people due to polluted water at Bhayandar,

Ten people are serious because of polluted water

13th May Bhayandar, Mumbai

Bhayandar, an overpopulated part of Mumbai has been facing water problem since the previous decade. There is no source of direct supply for drinking water. So the people are compelled to use water whatever is supplied to them through water tankers. Yesterday 10 people were admitted at J. J. Hospital and after the medical checkup, the doctors concluded that the only reason was; the use of contaminated drinking water. All the patients are under medical treatment but no action has been taken till now against the culprits.

4. Prepare a report on the cricket match held between film industry and cricket stars.

Cricket Match: Bollywood Vs Cricketwood

19th May: Mumbai

A cricket match had been organised at Wankhede Stadium in order to collect the drought relief fund for Rajasthan. The match started at 5 :00 p.m. Most of the famous film personalities were present. Hritik Roshan won the toss and decided to bat first. His team did well and scored 223 runs in 40 overs. Then Sachin came to bat and his team scored 225 runs in only 36 overs and won the match.

5. Prepare a report on a building collapsed at Thane and death of 54 people.

54 injured as building collapses in Thane

12 th May, Thane

54 people were killed when a 5-storey building collapsed in the morning. According to the fire brigade sources, the incident occurred at 7:10 am. Most of the victims were women and children. More than 50 persons were injured in this collapse and were admitted to Thane Government Hospital. The other occupants of the building have been evacuated. Senior officers rushed to the spot to supervise the rescue activities. The building was built by a reputed group of construction company. Still the cause of collapse is unknown. The ward officer is investigating the causes of the incident.

The builder has been criticized for this collapse. The legal authorities have assured to take strict action against the builder concerned. Items, used by the builder for the building construction, have been seized. The builder is yet to be arrested.

6. Customs officers seize drugs from a foreigner

New Delhi – The air intelligence unit (AIU) of the Customs Department on Sunday evening arrested one Belgian national Smith Francis, at the Indira Gandhi International Airport and seized narcotic substance from him. The officials seized 1,100 gms of morphine and 750 gms. of heroin, totally valued Rs.1.5 crore in the international market. According to the officials, Smith had declared that he was carrying food items.

7. Convocation ceremony of Vishwabharati University

Shantiniketan – The convocation ceremony of Vishwabharati University was celebrated on July 26. The President, Dr. K.R. Narayanan, and the West Bengal Chief Minister Mr. Jyoti Basu, graced the occasion. The President emphasized on the traditional heritage of the Gurukula and to fulfil the dreams of R.N. Tagore, the father of this temple of learning. Mr. Jyoti Basu, in his speech emphasized on the importance of value education. He appealed the students for introspection. A painting exhibition based on ancient history was held there. It was organised by the Dept. of History where historical paintings were exhibited to the people.